WA 1229516 7

... Methodology
in Finance and
Accounting

D1103591

Research Method and Methodology in Finance and Accounting

Second Edition

Bob Ryan
Robert W. Scapens
Michael Theobold

THOMSON ™

Australia • Canada • Mexico • Singapore • Spain • United Kingdom • United States

THOMSON

Research Method and Methodology in Finance and Accounting – Second Edition

Copyright © Bob Ryan, Robert W. Scapens and Michael Theobold 2002

The Thomson logo is a registered trademark used herein under licence.

For more information, contact Thomson, High Holborn House, 50/51 Bedford Row, London, WC1R 4LR or visit us on the World Wide Web at:
http://www.thomsonlearning.co.uk

All rights reserved by Thomson 2002. The text of this publication, or any part thereof, may not be reproduced or transmitted in any form or by any means, electronic or mechanical, including photocopying, recording, storage in an information retrieval system, or otherwise, without prior permission of the publisher.

Whilst the Publisher has taken all reasonable care in the preparation of this book the Publisher makes no representation, express or implied, with regard to the accuracy of the information contained in this book and cannot accept any legal responsibility or liability for any errors or omissions from the book or the consequences thereof.

Products and services that are referred to in this book may be either trademarks and/or registered trademarks of their respective owners. The publishers and author/s make no claim to these trademarks.

British Library Cataloguing-in-Publication Data
A catalogue record for this book is available from the British Library

ISBN 1–86152–881–7

First edition published by Academic Press Limited 1992
This edition published by Thomson

Typeset by LaserScript, Mitcham, Surrey
Printed in Great Britain by TJ International, Padstow, Cornwall

Learning Resources
Centre
1229516 7

Contents

List of figures

List of tables

Preface to the second edition

In the introduction to the first edition of this book we made some remarks about research that have stood the test of time. In particular we emphasized the point that research is uniquely about discovery and that research entails disagreement, criticism, chance and error. In working together to produce this text we have had many debates about the fundamentals of our subject and tested the truth of that statement. As we said in our first introduction, accounting and financial research cuts across many boundaries – it divides researchers into political and philosophical camps, it brings world views into sharp conflict and it is tied to the paradoxes of our uncertain social and value systems.

We are pleased to say that we have managed to join camps again and have written what we believe to be of importance in understanding research in accounting and finance. The principal differences to the first edition are in Part One, which has been extended to include a new chapter 'Alternative philosophies of accounting research'. This chapter is designed to be read in juxtaposition to Chapter 1 where, as before, we explore the philosophy which underpins accounting and finance. Chapter 1 covers the areas of epistemological and ontological significance to the researcher in greater depth than in the first edition but it misses the complementary perspective supplied by the many social philosophers who have written on the subject. It is this perspective which Chapter 2 provides.

Chapters 3, 4 and 5 review the history of research in finance, management accounting and financial accounting. These chapters have been thoroughly revised and updated and we were delighted, and much relieved, when Vivien Beattie agreed to revise her chapter from the first edition on financial accounting. Obviously, in a few thousand words, it proved impossible to address all that has been of significance in the research literature in these three areas, and certain topics such as auditing and information systems have not been covered. However, we hope that what we have written in these chapters will provide an interesting and stimulating overview of the research in each area.

Apart from the final two chapters on the formal analysis of arguments we have taken the opportunity to update and clarify the text. We have, however, taken a more general approach to the discussion of the literature, and particularly the role of academic journals, in Chapter 9. In the early 1970s when we entered academic life, finance and accounting was dominated by less than a dozen journals. Now, that situation has dramatically altered with the establishment of many new journals of outstanding quality. We are now seeing the emergence in other fields of electronic journals which offer the researcher desktop access to the literature. If there is a third edition of this book, we are sure that there will be some recognition of this new means of publication in our discipline too and, we hope, positive moves towards open and free access to the intellectual property of the research community through online libraries.

Finally, we were surprised and delighted by the reception which the first edition received. As we discussed the reasons for its success with fellow academics and students, we achieved a clearer idea of the position which our book had taken in the market. The market clearly recognized that the first edition of our book was not a primer on quantitative or qualitative methods but, rather, an exploration of the methods and methodology of our subject written in a way which was designed to stimulate and motivate research. Our market told us that we had got the message about right. We have taken care to ensure that this new edition does not attempt to do more than achieve this limited but important objective.

We apologize to all those who have written to us for the long delay in the production of this second edition; we blame that on the contingencies of the Research Assessment Exercise which does not, in our subject, reward book production. We also apologize to Jennifer Pegg, our long-suffering editor, whose reaction when she heard that the manuscript for this edition was approaching completion was to say that 'pigs don't fly'. Well Jennifer, pigs do, and many thanks for staying with it and providing us with the motivation to get the job done!

Introduction

Research is an activity that we all undertake to learn more about our environment and the impact we have upon it. Research is labelled in many different ways: 'academic', 'scientific', 'fundamental' and 'applied', to give just four examples. However, none of these labels changes the most important aspect of research itself – namely, that research is about discovery. Research entails disagreement, criticism, chance and error. In the disciplines discussed in this text all four feature in abundance. One of the great attractions of accounting and financial research to those who pursue it is that it cuts across many boundaries – it divides researchers into political and philosophical camps, it brings world views into sharp conflict and it is tied to the paradoxes of our uncertain social and value systems.

Accounting and finance are relatively new academic disciplines, although certain aspects of accounting have an ancient pedigree. Accounting has been taught within European universities since the fourteenth century and formed an essential part of the mathematics tripos at Oxford and Cambridge until the nineteenth century. Finance as a subject area developed as a strong academic discipline in the USA principally at the University of Chicago Graduate School of Business and in the UK at the London Business School.

Both accounting and finance present rich areas of study for researchers of widely different intellectual persuasion. Certain aspects of finance provide rigorous formal and mathematical problems in the treatment of individual behaviour, while others provide unique challenges for those who enjoy the arcane mysteries of the legal and regulatory environments which accountants and financiers inhabit. There is no need to be highly numerate to contribute to advanced research in these subject areas. Accounting and finance offer even the most innumerate of researchers ample scope for their other intellectual skills.

This text offers an introduction to the research process for scholars in accounting and finance. All three of us have for a large part of our working careers been involved in research both directly and through supervision, and we all have offered programmes in research method and methodology. Our first attempts in this latter area were offered at the University of Manchester in the mid to late 1970s through a postgraduate course in methodology. As we went our separate ways in the early 1980s we took many of the ideas we had developed in this area at Manchester with us to our new institutions. Although our actual research interests have lain in different directions, we do believe that the process of research is as important as the output. Within a research community, whether it be in a university or professional organization, the cultivation of sound method and a strong critical approach are necessary conditions for healthy and productive research to flourish. Furthermore, we believe that there is a place within every research community for continuous reappraisal of the methodological preconceptions upon which its work is based. In writing this text we hope that we can stimulate thinking about the process of research in accounting and finance and also offer our own appraisal about the stage it has reached in its development.

In Part One we initiate our treatise with two chapters that examine the philosophical debates which condition research in our subject areas. For many, philosophy is an instant 'turn-off'. We beg them to stay the course – philosophy raises a number of issues that strike hard at the roots of even the most hard-edged empirical work. Libraries have been written on the philosophical disputes within the natural sciences and yet for many the natural sciences are still considered object lessons in how truth should be uncovered. On the other hand, the social sciences (of which, we argue, accounting and finance are a part) raise countless issues concerning the nature of truth and knowledge, the role of empirical testing, the distinction between mental and real constructs and so on. At the more pragmatic level, an understanding of certain philosophical issues can greatly aid the researcher in areas as diverse as conducting effective literature reviews to determining the relative quality of arguments.

Part One continues with three chapters explaining our understanding of the scope of accounting and financial research. It is not our intention in these three chapters to provide a knowledge base from which further research can be developed but rather to indicate what we perceive to be the most important threads of research in our subject areas. We address these three chapters to two principal audiences: the students of research who are attempting to pick up clues as to what may be interesting and important in accounting and finance and those professionals within the areas who have much to offer the research community through critical involvement and debate but who do not perceive the scope of research which has already been undertaken.

Part Two provides three chapters on research methods. Many books on research in the social sciences generally, and in our areas particularly, confuse research 'methods' with statistical techniques. Statistical techniques are important, but are only a part of the competent researcher's methods. In our chapters, we devote considerable space to discussion of the power and application of different methods and, in particular, we hope we do justice to the important, but often neglected, topic of case study research. In Chapter 6 we examine the problems of interpreting empirical research in some detail. This is a common area of difficulty for new researchers and we hope that the guidance we give may be of some assistance.

In Part Three we take a 'top-down' approach to critical analysis. In the first chapter of this part we bring the philosophical discussion started in Chapters 1 and 2

Chap. 10

Chap. 2 (good but diff to read)

Customer name: MRS HEATHER JULIE ROPER
Customer ID: ***********002

Title: Research method and methodology in finance and
ID: 7312295167
Due: 28/10/2010 23:59

Total items: 1
21/10/2010 14:40

Thank you for using the Self-Service system
Diolch yn fawr

University of Glamorgan
Learning Resources Centre -
Treforest
Self Issue Receipt (TR2)

**Customer name: MRS HEATHER
JULIE ROPER**
Customer ID: **********002

Title: Research method and
methodology in finance and
ID: 7312295167
Due: 28/10/2010 23:59

Total items: 1
21/10/2010 14:40

Thank you for using the Self-
Service system
Diolch yn fawr

down to earth and throw light on what we believe to be a substantial stumbling block for many researchers – namely, how to conduct an effective, coherent and original literature review. In the second chapter we introduce some powerful techniques in the critical analysis of natural language reasoning and, finally, we close with a discussion of the power and scope of formal, logical method in criticism.

This text is aimed at all those who are interested in understanding the research process and improving their performance in research. Both new researchers and more seasoned campaigners should find something of interest, even if only to argue against our position. In our experience first-year research students need clear guidance on methodological principles and we hope that our text will find a place on the reading lists of the numerous faculty courses which exist to serve such students. New academics face a different problem in that while undertaking research is given very high priority for career development there are very few sources of information on how to go about it and how to avoid the obvious pitfalls. Sometimes academic colleagues are not as helpful in this respect as they might be because for many of them research has been a rather hit and miss process over a number of years. We hope that our text will help in this respect. Finally, our text should be of interest to all those who are interested in accounting and financial research as bystanders and as the consumers of results. We are therefore looking for a large sale to the professional community who can make yet another contribution to the academic community (at least three members of it) by buying this book in large numbers!

Finally, we have a number of important acknowledgements to make. When we wrote the first edition we tried to muster our combined knowledge about research in financial accounting only to discover the true depths of our combined ignorance. We were fortunate indeed that Vivien Beattie agreed to draft that chapter for us. We are deeply indebted to Vivien for coming to our rescue again and producing a revised chapter (Chapter 5) that not only fits with the tenor of our text but also is of far higher quality than we could have hoped to produce. For this edition, we have not presumed to either add or subtract from what Vivien has written and so that chapter now stands as her own contribution to the literature in the field. We believe it is an important contribution and Vivien has our heartfelt thanks.

In many chapters, we have used examples, which have been drawn from the work of our research students, and we thank them. They, throughout the years, have taught us all we know about good research supervision. All the mistakes, errors and misconceptions in this text are ours; we have not yet managed to convince ourselves, nor anybody else for that matter, of the extreme relativist view that the concept of error has no meaning (see Chapter 1).

Part One

Traditions of Research in Finance and Accounting

1

The philosophy of financial research

Research is a process of intellectual discovery, which has the potential to transform our knowledge and understanding of the world around us. In this chapter we examine some of the fundamental assumptions upon which research in the financial disciplines is based. These disciplines, like most others within the social sciences, are methodologically highly diverse. Scholars in these disciplines come from a variety of different backgrounds and sometimes make implicit but different methodological assumptions about the nature of reality, the role of theory and the significance of empirical experimentation.

Part of our task in this chapter is to make clear what those assumptions are and how they influence the research process. We start our discussions about research at a somewhat abstract level but, as we will demonstrate in later chapters, the issues we raise here condition much of what we have to say later about such questions as:

- What are the different assumptions about the nature of financial reality that inform research?
- What is the role of theory in acquiring knowledge about financial and accounting reality?
- How does research progress?

Given that research is fundamentally about the discovery, interpretation and communication of new knowledge there is still little agreement about the source of knowledge itself. The financial disciplines have, over the last 40 years, provided a new intellectual arena for some very old debates, and our purpose here is to discuss the range of issues and debates, which are of importance to the practising researcher.

To illustrate the methodological issues presented by financial research, consider two studies recently published in the accounting literature. The first by Maines and McDaniel (2000) is typical of the type of article found in the mainstream US literature and examines the effect of a disclosure requirement on the processing of financial information by investors. This article draws upon prior work in psychology (Hogarth, 1987), which asserts that performance–assessment judgments are formed by individuals from a linear combination of cues. On the basis of this the researchers create two empirical hypotheses, which are tested in the controlled research environment of 90 Master of Business Administration (MBA) students. Their performance is analysed and the hypotheses empirically confirmed through a variety of statistical tests which allow the authors to conclude: 'the results of our experiment show... the financial statement format... did not significantly affect nonprofessional investors' ... evaluation of that information ... but generally did significantly influence their information weighting and resulting performance judgments' (Maines and McDaniel, 2000: 199). Note that the conclusion drawn from an empirical domain of 90 MBA students has been generalized to include all non-professional investors.

This type of research is generally called 'positive' accounting research in that it claims to give reliable and empirically sustainable answers to questions that policy-makers regard to be important. This type of research is contested by many researchers, not on grounds of method, but because they do not agree with the philosophical premises upon which the research is based.

Our second example was recently published in *Economy and Society* by Froud *et al.* (2000). This paper addresses the issue of whether maximizing shareholder value results in superior business perfomance. The authors combine a limited but critical review of the literature before presenting a range of evidence ('empirics on micro performance and the meso limits to shareholder value') to support their case. The evidence cited is in the form of a listing of the value-added performance of a range of companies as illustration of a thread of argument drawn from the author's social and political framework. This research is developed through a lengthy series of natural language arguments (see Chapter 11) containing numerous suppositions and assertions (we use these words in a non-pejorative sense). The paper emphasizes 'interpretation' rather than 'explanation' or 'prediction' when studying social phenomena. No appeal is made to the use of statistical or other formal method although, as was the case with the first example discussed above, a wide range of generalizations are made in the conclusion to the paper.

However, our point is that research of either type, whilst being acceptable in terms of the methods employed, may be subject to hostile and fundamentally non-comprehending criticism because of underlying disputes at the philosophical level. When a piece of research is characterized by poor technique, a critic may argue that the research is 'defective', 'weak' or 'misapplied', however, when a methodological dispute is involved the research is simply labelled as 'nonsensical'.

Notwithstanding the fundamental nature of the debates that permeate much research in accounting and finance, historically the methodological position adopted by the large majority of active researchers in these disciplines has inclined towards the position exemplified by the first of our examples above. That is, they demonstrate a strong commitment to what we would label 'objective' research. By this they view research as a process of constructing precise and economical theories validated by well-designed tests using large and, as far as possible, unbiased samples. Replicability and critical evaluation of method and results are the hallmark of this type of research. We will spend considerable time in this chapter evaluating the 'empiricist' philosophical tradition which informs this type of research and the most important variants of that tradition.

This chapter has a strong philosophical bias as we explore some of the issues which underpin debates in finance and accounting. We have knowledge of the work of philosophers stretching back over 3000 years. This history has two important consequences: first, the language of the subject has become progressively more technical as philosophers, like most other branches of scholarship, tend to talk among themselves and, second, many of the arguments within the subject are returned to time and time again. Obviously, we must be very selective and in this chapter we concentrate on a very limited set of issues. Our principal target will be to show how the dominant methodologies within research in finance and accounting have developed and, in particular, how the empiricist tradition has acquired its current supremacy. We will, however, consider other positions and seek to explain from a philosophical perspective the more important methodological alternatives adopted by other researchers. These alternative methodologies now command a significant literature with a number of journals (*Accounting, Organizations and Society, Critical Perspectives in Accounting* and others) editorially sympathetic to this type of research. This chapter is an important precursor to Chapter 2, where we consider in more detail how scholars within the social sciences, and accounting researchers who draw upon the work of such scholars, have sought to categorize their own and alternative positions and, in particular, we will discuss the important contribution made by two organizational theorists, Burrell and Morgan, to the methodological debate.

The duality within western thought

Research in accounting and finance is generally accepted as being social scientific, as appropriate standards of scientific enquiry are applied to social issues rather than natural phenomena, which is taken to be the domain of the natural sciences and of physics in particular. Many philosophers, such as Bertrand Russell in his *History of Western Philosophy*, argue that the origins of western thought can be traced back to the Greeks, who in their turn almost certainly drew upon and rationalized ideas from their own social and religious inheritance as well as those other Eastern Mediterranean cultures with which they came in contact. Possibly the most important idea contributed by the Greeks was that reality could be characterized by opposites and that there is an essential duality in all things. To give two important examples: statements are either true or false (in Aristotelian logic: the Law of Excluded Middle) and each individual is a subject in a 'subject–object' relationship with the external world.

Although deeply rooted in our social and cultural heritage, these dualities of thought and understanding do have limitations and have provoked debate within their own terms about the nature of knowledge, truth and reality and, more recently, in terms of their own validity. The Greek perception of opposites endowed western thought with great power, especially when dealing with the natural order or with the development of logic and mathematics. Where they have been less successful is in helping us to gain mastery of our social world where truth and falsity are much more ambiguous concepts and where relationships which are objectified often cease to be relationships. However, the dualist perspective does permit the ready abstraction of ideas and concepts at one level and the 'objectification' of domains of enquiry at the other.

By characterizing individuals as subjects in subject–object relationships with everyone and everything around them it makes sense to propose that individuals must have beliefs about what is true or false in their objective world. But, it is important to ask what forms these beliefs? One view is that they are formed from the *perceptions* individuals have about the objects that confront them. But do they perceive objects, or as many philosophers argue, the '*appearance*' of objects? We can then propose that the appearance of what we observe should be distinguished from the fundamental nature (if such exists) of what we observe. We might also argue that we can come to know things about objects through reason and thus bypass the problem of appearances and perception altogether.

Before long, the dualism represented in Figure 1.1 leads to a range of derived questions which all nevertheless presuppose the seductively obvious distinction between subject and object. One view that we will discuss is that the knowledge possessed by the subject of an external object is driven by the perception of appearances, another view is that such knowledge is not driven by perception but by the exercise of reason. We will turn to this debate about the source of knowledge in the next section.

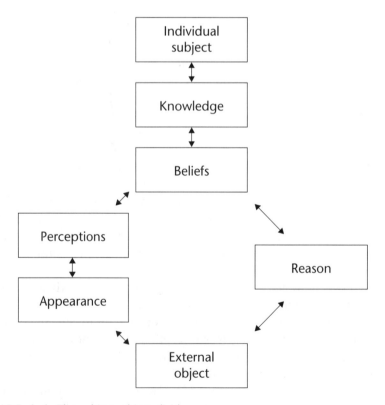

FIGURE 1.1 The subject–object divide

Epistemology or what is knowledge?

The central problem of epistemology is to decide how we can acquire knowledge which Plato and others following him have defined as *justified true belief*. This definition of knowledge creates three substantive issues: the nature of belief, the basis of truth and the problem of justification. When we reflect upon the statement made in the Maines and McDaniel (2000) article quoted above: 'the financial statement format ... did not significantly affect nonprofessional investors'... evaluation of that information' it is pertinent to ask how this conclusion is justified even assuming the truth of the empirical data upon which it is based. This definition of knowledge is widely accepted, and for now we will discuss its implications in its own terms by addressing such questions as what is the source of our belief, how we determine what is true and how we justify our belief? These weighty issues each have their own branch of philosophical enquiry.

Empiricism and rationalism

There are a number of sources of our beliefs (see Audi, 1998): we may perceive objects or events (perceptual belief); we may remember facts (memorial belief), we may come to believe by a process of introspection (introspective belief) or we may come to believe by a process of reason (rational belief). We may come to believe through induction (inductive belief), which is a process of inferring general truths from perceptual and/or memorial belief, and we may also come to believe because of the testimony of others (testimonial belief). In principal, however, all of these reduce to two distinct sources: first, that which is grounded within our own rational processes as the enquiring subjects, that is, rational belief, and, second, that which is grounded in the object of our enquiry, that is, perceptual belief.

The first of these two sources of belief (and hence knowledge) assumes that we do not need to look beyond ourselves to form a *justified true belief* about the world. In other words propositional knowledge, that is, knowledge about what *is* can be known a priori and does not have to be perceived. This idea can be traced back to Socrates and Plato who argued the existence of abstract forms of knowledge. Socrates believed that all knowledge is innate and the wise teacher could draw that knowledge from others through the use of leading questions. This is the basis of what is often referred to as the 'Socratic method' in teaching. His pupil, Plato, extended these ideas and taught that there exists a realm of ideas which contain the essence of things (their form). Platonic *ideal forms*, as they became known, could include the abstractions of pure geometry at one extreme to the ideal society (the republic) at the other. Plato believed that these ideal forms were real, in the sense that they had an existence as abstractions independently of any enquiring mind, but that they could be accessed only through the exercise of reason. In this sense Plato was a 'rationalist' in that he held that true belief is accessible only through reason. However, he was also a realist (see below) in that he believed that the world of ideal forms had an objective existence.

In finance, which takes much of its intellectual basis from economics, the concepts of ideal or perfect markets are Platonic abstractions. If Plato had bothered with perfectly efficient capital markets (whether this was a side interest of his, history does not record) he would have argued that what he had conceptualized was a real entity, which does not exist in space or time, but which can be understood and reflected upon by the exercise of reason alone.

Platonic abstraction and its modern variant, rationalism, has proved particularly tenacious in western culture – especially for those who have spent considerable time throughout their education improving their powers of reason (as opposed to their power of observation, for example). A second tradition of thought is derived from Aristotle and is quite different.

Aristotle did not accept the arguments of the academicians and entered into a long dispute with Plato, which led to his expulsion from the Academy. Given the dearth of other institutions of learning at the time, Aristotle formed a rival school called the Lyceum in 366 BC. Aristotle argued that we gather knowledge by observation and categorization, and he challenged the existence of ideal forms. In as far as they do exist, Aristotle saw them as embedded within objects that have a spatio-temporal existence. For example, as we reflect upon different types of market we note that each has certain characteristics that recur in different situations. Through repeated observation of particulars we begin to form an understanding of the properties of a general class of markets and these general properties, in their turn, are amenable to logical extension and analysis.

We can find elements of these two traditions in the writings of St Augustine (354–430) and the thirteenth-century scholastics: St Thomas Aquinas (on the Platonic side) and William of Ockham (on the Aristotelian). However, it was not until the seventeenth and eighteenth centuries that the ideas we now describe as 'rationalism' and 'empiricism' were fully articulated. 'Rationalism' as a term was first used to describe the world view of the French philosopher-mathematician René Descartes (1596–1650). However, as a tradition it underpins much of modern continental philosophy and particularly the work of Hegel and Marx. Empiricism, however, became dominant in Britain where the trade guilds and the professions in the seventeenth, eighteenth and nineteenth centuries created a new social milieu. The entrants to these trades were not generally the product of a classical education system, and their expertise relied on the transfer of skills by word of mouth – master to apprentice. In such a system, the educational tradition relied very heavily on the careful observation and practice of what the apprentice observed. This was also the time of the emergence of the 'scientific method' with its foremost champion, Sir Isaac Newton, harnessing the discipline and observational skills of an alchemist with a formidable theoretical and mathematical ability.

Much has been argued and written about the merits and defects of empiricism. Modern empiricists by and large now accept as untenable the idea that knowledge is uniquely determined by experience, but they would claim that experience can represent a *justification* for our beliefs about what we know. The term 'empiricism' is the name we now give to a family of philosophies. Traditionally, classical empiricists accepted that:

(1) Certainty of belief in what we know can only be approached through perception.
(2) Ultimately all knowledge is derived from perception through our senses, as Locke said: 'We are all born with a blank sheet upon which sense impressions are written.'
(3) In the realm of discourse statements are either true or false because of the way the world is or because of some formal properties of the language we use.

These three tenets of the empiricist position lead to the following conclusions: from (1), beliefs based upon non-experiential grounds (that is, not justified by experience or by logically or mathematically derived implications of experience) are termed metaphysical and are meaningless, and from (2) and (3), beliefs about the world cannot be justified by the use of reason alone. The empiricist position leads quite naturally to the idea that science (natural or social) should be 'value free'; that is, free from beliefs and ideologies which cannot be justified in terms of the objects of experience under study.

The influence of empiricism has been extremely pervasive and has led to one of the most significant philosophical movements of modem times: positivism. Positivism is now regarded as rather passé in certain quarters, although it has been particularly influential in the recent development of the disciplines of finance, economics and accounting. However, before we consider positivism in detail it is worth while considering two other important and related areas of philosophical debate: to what extent can we be truly objective in the statements we make about the world and to what extent are scientific beliefs conditioned by or relative to the social context of the researcher?

Realism versus idealism

Empiricism and rationalism is a classical distinction which focuses on the *source* of knowledge. Realism and idealism are terms used to describe the *ontology* of what we know. Ontology is the study of existence and in this context is concerned with what we discern to be 'real'. Reality is a difficult concept but is concerned with the construction of existence in objects. The questions we now pose is how do we know what is real and how do we know when statements about the world are true or false? Following the ancient Greeks there are two opposite positions: that of the *realists* who hold that reality subsists within objects, and that of the *idealists* who hold that it exists within the mind of the subject. However, the empiricist–rationalist distinction still holds. As we noted before, Plato was a realist in that he believed that his perfect worlds were real but only accessible to reason. Bishop George Berkeley, an eighteenth-century cleric and highly influential idealist philosopher, proposed that, even though knowledge is derived from perception, the objects of perception are mentally constructed and only continue to exist in the presence of a perceiving mind.[1]

At its simplest, realism represents the common-sense view that, when we describe something, that thing has a reality which is independent of our perception of it. As Popper and numerous other philosophers have pointed out, our belief in a mind-independent reality, which impacts upon our senses and forms our perceptions, is a strong one. The difficulty is that we are not conscious of reality as such, but following the empiricist's account, we are conscious only of our perceptions of what our senses present to us. Naive or empirical realists such as the Scottish empirical philosopher David Hume (1711–76) hold that reality subsists within the objects of perception, and that we construct reality behaviourally as we make conjunctions between different events. Belief in causality (the idea that effect B must have a cause A), and in general laws of behaviour, such as Newton's laws of motion, are 'induced' or inferred from the observation of the repeated conjunction of events. Likewise, for the empirical realist the way to determine whether a statement is true is to compare what is claimed with 'empirical evidence' – this creates what is known as a 'correspondence theory' of truth.

The first coherent account of idealism was given by Bishop Berkeley, who like Hume and Locke was an empiricist, but who argued that the qualities that we perceive, such as colour or texture, are mental representations of sense-data and it is these mental representations which form the 'reality' of what we experience. Knowledge is therefore mentally constructed and the truth or falsity of statements are checked, not in terms of their correspondence with reality but, rather, in terms of their 'coherence' either with the other beliefs of the individual or with the beliefs of others. This leads to the notion that knowledge and, more importantly, reality can be socially constructed. Some social scientists conclude that it follows from the idealist position that all knowledge is socially constructed. However, this conclusion does not follow from idealism: reality is a construction of minds (singular or plural) and is tested for coherence at either the individual or the social level or, indeed, both.

Few philosophers would agree that realism or idealism in their extreme form as described above are tenable. The central problem with empirical or naive realism is bridging the gap between the appearances of reality, which we perceive, and the reality of the *thing in itself*. The problem with idealism is that it takes us to the position that what is true is either what we choose to believe is true or what society believes to be true. The proposition that truth has no objective basis is necessarily true if knowledge is purely a product of minds. However, few would be prepared to go that far – surely there must be some external justification for what we believe and some role for external verification through experimentation or observation? Indeed, in its brute form it is difficult to understand what the term 'observation' would mean to the idealist because to observe implies an object of observation. There have been a number of (more or less successful attempts) to resolve the problem posed by the realist–idealist distinction.

Kantian philosophy

Immanuel Kant (1724–1804) attempted to resolve the problems posed by both empiricism and rationalism and realism and idealism. He tried to establish the meta-principles which allow us to relate to, and make sense of, the empirical world. In this sense he challenged both the empiricists who denied the possibility of such meta-principles and the rationalists in that he believed that we had to make sense of our relationship with the world we experience.

Kant's 'transcendental idealism' was his attempt to resolve these four positions. Kant did not deny that there is an objective world of experience to which we relate and ultimately test our claims to knowledge of what is true or false. However, Kant argued that the notion of discrete objects as knowable in an absolute sense is wrong but rather we can know them by the application of certain principles of causality, space and time. These principles are knowable a priori through the use of pure reason and are also *synthetic* in that they are true propositions about the world. These principles are transcendent, in that they are not properties of objects themselves nor are they real objects themselves, rather they are produced through the agency of the thinking mind.

Few philosophers now accept that Kant's transcendental idealism was the final answer, although he has had a profound effect on many social thinkers and philosophers including Hegel and Marx and, more recently, the influential German philosopher Jürgen Habermas. For Kant reality is mentally *constructed* whereas the common orthodoxy in the social sciences is that reality is socially constructed. What is clear, whether we accept Kant's version of idealism or its more modern version in the social sciences, is that reality is a concept which is *constructed* rather than *discovered* and it is this distinction which demarcates idealist philosophies from those of the realists.

The realist alternative

Roy Bhaskar (1997) employed Kant's transcendental method but argued for a version of realism which has many similarities to that of Plato. Bhaskar and the critical realist school founded on his work argue that naive realism is clearly problematic for the reasons that we have outlined above and that reality does not subsist in the 'surface layer' of objects. Critical realists further argue that Kantian idealism is also problematic: they question whether it is credible to believe that the laws of physical motion or the equations of quantum mechanics would cease to apply if there were no human beings to think about them. The critical realists argue that these laws of behaviour have always existed – they are real descriptions of the world irrespective of their discovery by human beings. For Bhaskar, these laws are discovered not constructed aspects of reality. In many respects Bhaskar is close to the current orthodoxy in cosmology which argues that our existence is made possible because of certain initial conditions (the magnitude of Planck's constant, for example) and the operation of certain key universal laws which took effect at the moment of the Big Bang.

It may be that the natural laws of physics and biology are permanent features of existence irrespective of the minds that perceive them. However, is this also true of social systems? Some would argue that the laws controlling social systems only hold until the point that the social scientist attempts to test them. The mere intervention of the social observer changes the system which he or she is attempting to observe. In what sense, therefore, can we argue for the existence of laws which transcend the objects of social systems? One essential problem is that the so-called laws of social behaviour fail as soon as one attempts to observe them in operation. However, critical realists do not regard this problem as insurmountable.

One way of explaining the critical realist position is through an understanding of time. We can argue that our notion of the present and what is currently real is an illusion. The present is simply the objective point of our existence, which is the point at which the future is being translated into the past. Our perception is thus revealed as a memory of a reality which has passed rather than an experience of the present. This radically reduces the range of beliefs described above; perceptual belief is always memorial belief because even if we look in a mirror what we are observing is not our face as it is now but our face as it once was. But how does this affect the problem of social laws?

As far as the future is concerned we tend to believe two things: first, we can change the course of events and, second, that the translation of the future into the past is governed by laws of behaviour which we cannot change. I see a glass just about to fall from the edge of a table and I jump forward and catch it. In doing that I have changed what appeared to be an inevitable sequence of events where the spatial stability of the glass was about to be radically altered by the gravity acting in accordance with Newton's Law. However, a moment's reflection shows that all I have done is to bring into play, through my intended act, a whole range of other laws to do with catching and holding. Therefore, the mutability of events is, in reality, the summation through my action of a different set of physical laws, which would not have been brought into play if I had not so acted. Arguably, it is exactly the same with social systems, which by their nature tend to exhibit much higher degrees of complexity than natural systems. Our acting in the social domain where observation and experiment are themselves a form of social interaction brings yet more laws into play all of which are very real but currently, and perhaps forever, are beyond our scientific powers to understand.

Relativism

'Relativism' is a term given to a group of ideas which argue that truth is relative to the beliefs of the observer. It is not quite the same as arguing that beliefs are individually or socially constructed because it is possible for the social constructionist to argue from a critical realist perspective that truth is constructed on the basis of transcendent laws of human or social behaviour. Relativists argue that these laws are socially constructed as well and that all belief is relative to the social value system and norms that transcend the individual level, but not the social level. There is one paradox with relativism which is apparent as soon as we recast their governing theory of truth as follows: *all truth statements are relative to X or Y*, where X and Y are whatever the relativist proposes to ground their concept of truth. The obvious problem is that this statement is contradictory – a contradiction that is revealed as soon as we extend its logical form: *all truth statements are relative to X or Y except this one*. Thus there must be at least one universally true statement, namely, that *all* true statements are relative. But why should this one statement be privileged? It can be privileged if we deny the applicability of the laws of logic but where does that leave us? This is an issue we will consider when we return to the claims of *postmodernist* philosophers towards the end of this chapter.

Logical positivism and instrumentalism

A variant of empiricism called 'logical positivism' became a major force in the early part of the twentieth century through the work of the Vienna Circle of Philosophers – Schlick, Carnap, Feigl and others. Logical positivism[2] is a linguistic derivative of empiricism where the world of 'meaningful discourse' is controlled by a particular variety of the correspondence theory of truth. Positivists, like empiricists, argue that true belief is grounded in what we perceive and that what we perceive is derived from a value-free, independent reality. However, their most significant innovation was to propose that meaningful statements are only those which can, in principle at least, be verified by appeal to observation. This is the correspondence theory of truth recast in the form of observation statements (which are, for the logical positivists, the substance of 'observation language').

Apart from the verification principle, logical positivism is very similar to the philosophy articulated by Mill, Locke and Hume. In the UK, Alfred Ayer (1936) in his brilliant book *Language, Truth and Logic* popularized the ideas developed by the Vienna Circle. Both Popper and Wittgenstein visited the circle and were influenced by the discussions that took place, although both developed their own particular philosophical positions which were different in a number of crucial respects from logical positivism. In economics, Milton Friedman (1953), at Chicago, produced a very influential positivist essay: 'The methodology of positive economics'. This essay has had a significant impact on economic thought and especially on the thinking of the early writers in the theory of finance. There is no doubt that positivism has had a profound effect on the development of finance and accounting.

For many scholars in the social sciences and, in particular, in accounting, the positivists' appeal to value-free knowledge and their rejection of metaphysics coupled with a hard-nosed instrumentality has led to a polarization of debate and a degree of mutual incomprehension. In part, the issue of value-free knowledge is derived from the British Empiricist School, particularly Mill and Hume, who also held to the correspondence theory of truth (realism). Hume in particular argued that injunctive statements cannot be reduced to existential statements. In other words because I believe that X *ought* to be true I cannot infer that it *is* true.[3] This logical inference from the correspondence theory coupled with exclusion of synthetic a priori statements within empiricism led to the logical positivist position that metaphysical statements are meaningless.

At one level our examination of the alternatives to empiricism and realism has probed the weakness behind the 'value-free' debate. However, even accepting the correspondence theory of truth which entails that there is an objective domain of scientific enquiry which can legitimate beliefs, the question still remains as to what motivates the scientific enquiry in the first place. Clearly, scientists are motivated by what they deem, for whatever reason, to be important and it is at this level that the question of the values embedded within scientific research become important, even accepting for a moment the argument that scientific facts are value neutral.

We have already dealt with many of the central issues within positivism. However, it does present two further difficulties: first, concerning the validity of the verification principle itself and, second, the logical positivists approach to general laws and theoretical terms.

A law in the sciences (both natural and social) always makes some appeal to a universal generalization. The law of demand, for example, asserts that reducing the price of a commodity always increases its demand – note not 'sometimes' or 'usually' but *always*. Scientific theories, in particular, contain many of these laws and apart from testing all possible instances of the operation of that law its truth cannot be definitively established. So, in the case of laws the verification principle breaks down. Furthermore, a law cannot be extrapolated with certainty from any number of singular observations (induction) and, therefore, propositions containing laws expressing universal generalizations exist in a different logical realm, as they are neither analytically derivable from observation nor provable as contingent propositions.

Theoretical terms pose another severe difficulty for logical positivism and the verification principle. Take, for example, the word 'value'. This is a common word used in everyday discourse and most people would say that they have, at least, an intuitive notion of its meaning. However, when we attempt (following logical positivist principles) to define the meaning of the term 'value' in purely observational terms we run into difficulties. The term 'value' is both *under* and *over*defined observationally, which renders impossible a direct reduction of the term to observational language.

When we use a term such as 'value' we believe it to be meaningful with respect to a given asset even though no direct observation of that asset's value is being made. Most corporate assets, for example, would only be valued for accounting purposes at each year end and, even assuming that such valuations are objective observation statements concerning the assets, no direct observation of value is made when we use the term at intermediate points. In this sense the meaning of the term 'value' is observationally underdefined.

At another level the term 'value' subsumes a variety of different measurement systems. When valuing corporate assets, for instance, we have a wide choice of valuation bases: historic cost, replacement cost, realizable value, current cost (to name just a few of the possibilities). We would also have to include some definition of the amortization principle we deem appropriate. In this sense, the term 'value' is observationally overdefined in that any one of a number of observational criteria would give it meaning. It is for this reason that auditors can certify any number of different valuation bases as presenting a true and fair view of the affairs of a given company.

Therefore, at the heart of empiricism in general, and positivism in particular, lies a significant difficulty concerning the ontological status of theoretical terms which are non-observable and the language we use to describe those entities which has no direct observational reference. There have been two broad strategies for dealing with these difficulties: the first simply denies the distinction between observational and theoretical terms (that is, it embraces the strongest form of realism outlined above). The second accepts the distinction between theoretical and observational terms but argues that theoretical terms have no real observational meaning. In this view, theoretical terms are merely convenient analytical constructions of observational terms whose purpose is to help in the derivation of novel observational implications and predictions. This latter approach has become known as 'instrumentalism', although it is Kantian idealism in yet another disguise.

Like Kant, instrumentalists would argue that belief is grounded in observables. However, they also hold the view that theoretical language, and especially language that appeals to universal laws of behaviour, are purely mental artefacts or linguistic conventions which allow us to tie up observational terms into loose 'bundles of thought' which we can carry around while they serve their purpose and abandon when they do not. At the observational level, logical positivists argue through the verification principle for a correspondence theory of truth, while at the theoretical level they would argue that truth is what is convenient rather than what is coherent at either the individual or social level.

The point at issue here is that in the instrumentalist programme the realism of given theoretical terms is quite irrelevant in determining the validity of any theoretical constructions (what we term 'theories') derived from them or in which they are embedded. The purpose of theories is to enable us make predictions which can be verified. If they fail in that task then they can be abandoned once a more satisfactory alternative becomes available. The fact that a theory (or perhaps the assumptions which make it up) is unreal is quite irrelevant provided that it works in practice. This was the general thrust of Friedman's (1953) essay which provides an excellent exposition of the instrumentalist position. It is also easy to see why such a philosophical position was so attractive to economists. For the first time they could rebut the often repeated charge that their theories were unreal with the rejoinder, 'it doesn't matter!'

Prediction and explanation

The principal thrust of the instrumentalist position is the use of theories as convenient artefacts for the generation of observational predictions. Given any law-like generalization it is possible, by invoking certain qualifying assumptions, to produce a consequence or implication. If the argument is couched in conditional form (that is, *if* X is true *then* Y is true) a prediction is produced. The problem of course is that the qualifying assumptions must be such that the terms contained within the generalizations used to create the predictions are translated into implications that have clear observational reference.

Positivists usually regard explanation as a process of discovering the necessary law-like generalizations that 'cover' the singular instance to be explained. However, the process of explanation is not symmetrical with prediction. Laws that appear to have good predictive power often have poor explanatory power, and vice versa. This is usually because the qualifying assumptions required to yield an adequate prediction are invariably much more stringent than those required to match a covering law in explanation. Numerous, and quite trivial examples can be cited. Generalizations linking sex and pregnancy, clouds and rain, illiquidity and bankruptcy are often sufficient to produce explanations of particular observations of pregnancy, rain or bankruptcy but are insufficient to generate predictions of these phenomena. With more complex, scientific examples, the qualifying assumptions necessary to generate a prediction reduce its scope considerably and the same is true in reverse with explanation – the greater the number of qualifying assumptions the more specific the scope of the explanatory laws must be.

Explanation in finance and accounting is rarely a technical problem of identifying some particular law of behaviour as is usually the case with explanation in the natural sciences. Explanation in the social sciences invariably entails interpretation. We will discuss the interpretive element of the social science disciplines later in this chapter and in the chapter that follows.

Popper and falsificationism

Up until this point we have been particularly concerned to identify the crucial features and weaknesses of empiricism and its derivative – positivism. All the time, however, we have had to bear in mind the issue of realism in its varying degrees and the extent to which the realist–idealist distinction informs or clouds the issues discussed. At this point, however, it is appropriate to discuss a major attempt to sidestep at least one of the crucial difficulties of empiricism and positivism.

Karl Popper (1959) in his book *The Logic of Scientific Discovery* was particularly concerned with finding an unambiguous role for observation in the testing of theories and for eliminating the problem of induction. Popper's position entails realism with respect to theoretical entities and can be summarized as follows:

- Science progresses through the creation of conjectured hypotheses which in simple form can be described as one or more universal generalizations acting as premises in a logical argument from which conditional and refutable implications can be deductively drawn. The theoretical endeavour is to formulate theories in such a form that refutable instances can be derived from them. Theories, which do not admit refutation, are deemed non-scientific.
- The role of experimental science is to design suitably punishing tests which will, if at all possible, demonstrate the falsity of the theoretical implications and hence refute the theory concerned.
- A theory which survives a number of attempts to refute it is said to be 'well corroborated' by experiment. Note, however, that a theory can never be said to be proven; it can be well corroborated by the facts but refutation is always fatal. Theories progress accumulating 'truth value' through an almost Darwinian notion of the survival of the fittest. Absolute theoretical truth is an unobtainable ideal but is the ultimate aim of all science.

- Ad hoc modification of a theory as a tactic designed to remove the possibility of refutation is inadmissible. A theory which can never be falsified is useless.

Popper demarcates science from pseudo-science by the falsifiability of the theories produced and argues that science progresses through the attempt to replace refuted theories by ones which perform as well as their predecessors but which survive all refuting instances so far identified. Freudian psychology and Marx's 'scientific' view of history both fell victim to Popper's criterion as both can be used to defend any particular state of the world their protagonists may wish.

Note that Popper's falsificationism contains a strong prescriptive element and is particularly theory orientated. By following his principle of demarcation scientists can hope to produce better theories, that is, better descriptions 'of entities conjectured to be real'. Popper is not particularly concerned with whether or not this is how science really proceeds. As a methodology of science, falsificationism is strongly instrumentalist in tone and Popper showed no inclination to abandon his position in the face of the many refuting instances in the history of science. At one level Popper is advancing a criterion for how science should progress in the search for a better theory.

Popper's ideas have been extremely influential and, although he was not a logical positivist, his falsifiability criterion has some symmetry with the verification principle. It is a seductive notion that any statement which cannot be demonstrated to be false is meaningless and any theory which cannot be falsified is devoid of empirical content. It is true that Popper had surmounted one problem faced by the logical positivists, as any contrary case falsifies a universal law. If the sun fails to rise in the morning the universal generalization that it always will is indeed falsified, and presumably much else that we regard as important as well! Popper, however, did not manage to defeat the problem of theoretical terms – a fact which was pounced upon by his friends as well as his enemies.

Methodology as history

Popper's falsificationism came under sustained attack from one of his students – Imre Lakatos – and from Thomas Kuhn, both of whom rejected the possibility that a single observation could refute or confirm any given theory. The two planks of their argument were, first, that observation statements are intrinsically 'theory laden' and, second, that all theoretical predictions are so conditioned by qualifying assumptions that no test can uniquely determine whether a given theory is valid or whether one of its qualifying assumptions is at fault. In addition, they held the view that the meaning attributed to all observation terms is solely determined by their particular theoretical context.

In 1962 Kuhn published one of the most influential texts in the modern philosophy of science: *The Structure of Scientific Revolutions*. Kuhn's work is highly derivative and from a philosophical perspective relies heavily upon the work of Fleck who published his *Genesis and Development of a Scientific Fact* in 1935. Kuhn, however, took a particularly socio-historic view of science and was opposed to the view that a definitive, prescriptive methodology of science could ever be constructed. Kuhn viewed science as a process where 'paradigms' consisting of the corpus of theories and observations within a particular subject area pass through a definable 'life cycle'. During the life of a paradigm scientists engage in 'normal' science which consists of relatively minor problem-solving and experimentation. However, as the weight of anomalous evidence piles up, some scientists (particularly young ones!) will create a new theoretical structure with greater explanatory power and through an intellectual revolution supplant the old paradigm with the new. Once established, the new paradigm will itself settle into a 'normal' science stage until the time comes when it too becomes overburdened with anomalies (theoretical and empirical) and is replaced with something new.

Kuhn's methodology has little prescriptive content in that it does not help us decide between what is good and what is bad science and it gives us no rules for judging between competing hypotheses. At best, Kuhn has produced an interpretation of historical processes in the development of science but does not explain why it should happen in the way he describes rather than in any other. Kuhn's *Structure of Scientific Revolutions* offers a description of a process, which may be an approximation of what has happened in the past, but it has come under sustained criticism because it does not provide the necessary tools to either allow us to predict the future or to establish rules for demarcating good from bad science.

Lakatos's (1970) methodology contained a greater prescriptive element than Kuhn's. According to Lakatos, scientists commit themselves to a group of 'core terms', which they hold as irrefutable. An example of a core term in most of the economic and financial disciplines would be the notion of rationality – the idea that individuals are rational utility maximizers. Lakatos referred to the adherence to core terms as the 'negative heuristic' of the research programme. Throughout the life of the programme, researchers attempt to create a shell of ad hoc modifications consisting of confirmatory experimental evidence and theoretical adjustments to 'protect' the core from refutation. This process he referred to as the 'positive heuristic' of the research programme. Finally, a research programme is said to be progressing if the ad hoc modifications enhance its empirical content (that is, make it richer in predictive power) and degenerating if they reduce its empirical content. So, a research life cycle comprises innovation, progression and degeneration. But research programmes never die – they merely fade away. Some later finding or theoretical innovation may well reactivate a programme and renew interest in it within the scientific community.

The theory dependence of observation

The meta-theoretical presupposition which underpins the work of Kuhn and Lakatos is the notion that observation is overwhelmingly conditioned by theory. This nullifies any attempts to use empirical work as a final 'court of appeal' for any theory and, therefore, undermines any attempt to put theory construction and testing at the heart of the philosophy of science. But, to get to their position it is necessary to backtrack a little to 1959 and consider for the moment Hanson's (1958) *Patterns of Discovery*.

In that text Hanson coined the term 'theory laden' to express the idea that the language we use to describe observation is conditional upon a wide variety of linguistic rules and held theories. The fact that all linguistic terms depend, to a certain extent, for their meaning on the rules of the language concerned and on a variety of implicit theoretical assumptions is not surprising. What is surprising is the view held by Kuhn and Lakatos that observation is so completely theory dependent that the distinction between theory and observation is rendered meaningless. Indeed, both argued that any methodology of scientific development is intrinsically flawed if it presupposes that science proceeds through theory construction and experimental testing (by verification or falsification). Both challenged any methodological dependency upon experimental results, which they argued are conditioned by the theoretical presuppositions of the observer. We can never tell, according to them, whether any given observation is refuting a particular theory or the particular theoretical presuppositions of the observer.

The interesting point to note about Kuhn's concept of paradigm is that different paradigms represent quite separate and largely incommensurable ways of viewing the world. Scientists' interpretations of the empirical world are, for Kuhn, intensely theory (or rather 'paradigm') laden. Interpretations of reality, indeed the very meaning imputed to reality, change when one paradigm overthrows another. The revolution to which Kuhn alluded in the title of his book is not just a revolution in the range of possible explanations of a given reality, but a fundamental shift in the way scientists perceive that reality.

The problem of the theory dependence of observation has taken its most extreme form in the 'meaning variance hypothesis' that proposes that as we change a theory so all of the meanings attached to any related observation also change.

Our observation of reality and the meaning we attach to that observation is dependent upon our intellectual constructs (or theories). However, the meaning variance hypothesis can be shown to produce a paradox. If we accept that any term changes its meaning given a different theoretical context, then we would not expect to be able to use a given observation statement in more than one competing theory. Put another way, we would never be able to use an observation statement to test the rival claims of conflicting theories. This is a rather uncomfortable consequence as well as apparently conflicting with the history and practice of science.

Often, scientists are able to distinguish between the raw data of experiment (where objectivity can be checked by replication) and the admittedly fallible and conditional language we use to interpret that reality. Indeed, the history of science gives many examples of observation reports which have survived cultures and changes in explanation and theory. One example of this was the planetary and stellar observations made by Persian astronomers 1000 years before Christ. Their observations were regarded as definitive up until the eighteenth century. Scientists have used these observations to adjudicate between one theory and another, and have been able to interpret their meaning for theory changes. In the field of finance, price data observations support many different and largely incommensurate theories of the nature of the market and, in particular, the ability of such share price data to predict future price data and hence returns. It may be objected that price itself is a theory laden concept – which it is – however, when we talk about share price data what we are referring to is the reports of share prices which, once posted, become part of a historical record. It is this historical record which becomes the objective 'raw data' for research and the reading of that data can be conducted with a high degree of objectivity.[4] What is conjectural, however, is the theoretical meaning that is attached to that data not the verisimilitude of the data itself.

As you reflect on this debate and ponder the linkages between theory and observation it is worth noting that we are dealing with the ontological location of reality and the location of truth. Popper was an empirical realist who believed in the possibility of objective knowledge at the observational and the theoretical level of discourse. Lakatos and Kuhn proposed a meta-theoretical reality where theories are socially constructed by the community of relevant scholars although Lakatos was a realist as far as observables were concerned, and Kuhn[5] was not even prepared to concede that.

A critique of Kuhn's relativism

The writings of Kuhn and in particular those of Paul Feyerabend present a strong form of theoretical relativism which we can summarize as follows:

- All observation statements are theory laden and thus, in contradiction to Popper, provisional.
- Theory development is a competitive social process and is embedded within the social structure of science.
- Theories or paradigms are more or less internally coherent within the terms of the language in which they are constructed but represent incommensurable ways of describing reality (the meaning variance hypothesis).

However, Kuhn did not go as far as Feyerabend (1970) whose theoretical relativism led him to argue that there is no way of deciding which competing theory is better except in terms of its political success. In science, he argued, 'anything goes' and as scientific descriptions of reality medical science and witchcraft are of equal value.

The theory dependence argument assumes that reality subsists within the object, which is impenetrable because observation is theoretically determined, and Kuhn and Feyerabend would argue that theories are socially constructed. The circle has thus returned us to the idealism of Berkeley whom we have discussed before. However, the argument is problematic because as we move from observation to theory, and back again, and from theory to theory we discover rules which form a type of 'linking language' which allow us to translate from one to another. In both the social and natural sciences, logic and mathematics often provide the bridge. Kuhn was mistaken in believing that paradigmatic revolutions completely restructure the language of the science concerned – if that had been the case scientists embedded within the Newtonian 'paradigm' would have been completely unable to understand

Einstein's papers on relativity when they were published. However, even within its own terms this form of theoretical relativity ignores the fact that observation is itself a social phenomenon where groups of scientists confirm observation reports through replication.

Replication is a well-known scientific strategy both in the natural and social sciences. By replication, observational claims are tested sometimes using the same control conditions and sometimes others. This strategy sifts out those claims which are spurious and should not be admitted into the accepted canon of scientific knowledge. For example, in 1990 two chemists, Fleischman and Pons, reported that they had achieved nuclear fusion at room temperature – this was a novel discovery and if true would have revolutionized nuclear physics and the electricity generation-industry. The scientific community engaged in a systematic attempt using the reported experimental conditions to replicate their results. They failed and cold-fusion has been consigned to the scientific waste basket entitled 'embarrassing mistakes'. In finance, in the late 1980s a number of papers cast doubt upon the prevailing academic orthodoxy that capital markets are information efficient. Gradually papers emerged reporting anomalies such as seasonal, day of the week and small-firm effects. These experiments were repeated using different data-sets and in different countries, and have been confirmed to the satisfaction of most scholars working in the field.

In the natural sciences and the social sciences the reality which subsists within objects can be argued to be the product of collective observation and can become so robust in its meaning that it supports more than one theoretical structure. Observations of share price data by many different researchers often working with the same databases have been used to support different theories of price behaviour – some supporting efficiency models and others supporting chart-based prediction techniques.

Postmodernism and post-structuralism[6]

In recent years there has been an attempt by many social and political thinkers to draw a line under what they term 'modernity' which, they argue, is the era of time which commenced with the Enlightenment and came to its apotheosis with the Holocaust in Nazi Germany. As a philosophical tradition, postmodernism traces its roots to the German critical-philosopher, Freidrich Nietzsche, and the founder of modern existentialism, Martin Heidegger. However, as a movement it has been profoundly influenced by architecture, art and linguistics. More recently, postmodern philosophers have drawn inspiration from the attacks on conventional epistemology by the neo-pragmatist Richard Rorty, who argues that philosophy has no privileged access to knowledge, nor is it a superior way of arguing but it is simply another way in which people talk to one another.

Postmodernists argue that the flowering of the sciences during the Enlightenment and the advancement of technology that followed was coercive in that it not only led to a greater understanding of the world but it also led to the creation of more powerful instruments for individual and social control. Postmodernists have pointed to the contradictions of meaning and the absurdities which modernism has generated, and in particular they denounce the objectification of language, relationships and society. There is now a substantial body of writing within this tradition much of which is difficult to characterize. However, many would maintain, that the postmodernism and the post-structuralism of philosophers such as Foucault and Derrida is a form of unconstrained relativism, although postmodernists reject this along with the charges of nihilism or scepticism.

Derrida argues that there is no absolute foundation for beliefs and that no belief is more fundamental than any other. In this, he is making the same point that Paul Feyerabend made in his claim that all theories are equally valuable (or valueless) and for Derrida the maxim 'anything goes' holds for what we choose to believe. Post-structuralism, the term given to the French school of linguistic philosophy which encompasses the work of Michel Foucault and Jacques Derrida, argues that truth is linguistically constructed within a particular cultural discourse. For Derrida, meaning subsists in the reading and not in the intentions of the author. Deconstruction is a tool to subvert the text and to show that the meaning, which is signified, can be reinterpreted in ways that subvert the intention of the author. More generally, deconstruction is now seen as a 'method' where the critic assumes the position proposed by the subject of the criticism and then within its own terms proceeds to subvert the intended message.

This is a relativist position in that the meaning, which is imputed by the reader, is socially and culturally determined, and that the product of deconstruction succeeds in subverting the surface meaning of the text within the mind of the reader. In its turn, any reading of the text itself can be deconstructed and an endless fabric of alternatives created. Within its own terms, postmodern criticism rejects any attempt at refutation either empirically (by pointing to the facts) or analytically (by the attack of logic). Both, it is argued, fundamentally hinge on the artificial distinctions that pervade philosophy and modernity. The problem that this presents is that we are soon forced to abandon any critical standards and confront an infinite regress of thought with no possibility of achieving any knowledge that can form the basis for future progress.

In some respects, postmodernism is a rebellion against philosophical debates about the nature of knowledge, which as we have already suggested, are incapable of resolution. However, postmodernists do not provide any answers – they would argue there are none – but rather they privilege critical discourse as the only alternative open to us. Whatever one thinks of postmodernism as a philosophical position it is an interesting demonstration of the meaning variance hypothesis where the incommensurable paradigms of conventional and postmodern philosophy indeed appear incomprehensible to proponents from the other camp. However, we have already given some clues as to how its philosophical position can be attacked. Nevertheless, one of the most attractive aspects of postmodernism is that it is an abundant source of frivolity and humour, and although, as we have argued before, extreme relativism leads to absurdity, it has put the fun back into philosophy!

The dominant methodology of the financial disciplines

Our previous discussion has emphasized the difficulty of constructing a methodology for scientific development based upon theory construction and testing. However, within the financial disciplines, and particularly the field of finance itself, a dominant methodology has emerged. Much of this methodology is implicit rather than explicit within the writings of scholars within the area but, because criticism and historical analysis of the literature of any discipline is an important component of research, it is important to establish that set of methodological principles which appears to form the dominant view of how research should be conducted in the financial disciplines.

Certain key philosophical threads appear in this reconstruction of what we argue is the dominant methodology of the financial disciplines. First, it is empiricist in nature and accepts the distinction between theoretical and empirical domains of discovery. In this respect there appears to be an implicit acceptance of the 'double language model' discussed above. There also appears to be a recognition of the distinct existence of 'models' as abstract theoretical descriptions of reality which are developed through an exhaustive process of refinement and validation. In this respect, therefore, the dominant methodology is Lakatosian but where the focus is on the development of research programmes based upon models rather than theories.

The key to what we argue is the dominant methodology lies in the nature of assumptions and in the linkage between observation and theoretical terms. In a previous section we argued that observational data can be linked to theoretical classes through a 'linking language' which gives meaning to that data in terms of the theories concerned. There are, for any particular attested observational data, a number of inevitably ambiguous linkages that can be created to different theoretical terms. This reflects the well-known fact that observational data can take on radically different interpretations from different theoretical standpoints even though different scientists with those different standpoints may well agree or the fundamental veracity of the data itself.

We now turn our attention to how financial disciplines have progressed over time. The essence of this development starts in a way similar to that proposed by Lakatos except that in the methodology we propose here the negative heuristic consists initially of a theoretical model of behaviour (individual or social) which, in its preliminary form, is invariably specified in terms of a list of assumptions representing limiting behaviour. Indeed, an assumption in this type of model can be characterized as a universal generalization representing, along a single definable vector, extreme behaviour.

Certain of the assumptions will be regarded as crucial to the status of the model (for example, rational utility maximization across risk and return within capital asset pricing). Others will be regarded as purely instruments for the necessary delivery of implications and, as such, will be regarded as less crucial for the status of the model and revisable in the light of empirical research.

It appears that the notion of the 'model' as an abstraction of reality is a more meaningful concept for practising researchers to handle than the notion of theory. In the financial disciplines, as in the natural sciences, the model is central to the development of any research programme, and it is evident in the literature of these various disciplines that schools of researchers develop around particular 'primary' or 'core' models and later subdivide into schools associated with examining the implications and variations of particular assumptions.

For this primary model to succeed as the core of a research programme it must possess a certain number of crucial characteristics:

- It must be possible to generate theoretical implications from which observational predictions can be drawn. These observational predictions should permit as well-targeted tests as possible. The more successful a model is at generating testable implications the greater its theoretical credibility.
- The assumptions within the model should be internally consistent in the logical sense and as simple as the logical integrity of the model will permit. This belief in the importance of logical rigour within arguments has been argued (Harre, 1986) to be an important rhetorical device in the construction of the academic literature. We will return to the importance of logic and its role within the literature in a later chapter.
- The model should be theoretically commensurate with any known empirical facts within its domain. Invariably, the creation of a new theoretical model will entail changes in the 'exchange syntax' through which established observational 'facts' are interpreted. In addition, we would expect these interpretations to change as a model develops.
- The model's theoretical scope is defined by the model and its attendant set of explanatory and predictive implications. So, within the finance literature the capital asset pricing model, the Black and Scholes's option pricing model and the arbitrage pricing model each form the core of an individual research programme.
- The combination of a set of related models (related in the sense that they cover the same empirical domain) form, with the relevant observation reports, the literary domain of a particular research programme. Those who control this literature will have a range of both local (domain specific) and general (methodological) criteria for assessing new contributions. A mapping of any research literature can be constructed as an expanding network of theoretical and observational connections where provisional and temporary linkages of meaning are made via the 'exchange syntax'.

From the initial stage of model formulation researchers described above, appear to undertake the following activities:

- They will seek internal economy within the core model attempting, as they do so, to reformulate it in terms of the minimal set of assumptions required to yield the same set of implications (this is sometimes referred to as the application of Occam's Razor or the Law of Parsimony in Logical Inference).

- Empirical research will be conducted to test the primary implications of the model and the range of divergence. Such tests will be rarely fatal to the model but can be highly confirmatory. The impact of falsifying tests will weaken the status of the model itself but may speed up the generation of alternatives.
- Theoretical researchers will attempt to create competing models of the same or greater scope but relying on fewer assumptions or on assumptions which make weaker behavioural claims. This we would equate with the 'positive heuristic' of Lakatos's Methodology of Research programmes.
- Researchers will attempt to formalize the relationships between assumptions to generate indirect areas of implication. For example, the interconnection between informational efficiency, information costs and the bid–ask spread (transactions costs) has become a fruitful area of research.

Through time, by adopting these strategies a subject network will form in the literature with 'nodes' where major assumption shifts have occurred or particular observational data of importance in the development of the literature have been discovered. Major nodes in a literature net occur when alternative models are generated from modified assumption sets. From these nodes, meaning linkages will be created (via the exchange syntax discussed above) radiating to observational data positioned throughout the network. A literature reconstruction, at any point in time will only provide a snapshot of the agreed network of theory – observation meanings existing at any point in time. At the lowest level, the meaning attached to particular observation data reports may appear to be very stable although in other cases there may be considerable divergences on the significance attached to such reports for different models existing in the literature.

Finally, the question arises as to how we determine the state of health of particular research programmes. There are a number of key indicators: the first, and most obvious, consists of a simple headcount of the number of active researchers publishing within a particular research programme. This gives a straightforward indication of the degree of commitment to the programme and the point it has arrived at in its life cycle. Second, individual research programmes become moribund when:

- the process of exploration of all of the assumptions within the model has been worked through, Occam's Razor has been applied to the full, and
- all linkages have been explored and the theoretical and empirical anomalies exposed and discussed.

Although no one can be sure that a programme has reached this stage, a consensus will materialize in the scientific community and the number of research papers relying on that model will dwindle away. Third, new models covering the same empirical domain will be developed but with greater scope (assuming more vectors of reality) and greater explanatory and predictive power.

Summary

In this chapter, we have considered a number of issues relating to the methodology of research in the financial disciplines. At some length, we have considered the realist and idealist positions in philosophy and how they have influenced the positivist, post-empiricist and critical theory schools, all of which have had a considerable influence upon research in the financial disciplines. In one sense our approach has been reductionist in that we have attempted to argue that many of the positions discussed in the literature of philosophy and the social sciences can be reduced two pairs of polar alternatives: empiricism and rationalism and, realism and idealism. As you will have discerned we have proposed the view that little is new within philosophy and that the methodological position that the researcher adopts is one of choice. However, whichever position is chosen leads to certain methodological implications which we will explore in subsequent chapters.

Having described the variety of epistemological and ontological positions which active researchers may adopt, it is legitimate to ask if we as scholars advocate any agreed positions. Proudly, we answer no to that question because, although we take varying positions on many of the debates discussed above, we believe that a plurality of methodologies is possible and each can lead to fruitful research. However, we would argue that rational debate and enquiry and the sensible use of evidence in the resolution of competing truth claims is most likely to lead to the advancement of knowledge, although every step in the research process is problematic and fallible. But that is as far as we would be prepared to go.

Notes

1   The obvious problem is what happens when there is no perceiving mind. Does the object of perception cease to exist? No, said Berkeley, there is always a perceiving mind – namely God. This led to a key idea in Christian philosophy that if God ceased to think about us then we would cease to exist. The following limerick expresses the idea nicely: There was a young man who said 'God / Must think it exceedingly odd/ If he finds that the tree/ Continues to be/ When there is no one about in the quad.' Reply: 'Dear Sir:/ Your astonishment's odd:/ I am always about in the quad/ And that's why the tree / Continues to be/ While observed by Yours faithfully, God'.
2   The term 'positivism' was first used by the social philosopher Auguste Comte (1798–1857) and, although his philosophical position was heavily influenced by the empiricism of John Stuart Mill and in particular the success of Newtonian mechanics, it was not developed into a distinctive epistemic theory. When positivism is used as a pejorative term it is usually logical positivism which is being attacked.
3   This is usually referred to as 'Hume's fork'.
4   This does not deny the need for data checking and, in the case of star maps and the positions of planets, Edmund Halley, the first Astronomer Royal, took much of the old data and carefully corrected it using the new measuring instruments which were then available. With share prices, the errors take another form in that the share price is simply wrongly reported. This is far less of a problem than it once was given the reduced reliance on manual transcription in modern markets.
5   Some have attempted an ex-post defence of Kuhn but it is quite clear from the *Structure of Scientific Revolutions* (Kuhn 1962) and his subsequent revisions that he did argue for

the incommensurability of paradigms. However, it is also fair to say that Kuhn has not fully articulated what the term 'paradigm' means and as Putnam and others have pointed out there are at least 23 discernible definitions in *Structure*.

6   Postmodernism is a movement with philosophical implications; post-structuralism is the antithesis of the French structuralist movement which made claims to a scientific model of language.

2

Alternative philosophies of accounting research

In the previous chapter we started by discussing the philosophy of science in general, without being too specific about the type of science in question, but we finished with a discussion of the dominant methodology of the financial disciplines. The term 'financial disciplines' was used to include both accounting and finance research. In this chapter, we will discuss alternative philosophies in accounting research. Here, we use the term 'accounting' deliberately, as the approaches which we will discuss were raised first in management accounting research and then also applied to financial accounting, but until recently have had limited impact on research in finance. This is not to say that these alternative approaches have, in any way, replaced the dominant methodology described in Chapter 1, but rather that there are sizeable groups of researchers who use them in accounting research.

A core issue raised in Chapter 1 was whether our discussion of the philosophy of science can be applied to social sciences as well as the natural sciences. An influential critique levelled against the application to the social (or human sciences) of methodology appropriate to the natural sciences was made by Habermas, a leading member of the Frankfurt Institute for Social Policy, which was strongly influenced by the idealism of Hegel and Marxist critical theory.

The root of this critique lies in what has become known as the 'hermeneutic circle'. Hermeneutics originated as a theological term concerning the interpretation of the spiritual truth of religious writing (most notably the Bible). Dilthey, a German philosopher-historian, transported the concept into social philosophy relating it to the interpretation of intentional human behaviour, language and institutions. The hermeneutic circle raises the problem of how we can use the language and conceptual frameworks of our own culture to understand the meanings and interpretations of a different culture and even other individuals and groups within our own culture.

Habermas, *inter alia*, argued that the problem of the hermeneutic circle arises particularly in the social sciences. Indeed, he takes a positivist and instrumentalist approach to natural science, believing that it is the technical value of natural science that is its guarantor of objectivity. However, as far as the social sciences are concerned he argues:

- Data cannot be separated from theory and facts can be reconstructed in the light of theory.
- Theories in the natural sciences are constructed from 'models' of reality, while in the social sciences theories mimic facts and are judged good or bad by the extent to which they allow us to understand and interpret meaning.
- Unlike the essentially external law-like relationships of the natural sciences, social laws relate to 'internal' mental states and can be imposed by the observer.
- The language of the social sciences is malleable, permitting a wide diversity of meaning.
- Facts in the natural sciences are independent of meaning; meanings are the facts of the social sciences.

You may notice that there are strong echoes of the 'theory dependence of observation' in the above list. However, Habermas has identified a substantial problem which does not affect the natural sciences to the same degree as the social sciences. In the natural sciences, the interplay between the subjective and objective does not relate to the world observed but, rather, to the observer. In the social sciences this interplay is two sided.

The articulation of those beliefs and values through language is imbued with meaning at one level but forms part of the objective world at another. The science of linguistics, for example, is devoted to the analysis of language. The sphere of action, is unambiguously in the objective world in that it can be measured in both degree and kind. But action stimulates perception which, like language, straddles both the objective and the subjective world. The critical theory approach attempts to understand the nature and meaning of human action in the context of, and as a contribution towards, social evolution.

In Habermas's view, social evolution emerges from the dialectical interplay between instrumental and communicative action. Through instrumental action individuals attempt to manipulate their environment in order to satisfy their needs and wants, and through communicative action they attempt to control their world through the institutionalization of rules and norms. Both technical development and progress towards less repressive forms of social interaction and the tendency towards greater autonomy in these two dimensions help create a third: social evolution.

An interesting development of this idea has appeared in the writings of George Soros who studied at the London School of Economics and was profoundly influenced by Popper and, more recently, by Giddens. However, Soros's own ideas and especially his concept of reflexivity in social knowledge owes much to the notion of the hermeneutic circle. To quote:

> the achievements of the social sciences do not compare well with those of the natural sciences ... the independence of the objective criterion – namely, the facts – is impaired. [Social] Facts can be influenced by forming beliefs or propounding theories about them. This is true not only for the participants but also the scientists. Reflexivity implies a short circuit

between statements and facts, and that short circuit is available to scientists as well as participants.

(Soros, 2000: 44)

A new academic literature has developed in accounting exploiting the critical theory approach, although up until this time much of that literature has been derivative rather than novel, relying on observation reports where the researcher attempts to comprehend the underlying logic of the subject's political, social and economic position. Habermas's writing is broadly idealist and is not far removed at the methodological (as opposed to the sociological) level from the position of the post-empiricists. It does, however, show the limits of science when applied to the human sphere and the limits of interpretation through the hermeneutic circle.

Habermas raises problems which have become a major issue for accounting researchers and together with other issues such as the nature of social reality, the role of the researcher and the social nature of the research process, have shaped alternative approaches to accounting research. To explore the nature of these alternative approaches we will trace how these issues came to be raised over the years.

In this chapter we will first explore differences between the dominant scientific method in accounting research and the alternative naturalistic approach. We will then identify underlying assumptions about the nature of the subject being researched, which shape the different methodological approaches. This leads us to a taxonomy of accounting research and to a discussion of three types of research: mainstream, interpretive and critical. We then look at some alternative dimensions of the research taxonomy and finish with a discussion of the social nature of the research process. In the summary of the chapter we call for a plurality of methodological approaches in accounting (and finance) research.

Scientific methods vs naturalistic methods

As will be pointed out in later chapters, the 1970s was a period of rapid growth and development in accounting research. Much of the impetus for this research had been the application of financial economics to accounting problems and, as such, the researchers were using the methods commonly used in economics. However, little explicit consideration was given to the methodology of accounting research. But in 1979 the American Accounting Association published a report titled *Empirical Research in Accounting: A Methodological Viewpoint* (see Abdel-khalik and Ajinkya, 1979). This report explored alternative methodological approaches (including naturalistic modes of research – see below), but concluded that scientific method should be the 'ideal' or preferred method of accounting research.

As *argued in this report*, scientific method starts from a well-formulated theory, usually derived from a review of the previous academic literature and expressed in the form of a mathematical model. This theory is used to formulate hypotheses which express relationships between sets of dependent and independent variables. A highly structured and predetermined set of procedures are then used to collect data, which is analysed by mathematical and statistical techniques, and almost inevitably validates the hypothesis.[1] The final stage is to generalize the results. Thus, the approach is based on abstraction, reductionism and statistical methods.

It may be argued that such a picture of scientific method is overly simplistic, for many of the reasons discussed in the previous chapter. However, it seems to represent the view of scientific method that was then, and still remains, widely accepted in mainstream accounting research.

Referring to the papers then being published in the *Accounting Review* and the *Journal of Accounting Research*, the foreword to Abdel-khalik and Ajinkya's (1979) report comments, 'Heavy use of mathematical notation, reliance on complex statistical methodologies and attention to intellectually tractable problems at the expense of direct realism are all characteristic of the bulk of the papers published in these journals' (ibid.: vii). Abdel-khalik and Ajinkya went on to argue that: 'In principle, we prefer the formal structure of the scientific method as the goal for researchers in accounting. [But] infeasibility and intractability may sometimes make it difficult to use that structure' (ibid.: 21). Nevertheless, for them, scientific method remains the most desirable approach – anything else being a 'poor' approximation to this ideal.

This conclusion, however, was challenged by Tomkins and Groves (1983). They believed that scientific methods have their place, but it should not be a privileged place. Other methods may be more appropriate for certain kinds of research, including many types of accounting research. For example, they argued that naturalistic research methods are more appropriate for studying the everyday behaviour of accountants. Such research would use field study methods, to study accounting in its natural settings, to explore the interactions with its broader organizational and social context. Researchers would then develop holistic theories to interpret day-to-day accounting practices in the context of the wider social systems of which they are part. In contrast to scientific method, which as pointed out above is based on abstraction, reductionism and statistical methods, naturalistic methods are based on realism, holism and analytical method.

Tomkins and Groves (1983) were careful to distinguish the use of the term 'naturalistic', in the sense of studying accounting in its natural setting, from the term 'naturalism', which Dilthey and others have used to mean quite the opposite – that is, the importing of the methods of the natural sciences into the social sciences (ibid.: 362).

The primary object of Tomkins and Groves's paper was to point out that the selection of the most appropriate research methodology is dependent on the nature of the phenomenon being researched. In particular, the assumptions which the researcher holds regarding the nature of the phenomenon's reality (ontology), will affect the way in which knowledge can be gained about that phenomenon (epistemology), and this in turn affects the process through which research can be conducted (methodology). Consequently, the selection of an appropriate research methodology cannot be done in isolation of a consideration of the ontological and epistemological assumptions which underpin the research in question. Also, it is relevant to note that methodology is concerned with the *process of doing research* and, as such, it has both ontological and epistemological dimensions. Furthermore, it is important to distinguish methodology from methods. The latter are the particular techniques used in the research. In this sense, statistical techniques are methods, not a methodology; although their use in a particular research process, with its implicit ontological and epistemological assumptions, is a methodology.[2]

Thus, in considering different methodological approaches we need to begin by looking at different ontological assumptions. Tomkins and Groves draw on the sixfold classification of the social world developed by Morgan and Smircich (1980). This provides the six fundamental ontological assumptions set out in Table 2.1 to which we have attached the classical descriptions introduced in the last chapter. Each of these assumptions can be associated with particular schools of thought in the social sciences, and has implications for the methodological approaches that we might use in accounting research. The nature of each of these assumptions is briefly outlined in the next section.

Ontological assumptions

As indicated above, Table 2.1 identifies six different ontological assumptions; each being associated with particular schools of thought in the social sciences. Another way of looking at these six assumptions is to regard them as six alternative ways of viewing the world, with (1) reality as a concrete structure being the most objective and (6) reality as a projection of human imagination being the most subjective. The other intermediate assumptions can then be regarded as points on an objective–subjective continuum. The more mainstream accounting researcher who uses the 'scientific method' described above will probably feel most comfortable with the objective end of the continuum, but as reality becomes more subjective we are likely to need naturalistic research methods.

(1) *Reality as concrete structure*: at this end of the continuum, the reality of the external world is taken for granted and is characterized by objective 'facts' about the world which can be discovered and then defined by an appropriate set of variables and tied together by general laws. The discovery of these laws is

TABLE 2.1 Six ontological assumptions

---

1 Reality as a concrete structure (naive realism)
2 Reality as a concrete process (transcendental realism)
3 Reality as a contextual field of information (contextual relativism)
4 Reality as a symbolic discourse (transcendental idealism [Kant])
5 Reality as a social construction (social constructionism [socially mediated idealism])
6 Reality as a projection of human imagination (idealism [Berkeley])

Source: Morgan and Smircich, 1980: 492

perceived to be the real object of scientific research, although not all researchers necessarily perceive these laws as anything more than instrumental conveniences (see Friedman, 1953). Here, we have a considerable overlap with the way in which the physical world might be viewed in physics and chemistry. Thus, the method of scientific research, as used in the physical sciences, is appropriate if the social world is characterized by this ontological assumption.

(2) *Reality as concrete process*: moving away slightly from reality as a concrete structure, we relax the assumption that reality is embedded within physical or social objects characterized by stable relationships. Instead reality is assumed to subsist within the relationships and general laws which describe how things change. This could be illustrated by the notions of evolution and 'survival of the fittest' in biology. In terms of accounting research, this takes us away from the closed systems view, characterized by concrete structures, to a more open systems view of the world. But we are still clearly within the mainstream of accounting research where scientific method can be applied.

(3) *Reality as contextual field of information*: in contrast to the predictable and contingent relations in concrete processes, we now acknowledge that human beings are continually processing information, learning and adapting to their environment. As a result, the artificial distinction between the 'subject' and the 'environment' is dropped, and replaced with a more cybernetic perspective. In accounting research this might involve modelling the interconnections between the environment and, say, accounting practices. Such a model would be assumed to be capable of simulating (possibly probabilistically) the behaviour of the constituent parts of the system. Again, it should be obvious, that we have not moved very far from the assumptions of mainstream accounting research. But with the next three ontological assumptions we will be in rather different territory.

(4) *Reality as symbolic discourse*: we now see the world as comprising human actors who make sense of their reality through a process of social interaction and negotiation, which is made possible through the shared meanings and norms they attach to people, things and situations. As such, reality is not a set of rules per se, but is embedded in the meanings and norms which are created through individual experiences of events and situations, and then shared through social interaction. Although these meanings and norms can be changed at any time, they can also be quite stable over time and thereby come to structure social activity. These meanings and norms are, therefore, the reality of social research and such an approach can be used to study the role of accounting in giving meanings to organizational activity, providing norms of behaviour and structuring day-to-day social practices in organizations and society. Here we can see a need for naturalistic research methods, because scientific method becomes inapplicable as the notion of providing generalizations is problematic when everything depends on subjective meanings.

(5) *Reality as social construction*: whereas in the previous category it is the meanings and norms which structure the social practices of individual human actors, here the social world is re-created by the actors with every encounter, and reality is the *accomplishment of individual sense-making*. Although Tomkins and Groves, following Morgan and Smircich, refer to this category as 'social construction', it might be better termed 'individual construction'. The term 'social construction of reality' is sometimes used for all the subjectivist approaches, to distinguish them from the assumption of an independent reality which is assumed by the more objectivist approaches. In the previous category we were concerned with the meanings and norms which comprise social structures and thereby shape individual actions. Here, it is the social actions which are the focus of the research, and researchers are concerned with *the procedures* through which the individual actors make sense of 'what is going on'. As such, multiple realities are possible, and researchers are concerned with how individuals make sense of their everyday existence. Accounting researchers could, for instance, seek to establish how individual actors make sense of accounting information they receive (for example, Boland, 1993).

(6) *Reality as projection of human imagination*: this is the extreme subjectivist position in which reality exists only in the individual consciousness that is, in human imagination. This position was developed from the ideas of Berkeley and more latterly the German philosopher, Edmund Husserl, who wanted to lift the level of enquiry to the consciousness of the individual thinker. As such, this approach does not allow the possibility of 'empirical' research, but would require the accounting researcher to try to capture the imagined events of the practitioners' world. However, in a slightly less extreme form it might be argued that the social world is so complex that all a researcher can do is seek to understand people's feelings as human beings. This is similar to the previous category, but places more emphasis on individual feelings. Here we might see some possibility for accounting research which explores the depth of feeling of individual actors as they are confronted with the complexity of their reactions to accounting information.

This brief outline of the range of ontological assumptions indicates the issues which are ignored by the simplistic belief that the so-called 'scientific method', as described by Abdel-khalik and Ajinkya or, indeed, some variation of the approach in the last chapter, is the ideal for, and should be the goal of, accounting research. Under certain ontological assumptions scientific method could be quite appropriate. But it is clearly inappropriate for research based on other ontological assumptions. In the more subjectivist research other ways of gaining knowledge about the subject of the research are needed. This is where Tomkins and Groves argue that naturalistic methods are required. But even here, there are a range of possibilities and the appropriate research methods need to reflect the particular ontological assumptions of the researcher. But for present purposes it is sufficient simply to recognize that ontological assumptions need to be considered in discussing research methodology. In the next section we will use the range of ontological assumptions outlined above to provide the basis for a classification of different types of accounting research.

Taxonomy of accounting research

In the previous section we outlined six ontological assumptions, ranging from the objective to the subjective, and indicated that they would give rises to quite different types of accounting research. Hopper and Powell (1985) used a subjective–objective continuum as one dimension of their taxonomy of accounting research. They added to this continuum another dimension, representing the stance which researchers adopt towards the society they are researching, and produced a four-way classification, as we will see later in Figure 2.1. But first we need to explain how they constructed their subjective–objective continuum.

Hopper and Powell drew on the earlier work of Burrell and Morgan (1979) who had produced a classification of organizational research. Burrell and Morgan used two independent dimensions: the nature of social sciences and the nature of society. As Hopper and Powell explain (1985: 431), the social science dimension consists of four distinct but related elements: assumptions about ontology, epistemology, human nature and methodology. As illustrated in Table 2.2, each of these elements is itself a continuum, but Burrell and Morgan collapsed them into the single subjective–objective continuum.

In the previous section, we described ontological assumptions ranging from individual consciousness where reality exists in the mind of the individual, to concrete construction where there is an external reality which is independent of the observer. We also mentioned that different methods of gaining knowledge may be needed for the different ontological assumptions – in other words, there is also an epistemological dimension. This ranges from interpretation when the knowledge of the world is essentially of a personal nature, to observation when there is a concrete external world.

Burrell and Morgan added assumptions about human nature to ontology and epistemology. At one extreme individuals are regarded as possessing free will and autonomy of action. At the other, their actions and their behaviour are completely determined by their environment.

These three sets of assumptions have direct methodological implications. As we argued in the previous section, when reality is concrete and objective, and human

TABLE 2.2 Burrell and Morgan's social science dimension

Ontology:	individual consciousness	....	concrete construction
Epistemology:	interpretation	....	observation
Human nature:	free will	....	determinism
Methodology:	hermeneutics	....	scientific method
Collapsed to:	subjective	....	objective

behaviour is deterministic, knowledge is gained through observation and, so, scientific method will be appropriate. But where reality is grounded in subjective experiences and individuals possess free will, knowledge is gained through interpretation, and hermeneutical methods are needed. As mentioned earlier, the term 'hermeneutics' has its origins in the interpretation of biblical texts, but it can be applied to social research methods which seek to interpret the subjective experiences of individual social actors.

Following the earlier work of Burrell and Morgan, Hopper and Powell collapsed the four dimensions of ontology, epistemology, human nature and methodology, into a single subjective–objective continuum which they used to characterize the range of approaches to the social sciences. They explicitly recognized, however, that the four dimensions are analytically distinct, but collapsing them into a single dimension simplifies the discussion. They then added a second dimension, representing the range of approaches which researchers take towards society. At one extreme, researchers may be concerned with *regulation* and the creation of order in society; explaining how society is held together. At the other extreme, researchers are interested in conflicts and inequalities in society, and are concerned with the potential for *radical change*. Again, this is a continuum, not a dichotomy. In between the two extremes, there are intermediate positions with researchers interested in, say, ordered change, or in facilitating discussions about directions of change. By combining the two continua, Hopper and Powell obtained the taxonomy of accounting research set out in Figure 2.1.

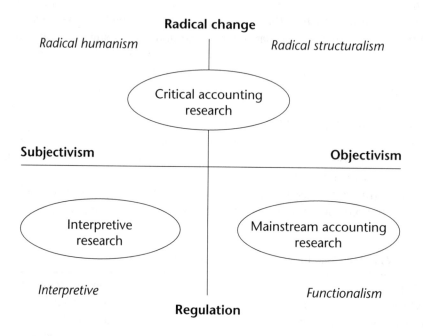

FIGURE 2.1 Hopper and Powell's taxonomy of accounting research

Source: adapted from Hopper and Powell, 1995

Categories of accounting research

The four sections of Figure 2.1 are labelled: functionalism, interpretive, radical humanism and radical structuralism. These are the terms used by Burrell and Morgan to categorize organizational research, but they can be linked to three categories of accounting research: mainstream research, interpretive research and critical research. Although, as Hopper and Powell point out (1985: 430–1), such a classification is useful for indicating the nature and range of alternative approaches, it would be wrong to claim that all accounting research can be neatly classified into one of these categories. Nevertheless, these three categories do provide a useful overview, which we will elaborate in the later chapters on the research traditions in management and financial accounting.

Mainstream accounting research

Burrell and Morgan used the term 'functionalism' to label the bottom-right quadrant of Figure 2.1, which combines an objectivist view of the world with a concern for regulation. This term is derived from work in sociology that regards society as a single system of interrelated elements, with each element of social life serving a specific function, and the role of the researcher being to discover the nature of those functions. This is similar to much of mainstream accounting research, which is primarily concerned with the functioning of accounting. Such work starts from an objective view of society, regards individual behaviour as deterministic, uses empirical observation and a positive research methodology.

In another paper which uses a similar classification of accounting research, Chua (1986) described the dominant assumptions of mainstream accounting research, interpretative research and critical theory. Table 2.3 contains an adapted version of Chua's categorization of the assumptions associated with mainstream accounting research. This aptly summarizes the epistemological and ontological

TABLE 2.3 Mainstream accounting research

A. Beliefs about knowledge

Theory and observation are independent of each other, and quantitative methods of data collection are favoured to provide a basis for generalizations.

B. Beliefs about physical and social reality

Empirical reality is objective and external to the subject (and the researcher). Human actors are essentially passive objects, who rationally pursue their assumed goals. Society and organizations are basically stable, and dysfunctional behaviour can be managed through the design of control systems.

C. Relationship between accounting theory and practice

Accounting is concerned with means, not ends – it is value neutral, and existing institutional structures are taken for granted.

Source: adapted from Chua, 1986

positions of mainstream accounting research, and adds some comments about the assumed relationship between accounting theory and practice.

Interpretive accounting research

The bottom-left quadrant of Figure 2.1 is labelled 'interpretive'. This research is concerned with understanding the social world, and includes work that seeks to understand the social nature of accounting practices. Some critical accounting researchers (see below) object to interpretive research because it does not seek to provide a social critique and promote radical change. Nevertheless, interpretive work is concerned with making sense of the social character of daily life. Such work has its origins in the work of social interactionists, such as Goffman (1959) and Blumer (1969). Some writers (for example, Roslender, 1992: 142) have classified accounting studies which use Giddens' structuration theory as interpretive (for example, Macintosh and Scapens, 1990), although Giddens himself would certainly claim that his work has a critical dimension (see Giddens, 1984). It may also be appropriate to classify recent accounting studies, which use the work of Latour, with interpretive research (see, for example, Preston, Cooper and Coombs, 1992). However, Latour's work is concerned with the sociology of science – to which we will return towards the end of this chapter.

Table 2.4 summarizes the dominant assumptions (slightly adapted) which Chua (1986) identified with interpretive accounting research.

Critical accounting research

Burrell and Morgan used the terms 'radical structuralism' and 'radical humanism' to distinguish between: (1) research which views society as shaped by social structures; and (2) research which puts the individual at the centre of the picture and views society as the creation of individual social actors. However, Hopper and Powell were

---

TABLE 2.4 Interpretive accounting research

A. Beliefs about knowledge

Theory is used to provide explanations of human intentions. Its adequacy is assessed via logical consistency, subjective interpretation, and agreement with the actors' common-sense interpretations.

B. Beliefs about physical and social reality

Reality is socially created and objectified through human interaction. Human action is intentional and has meaning grounded in the social and historical context. Social order is assumed and conflict mediated through shared meanings.

C. Relationship between accounting theory and practice

Accounting theory seeks to explain action and to understand how social order is produced and reproduced.

Source: adapted from Chua, 1986

reluctant to make such a distinction, preferring to discuss 'radical theories' as one category of accounting research. This is partly due to the problematic nature of the subjective–objective distinction and especially its manifestation in the action–structure debate, which will be discussed below.

Over the years the category which Hopper and Powell termed 'radical theories' has come to be labelled 'critical accounting research' – and we will use that term here. The term is derived from the 'critical theory' of the German philosopher Habermas, who was mentioned earlier. Together with his colleagues in the Frankfurt School, Habermas developed the earlier writings of Hegel and Marx to provide a critique of the social order of capitalist countries. Although broader than the labour process perspective of Braverman (1974), both were concerned with social critique intended to inform the class struggle. There are strands of accounting research that draw on the work of both Habermas and Braverman, as well as more directly on the work of Marx (for examples of these three strands of research see Puxty *et al.*, 1987; Hopper *et al.*, 1986; and Tinker and Neimark, 1987).

Another major strand of critical accounting research has been informed by the French post-structuralist philosopher Foucault (for example, Miller and O'Leary, 1987). Although not within the same Marxist tradition, Foucault was always politically engaged and as such has to be classified here. Table 2.5 contains an adapted list of the dominant assumptions of critical accounting research, as identified by Chua (1986).

As a comparison of Tables 2.3, 2.4 and 2.5 will indicate, there are underlying epistemological and ontological difference between mainstream accounting research and the interpretive and critical alternatives, as well as differences in political ideology. These alternatives will be further discussed in the later chapters dealing with the traditions of research in management accounting and financial accounting.

As already mentioned, it is important to emphasize that the above classification is useful in simplifying the discussion of a very complex area. But it carries with it the

---

TABLE 2.5 Critical accounting research

A. Beliefs about knowledge

Criteria for judging theories are always temporal and context bound. Social objects can only be understood through a study of their historical development and change within the totality of relations.

B. Beliefs about physical and social reality

Empirical reality is characterized by objective, real relations, but is transformed and reproduced through subjective interpretation. Human intention and rationality are accepted, but have to be critically analysed because human potential is alienated through false consciousness and ideology. Fundamental conflict is endemic in society because of social injustice.

C. Relationship between accounting theory and practice

Theory has a critical imperative; in particular the identification and removal of domination and ideological practices.

Source: adapted from Chua, 1986

risk of oversimplification. Furthermore, it may be difficult to classify individual pieces of work. Thus, the above discussion should be seen as providing a very broad overview of the range of methodological approaches used in accounting research and, in particular, emphasizing that the so-called scientific method should not be seen as the only, or even the ideal approach, across the whole range of accounting research.

In the following sections, we will explore a little further the debate about the nature of the subjective–objective continuum. Then, we will briefly mention another approach to classifying research in the social sciences which avoids that distinction. Finally, we will discuss the social process research.

Dissolving the subjective–objective debate

There has been a continuing debate within social theory over the relationship between individual action and social structures. At one extreme is structuralism, which maintains that social action is entirely determined by social structures. Individuals are 'pushed around' by the structures, which both constrain and shape their behaviour. Individualism is at the other extreme, and this maintains that all social action is voluntary and thus social structures, to the extent that they exist, are merely the reflection of accumulated individual action. However, it can be argued that these extremes are overly deterministic on the one hand, and overly voluntaristic on the other (Giddens, 1979).

In developing his structuration theory, Giddens wanted to replace this dualism of agency and structure with a duality (see also Giddens, 1984). Here agency refers to the individual's ability to make a difference in the world, that is, to act as a free human agent. This should be contrasted with the use of the term 'agent' in mainstream accounting research, where it means just the opposite. The agent in agency theory is perceived as driven by axioms of economically 'rational behaviour' to maximize expected utility. In this sense the 'agent's' behaviour is predictable and determined by the laws of rational choice. In social theory, however, agency refers to the ability of the individual to act autonomously. In the 'duality of structure', Giddens argues that agency and structure presuppose one another. Although structure is the medium which shapes action, it is itself the outcome of action (Giddens, 1979; 1984).

This relationship between action and structure can be illustrated in the use of language. Individual speech acts draw on the grammatical structure of the language. But this structure is created and re-created day by day through those very speech acts, which can and do bring about changes in the language. When applied to social actions more generally, we can argue the human agency is inherently subjective, but it can create social structures which then become externalized and, as such, capable of objective analysis. As a result the distinction between the subjective and the objective becomes problematic, as there are both subjective and objective elements within the duality of structure. This is the primary reason we did not distinguish between subjective and objective elements in our earlier discussion of critical accounting research. It also represents a criticism of the Burrell and Morgan classification (Willmott, 1990). In the next section we will describe an alternative taxonomy which seeks to build on Burrell and Morgan's work, but which avoids the simple subjective–objective dimension.

Other dimensions

Although the Burrell and Morgan framework, as used by Hopper and Powell, provides a useful overview and an initial categorization of accounting research, it does not identify certain other dimensions which need to be considered when discussing methodologies of accounting research. Laughlin (1995) starts from the Burrell and Morgan framework, but he avoids the subjective–objective dimension, and instead produces a three-dimensional framework labelled theory, methodology and change.

The change dimension is similar to Burrell and Morgan's approaches to society. Although Laughlin sees this dimension as a continuum, he singles out three levels: high, medium and low. Researchers who believe in a high level of change are of the view that society needs to be changed, while those who believe in a low level of change are quite happy with the status quo. Those who are in the middle are open to the possibilities for change, but do not automatically reject all aspects of the status quo.

Laughlin's other two dimensions, theory and methodology, are both concerned with the level of theorization. Again he uses three levels: high, medium and low. The theory dimension refers to the level of theorization prior to the research. High levels of prior theorizing are indicative of a world which the researcher assumes to be structured with high levels of generality and which has been well researched through previous studies. Low levels of prior theorization suggest a world where generalizations are difficult, or even impossible, and where it is inappropriate to derive insights from previous studies as they could potentially corrupt the present study.

The methodological dimension is concerned with the level of theorization in the research process itself – that is, in the methodology – and relates to the theoretical definition of how the researcher should 'see' the subject of the research. At the high end of the continuum, the nature of the research process is highly theorized and, as such, the observer has no substantive role other than the application of a predefined set of techniques. At the low end, however, the researcher is directly involved in the research and is encouraged to use his or her perceptual skills, uncluttered by a set of theoretical rules and procedures.

Laughlin combined these three dimensions into a framework, which he then used to classify the various social theories that have informed accounting research – as shown in Figure 2.2. Because of the difficulties of depicting a three-dimensional framework on a two-dimensional page, one of the dimensions has been embedded within the figure. The two dimensions of theory and methodology are shown on the horizontal and vertical axes, respectively, while the change dimension is indicated by the letters, H, M and L, in parentheses, shown along side each of the approaches identified within the framework. Mainstream accounting research is represented by the approaches shown in the top-left box, all indicated to be low on the change dimension. Such research would be classified as High, High, Low: in terms of theory, methodology and change, respectively.

Theory choice: levels of prior theorisation

		High	Medium	Low
Methodological choice: level of theorization in methods	High	Positivism (L) Realism (L) Instrumentalism (L) Conventionalism (L)		
	Medium		German critical theory (M)	Symbolic interactionism (Kuhn) (L)
	Low	Marxist (H)	Structuration (L) French critical theory (L)	Pragmatism (L) Symbolic interactionism (Blumer) (L) Ethnomethodology (L)

In parentheses (High/Medium/Low):
Change choice: level of emphasis given to critique of status quo and need for change

FIGURE 2.2 Laughlin's classifications of social research

Source: Laughlin (1995)

Laughlin contrasts the mainstream research with his favoured approach of middle-range thinking, which he derives from the work of Habermas (German critical theory in Figure 2.2), and with the more interpretive approaches shown in the bottom-left box and classified as Low, Low, Low. Table 2.6, which reproduces Laughlin's own table 1 (1995: 80), contrasts the nature of these three different approaches. This illustrates the importance of levels of theorization in distinguishing different methodological approaches in accounting research. It also emphasizes that researchers must consider whether their use of theory is appropriate for their research methodology.

Social process of research

As the above discussion indicates, the research process is not a value-neutral, objective search for the 'truth'. Such a view may be plausible in the natural sciences, but rarely if ever in the social sciences. Research is a social activity conducted by men and women who, by and large, are not so much concerned with obtaining financial rewards per se but, rather, with the accumulation of social credit or 'reputation'. As a social system, research communities exhibit strong social norms that are guarded by a rigorous procedure for the assessment and publication of 'writings'. The governing moral principle is that researchers only publish what they *honestly believe to be true* (Harre, 1986).

TABLE 2.6 Key characteristics of dominant schools of thought

	High/high/low[a]	Medium/medium/medium[a]	Low/low/low[a]
Theory characteristics			
Ontological belief	Generalizable world waiting to be discovered	'Skeletal' generalizations possible	Generalizations may not be there to be discovered
Role of theory	Definable theory with hypotheses to test	'Skeletal' theory with some broad understanding of relationships	Ill-defined theory – no prior hypotheses
Methodology characteristics			
Role of observer and human nature belief	Observer independent and irrelevant	Observer important and always part of the process of discovery	Observer important and always part of the process of discovery
Nature of method	Structured, quantitative method	Definable approach but subject to refinement in actual situations, invariably qualitative	Unstructured, ill-defined, qualitative approach
Data sought	Cross-sectional data used usually at one point in time and selectively gathered tied to hypotheses	Longitudinal, case study based. Heavily descriptive but also analytical	Longitudinal, case study based. Heavily descriptive
Conclusions derived	Tight conclusions about findings	Reasonably conclusive tied to 'skeletal' theory and empirical richness	Ill-defined and inconclusive conclusions but empirically rich in detail
Validity criteria	Statistical inference	Meanings: researchers + researched	Meanings: researched
Change characteristics			
	Low emphasis on changing status quo	Medium emphasis open to radical change and maintenance of status quo	Low emphasis on changing status quo

[a] Theory, methodology and change

Source: Laughlin 1995: 80

In a classical study of a natural science laboratory in which Nobel Prize winning work was being conducted, Latour and Woolgar observed:

> even insecure bureaucrats and compulsive novelists are less obsessed by inscriptions than scientists. Between scientists and chaos there is nothing but a wall of archives, labels, protocol books, figures and papers. But this

mass of documents provides the only means of creating more order, and scientific reality is a pocket of order created out of disorder by seizing on any signal which fits what has already been enclosed and by enclosing it, albeit at a cost.

(Latour and Woolgar, 1979: 245–6)

For the social theorist, the process of doing research appears to have many of the characteristics of other social productive systems. For example, reputation can be regarded as the symbolic capital of the productive process, published writings are the object of production, there is a rigid class structure of senior academics through to research assistants, and there is a rigorous procedure of social control. In a later chapter we will consider in detail the system of order and control in the finance and accounting literature, and the role of logic, mathematics and statistical method within that literature.

We will finish this chapter by mentioning a paper by two North Americans, Baker and Bettner (1997), who asked why interpretive and critical research is absent from the mainstream accounting research journals. They started by referencing Burrell and Morgan and proceeded to describe Laughlin's framework. After outlining the nature of mainstream, interpretive and critical research, as described earlier in this chapter, they produced an analysis of papers published in largely North American academic journals in 1995. If papers in the UK-based *Accounting, Organizations and Society* are excluded, they show that less than 1 per cent of the papers can be classified as interpretive or critical research.

The core of their question could be expressed as: why do North Americans (with some notable exceptions) do very little interpretive and critical research? They address this question by exploring the social construction of the accounting research community in North America, and point to the constraints which are imposed on researchers who try to move out of the mainstream. In particular, they argue that the doctoral programmes and the editorial policies of the main academic journals are controlled largely by mainstream researchers. This makes it very difficult for new researchers to be trained in critical and interpretive research, and so they build up their intellectual capital in mainstream research, which further reproduces the strength of the mainstream. Furthermore, it is very difficult to get papers published in North American journals if they do not meet the 'quality' standards of mainstream research – in other words if they do not use the 'scientific method' described above.

Thus, within the North American accounting research community, the mainstream exerts strong control. However, the alternative approaches have been able to develop in other parts of the world, especially where there is rather less social control over the research process. But even in North America there are notable examples of individuals using alternative accounting research methodologies.

Summary

In this chapter we have shown that there are a range of methodological approaches that can be, and are, used in accounting research. But we recognized that within finance research the mainstream approach outlined in the previous chapter still remains dominant, although there is a small but growing amount of literature that adopts affirmative methodological perspectives (see Chapter 6). The main point is that there are ontological and epistemological issues to be considered in deciding the appropriate methodology for accounting (and potentially also for finance) research. It is a mistake to see only one 'ideal' methodology, and to dismiss other methodologies as in some way inferior. If accounting and finance research are to explore fully all aspects and dimensions of the subject, we will need a plurality of methodological approaches and all researchers should be open minded about the contributions which alternative methodologies can make.

Notes

1 This bias towards positive outcomes is largely explained by the fact that it is generally difficult to get research published which does not validate the principal hypotheses.
2 This confusion between methodology and method is quite commonplace and is often caused by a desire to give a particular discussion more importance than it perhaps merits by describing it as 'methodological'.

3

Traditions of research in finance

The field of finance has generated a wealth of research in the last 50 years or so. This research has led to a considerable improvement in our understanding of issues in both capital markets and financial management, although many new questions and unresolved problems continue to arise. The research findings have, in a number of instances, brought about changes in working practices in financial institutions and companies. Inevitably, a discussion of the research traditions in finance will need to be somewhat selective due to the vast range of work that has been conducted in the finance area. Furthermore, in order to discuss these traditions a balance has to be achieved between current and past research; both are discussed since the roots of much of the more recent work lie in research conducted some time ago. (Duffie, 1992, for example, places considerable emphasis on the research achievements in the 1970s). Due to space constraints we will not discuss the corporate finance area in any depth, but refer interested readers to the many excellent surveys in that area by, for example, Harris and Raviv (1991), Shleifer and Vishny (1997) and Zingales (2000).

While the successes of research in finance are many, there are still interesting problems to be resolved and criticisms have been levelled at both the technical and methodological levels. Critics have, for example, focused upon the validity of the formal concept of rationality, which is embedded in much of the finance literature, and which has tended to exclude other behavioural and psychological factors in the explanation of investor behaviour. A 'behavioural' school of finance has developed since the 1980s, wherein certain features of irrational behaviour have been incorporated into the modelling structure and this approach has gained increasing acceptance in the 1990s. However, the rationality concept, as we noted in Chapter 2, still finds favour with the majority of researchers in the finance area. Empirical research has uncovered a number of anomalous results such as the size effect and long-run overreactions, which have thrown into relief many problems that would otherwise have been obscured if scholars had limited themselves purely to theory development. In many respects, the theoretical framework in finance has reached a very high degree of sophistication, although the linkages between theory and empirical results have not always been well articulated.

In this chapter we will describe the general framework of analysis and methodological criteria which have dominated much of the finance literature before proceeding to discuss the significance of the more important theoretical and empirical discoveries from both a methodological and technical standpoint. Finally, we will illustrate the dynamics of the research process with reference to examples from the capital asset pricing, options and market efficiency literature.

The general framework of analysis

In simple terms, the overall research framework in finance entails the development of theoretical models which are then tested by confronting hypotheses (which we can define as conjectural empirical propositions) derived from these models with empirical data. Although this opening statement reflects the strong positivist tradition within financial research, there are many examples of ultra-'rational' and ultra-'empirical' research within this area. The framework presented here strongly reflects the positivist methodology discussed in the previous two chapters but which represents a considerably more sophisticated position than that term would imply.

One approach to theory development in finance is based upon the 'neoclassical' research programme in economics; this programme is based upon a set of core terms which are taken as non-conjectural. We emphasize, however, as will be seen below, that there are other approaches followed in the finance literature. We can identify three such propositions which can form the basis of (at least) the initial phases of model development within such a framework:

- economic agents (investors and decision makers) are, at the individual level, formally rational
- financial markets are perfectly competitive
- information is freely available.

Investor (or decision-maker) rationality implies that the economic agent concerned seeks to maximize a utility function defined over a number of arguments (generally wealth or consumption related). By assuming that agents maximize their utility functions, classical calculus can be used to develop closed form pricing models and other models and relationships. Technically, such utility functions should be, *inter alia*, mathematically continuous and differentiable to any degree. No arbitrage approaches can remove the need to work with, or specify, utility functions; however, they are still generally predicated upon investor rationality. In the 'no arbitrage' approach a return or price generating process is posited and then a no arbitrage condition is imposed within the modelling structure (Black and Scholes, 1973; Ross, 1976). The no arbitrage approach to asset pricing has become the dominant paradigm within which most researchers now work (see, for example, Cochrane, 1999).

Much of the finance research literature has typically focused upon a capital market perspective rather than adopting an interfirm or managerial perspective. We will, accordingly, talk in terms of investors here, although agency and signalling models also incorporate managerial preferences and represent a significant component of the output in the finance area. Investors, then, may be presumed to behave in accordance with the von Neumann-Morgenstern axioms of rational choice which postulate, *inter alia*, that individuals have the ability to evaluate and rank the choices which confront them in terms of their preferences and are, furthermore, internally consistent in those rankings. The use of continuous time methods (Merton, 1990; Sundaresan, 2000) has greatly facilitated the development of intertemporal portfolio choice and asset pricing models.

The assumption of rationality is part and parcel of the abstraction process employed in both natural and social sciences. That is, in order that a particular phenomenon may be studied the researcher abstracts from reality. The 'grand problem' as it were, is broken down into manageable 'bits'. In finance we are interested in explaining overall market forces, phenomena or processes. The assumption that investors behave in a rational fashion enables us to focus upon market forces without getting embroiled in the individual investor's psychology which may, in any event, be better handled by other disciplines. The development of behavioural models of investor behaviour (Schleifer, 2000) and the increased interest in laboratory-type experiments of investor behaviour in capital market situations (see, for example, Glosten, 1999) indicates that a number of researchers identify this as a topic for the finance rather than, say, the psychology area, however.

Individual investor behaviour is often aggregated up to the market level to develop, among other things, pricing relationships, and it is through this aggregation process that the rationality assumption again manifests and reinforces itself. That is, rational investors' actions would dominate. This is often cited as a compelling rationale for the rationality assumption. Since the mid-1980s, a number of authors have discussed and analysed the topic of irrational investors and their varying impacts, for example, deBondt and Thaler (1985), Shefrin and Stratman (1985), Daniel, Hirshleifer and Subrahmanyam (1998), and pricing models have been developed which have irrational or noise traders figuring in the equilibrium pricing relationships (DeLong *et al.*, 1990). Effectively to prevent rational investors from generating arbitrage profits at the expense of irrational or 'noise' traders, factors have to exist to prevent this arbitrage. The major factor is risk related (see, for example, Campbell and Kyle (1993), DeLong *et al.* (1990)). DeBondt and Thaler (1995) and Schleifer (2000) provide excellent discussions of the behavioural finance field and its growing impact in enhancing our understanding of a variety of financial phenomena.

Returning to managerial motives, Roll (1986) provides a framework for rationalizing a number of merger-related phenomena employing irrational managerial behaviour (Roll emphasizes that in the scenario employed, aggregation will not eliminate irrational behaviour). Kleidon (1986) surveyed the finance field from the rationality perspective and discussed the inherent problems associated with the literature which indicate some degree of irrationality in the market. He argued against rejection of the existing rationality paradigm since so much, in his view, had been achieved by its use. Although the adoption of a different paradigm might alleviate some of the problems encountered in finance at the present time, much of what is a considerable body of knowledge could be lost by such a strategy. This viewpoint is also discussed in some detail by Merton (1987) and by Fama (1998). For example, Fama (1998) argues that 'market efficiency survives the challenge' from the apparent over and underreactions that have been documented in long run returns if limitations in the research designs employed in such studies are taken into account.

The second common feature of model development in finance is the assumption that capital markets are perfect. Capital markets are assumed, among other things, to be characterized by a large number of investors and an absence of frictions such as taxes and transactions costs. The perfect capital market assumption, however, is not as central to the theoretical structure as the rationality assumption was and, indeed, it has been relaxed in a large number of analyses. Perfect markets are often assumed as part of the initial phase of model development but are then relaxed as part of the subsequent development of the theoretical network. For example, in the classical Modigliani and Miller theories of capital structure and dividend policy (Miller and Modigliani, 1961; Modigliani and Miller, 1958) an ideal markets framework, incorporating rational investors and perfect capital markets, was used to demonstrate that under such 'ideal' conditions value depends only upon real phenomena such as the underlying earnings power of the firm, rather than financing or distributive phenomena. The next stage in the theoretical development arises from an analysis of the types of imperfections in capital markets that could lead to capital structure and/or dividend policy becoming relevant. A considerable amount of theoretical research has been directed at evaluating the impact of market imperfections (such as taxes, information asymmetries and bankruptcy costs, for example) upon the financing and distribution problem. The burgeoning microstructure literature (O'Hara, 1998), focuses upon a variety of frictions in the trading process. Indeed, many of the interesting areas of finance necessitate the study of capital markets which are imperfect (for example, bid–ask spread effects [Amihud and Mendelson, 1986], non-marketable assets such as human capital [Jagannathan and Wang, 1996; Mayers, 1972] and agency related costs [Jensen and Meckling, 1976].

A considerable amount of the theoretical development in finance has been achieved by abstracting from informational problems by assuming that prices 'fully' (in some sense) reflect information. Since the mid-1970s an increasing number of researchers have engaged in progressively more rigorous modelling of the informational aspects associated with markets and financial phenomena. The problems of fully revealing equilibria (that is, where prices both aggregate and communicate information) and costs of information processing are now well known and analysed. Indeed, a thriving microstructure literature has developed which models the interactions between informed investors, noise/liquidity traders and market traders (see, for example, O'Hara [1998] for a comprehensive overview of this literature). Similarly, the incentive-signalling literature originally developed by Spence (1973) is applied in a large number of areas such as new issues, debt maturity and dividends. While important developments have been achieved in modelling the informational processes in financial markets a number of theoretical analyses (such as much of the asset pricing literature) still invoke the full information assumption. Merton (1987) however, relaxes the assumption of the full dissemination of information across all investors by partitioning the market into segments where only a particular subset of (fully informed) investors takes positions and develops a number of implications for asset market prices.

The use of 'no arbitrage' arguments has become increasingly common and dominant in the development of pricing models due to the generality of the associated results and their wide applicability to both derivative and primary assets. In such 'no arbitrage' scenarios a stochastic discount factor exists which links prices to pay-offs across states. When markets are complete the stochastic discount factor is unique. (Campbell, 2000, provides a useful discussion of stochastic discount factor models.) The arbitrage pricing model, generally associated with Ross (1976), assumes a very central role in the asset pricing literature; the martingale pricing approach (Harrison and Pliska, 1979; Sundaram, 1997) provides the foundation for derivative and other pricing models (see also Duffie, 1992).

While this theoretical work is of great importance it cannot be considered in isolation from the problems of empirical testing. The theoretical propositions deduced from the axioms, postulates and definitions can be tested or matched with the real world from which the original theoretical structure was abstracted (provided, of course, that they have first been tested for internal consistency). The abstraction process entails making assumptions; in general, the stronger the assumptions the stronger the conclusions and hence, from a falsifications perspective, the easier that theory is to reject by empirical testing. Ideally there is a ready articulation between theories and facts, and vice versa. The word 'ideally' is used because in practice a number of interpretative or auxiliary statements generally have to be made before testable predictions can be generated or existing empirical work interpreted. The practicality of falsifying a theory is then limited by such statements with the result that 'crucial experiments' (Duhem, 1962) are regarded as not generally possible. That is, empirical tests of theories involve a test of a joint hypothesis: (1) the theoretical model and (2) the empirical constructs used in testing that theoretical model. Perhaps the most apparent instance of this situation has been in the testing of the capital asset pricing model where Roll (1977a) cogently pointed out the critical importance of identifying the market portfolio. Important insights into this issue are still being generated (see, for example, Roll and Ross, 1994).

The increasing analytical sophistication of the techniques employed in theory development has been matched by improvements in the quality of databases used and in the econometric techniques devised. The advent of databases with high-frequency price data, together with an increasing emphasis upon the efficiency of the statistical procedures employed, has led to the situation where very powerful tests of theories are now possible in the applied or empirical finance field.

Landmarks in the development of finance

Finance has evolved into a highly technical subject since the 1950s. Prior to that time it was largely institutionally oriented and a descriptive (in its broadest sense) subject. The two main precursors of the change in the scope of finance were the treatment of risk in the portfolio context by Markowitz (1953) and the mathematical economic analysis by Modigliani and Miller (1958) of capital structure. In a sense, it is relatively easy to identify the landmarks in finance development. The work by Markowitz, Modigliani, Miller, Sharpe, Scholes and Merton has led to them receiving Nobel Prizes for their contributions to the field of financial economics. The work of each is contained in the discussions presented below. Their work has provided the foundation for a very much more sophisticated approach to the finance field. It is also possible to trace the development of finance in terms of environmental factors. For example, the development of markets for new financial instruments, such as traded options and financial futures, has had a great impact upon the orientation and output of the academic finance profession. In this section we will discuss some of the landmark papers and concepts which assume considerable importance in contemporary finance work.

If we start in chronological order, the first landmark was Markowitz's portfolio theory. It was through Markowitz's work that the concept of diversification became operationalized in terms of portfolio variances and covariances between constitunent securities. While portfolio theory dealt with the individual investor's portfolio decision it provided the intuition and basis for an equilibrium asset pricing model – the capital asset pricing model (CAPM) – developed by Sharpe (1964), Lintner (1965) and Mossin (1966). Essentially, the only risk that is 'priced' at equilibrium in the capital market is covariance or systematic risk. Since much of the essence of finance is associated with risk and its interaction with time, the original contribution of Markowitz can hardly be overemphasized.

Modigliani and Miller (1958) introduced the rigours of neoclassical economic analysis into the finance field and subsequently applied it in a series of papers. This form of reasoning is now used extensively throughout the whole finance field. The analysis was originally carried out in the ideal market situation described in the previous section, and the irrelevance of capital structure for firm value was proven via a no arbitrage condition across firms in a homogeneous risk class. Modigliani and Miller then established that arbitrage opportunities would be available unless capital structure was irrelevant. Miller (1977) was able to demonstrate capital structure irrelevance even in a world of corporate taxes by analysing the corporate debt market at the aggregate level. The approach that he adopted formed the basis of a series of papers adopting a similar approach to corporate financial policy (see, for example, DeAngelo and Masulis, 1980a; 1980b). Much of the more recent work in the capital structure area has adopted an agency theory based approach (see Harris and Raviv, 1991, for a survey of more recent developments in the capital structure area).

The study of the processing of information by stock prices generated a considerable amount of empirical interest in the late 1950s and the 1960s, but the landmark paper in this area would seem to be the paper by Fama (1970) which was extensively updated in Fama (1991). The original paper discussed the notion of market efficiency in three forms (weak, semi-strong and strong). This classification is still widely used within the literature; although in the subsequent paper the terms were modified slightly by Fama, a similar form of classification scheme was adopted. A weak form-efficient market is one where prices reflect all past information, while in its semi-strong form prices reflect publicly available information. Strong form efficiency states that all information (whether publicly available or not) is reflected in prices. Although a number of experimental refinements have been developed, the major innovations in the field have been in the area of theoretical developments of the pricing mechanism in efficient or noisy rational expectations economies (see, for example, Brown and Jennings, 1989; Diamond and Verrecchia, 1981) and the discovery of anomalies, such as the firm size effect, the day of the week effect and long-run over/underreactions and attempts to rationalize their existence.

A very significant development in the early 1970s was the application of continuous time mathematics to the pricing problem under conditions of uncertainty (see Merton, 1990). The 'continuous time' approach is now commonly applied to problems across the whole finance spectrum. The level of mathematical sophistication necessary to contribute to certain areas of the theoretical finance literature is now very high indeed (a useful introduction is provided by Neftci [1996]). Perhaps the best known of all such developments is the Black and Scholes (1973) option pricing model. Until the development of the Black–Scholes model closed form pricing relationships for options under conditions of uncertainty had not been available. By using continuous time mathematics and forming instantaneously risk-free portfolios containing the underlying stock and options, Black and Scholes were able to derive a pricing model for options. Sundaresan (2000) provides a recent review of the applications of continuous time modelling in the finance area.

The highly important subsidiary effect of the development of the option pricing model has been the use of contingent claims logic and pricing models to study a number of areas quite distinct from traded options, such as capital structure, underwriting commissions and co-insurance effects in mergers. Another early application of continuous time mathematics/stochastic calculus was the development of an intertemporal asset pricing model by Merton (1973b); this has led to a variety of subsequent pricing applications. Cox, Ingersoll and Ross (1977) used similar techniques to develop models of the term structure of interest rates and, subsequently, they developed a pricing model for futures contracts which indicated how future prices may differ from forward prices (Cox, Ingersoll and Ross, 1981). Heath, Jarrow and Morton (1992) developed a model of the evolution of forward rates which is particularly appropriate for the pricing of interest rate derivative products. Many of the derivative pricing models are developed from the martingale pricing approach (Harrison and Pliska, 1979) mentioned in the previous section.

A paper which had a significant impact upon the finance profession was that by Roll (1977a) where he very cogently argued that tests of the CAPM which employed market portfolio proxies were flawed since in such cases an unambiguous test is only possible if the market portfolio is exactly identified. While Roll's paper was directed at the empirical aspects of asset pricing model testing, and indeed did inspire some alternative pricing testing methodologies, it also provided an incentive to develop alternative pricing models such as the arbitrage pricing model (APT) originally developed by Ross (1976). This shift of focus led to a large number of empirical tests of the arbitrage pricing model which have, themselves at times, been subject to considerable controversy. However, as we indicated previously, the no arbitrage approach to asset pricing is now the dominant paradigm.

Agency theory and incentive signalling theories have assumed increasing importance in the development of theoretical models of institutional and firm operations and characteristics. The seminal article in the finance area in agency theory was produced by Jensen and Meckling (1976) in which a theoretical structure was developed for the existence of an optimal debt/equity ratio in terms of the trade-offs between the agency costs associated with debt and equity. Since the Jensen and Meckling paper there have been numerous studies employing similar theoretical structures. The early papers using incentive signalling in finance were by Ross (1977) and Bhattacharya (1976) in the capital structure and dividend areas, respectively. Following these earlier papers the incentive signalling model has been widely employed throughout finance in such diverse areas as debt maturity and multivariate signalling. A comprehensive survey of theoretical applications in these areas is to be found in Harris and Raviv (1991), and Shleifer and Vishny (1997) provide an excellent survey of corporate governance applications.

Our brief overview of the developments in finance has, of necessity, been somewhat subjective and restrictive. However, our objective in this section has been to summarize the essentials of the finance literature and in such a diverse field it is not possible to cover fully all the relevant areas in great detail. However, a striking characteristic of all of this research is the development of highly rigorous models using, in many instances, certain narrowly specified assumptions about market or investor (agent) behaviour.

The dynamics of the research process – three examples

The discussion of the landmark papers in the previous section was necessarily conducted at a relatively superficial level in order that a broad perspective could be achieved. In this section we will attempt to rectify this superficiality to a degree by studying the dynamics of three important research areas in finance – the pricing of primary financial assets, option pricing and the assimilation of information by asset prices within financial markets. Again, however, due to space limitations our discussions will necessarily be restricted to an extent. We do, however, throughout refer the reader to the papers in question or more specialized and detailed surveys, where available.

The pricing of capital assets

We will start with the capital asset pricing literature in which there have been significant theoretical developments, a ready articulation between theory and empirical work and some considerable controversy! An excellent recent paper that surveys the asset pricing literature from a slightly different perspective and far more extensively than is possible in this section is provided by Campbell (2000). In particular, we will discuss the CAPM and APT in some detail as these provide an excellent case study for the articulation between theory development and empirical testing. Textbook coverage of this topic area is provided, for example, in Duffie (1992) and Campbell, Lo and MacKinlay (1997).

The roots of this particular area lie in Markowitz's modern portfolio theory (MPT). Modern portfolio theory, as such, did not provide a pricing model as its scope was limited to normative prescriptions as to how an investor should operate in order that a risk-averse wealth maximizer might maximize his or her utility. By identifying risk with the dispersion of returns it is possible to develop mean variance efficient sets and with the introduction of risk-free borrowing and lending opportunities a 'separation theorem' can be derived in mean-standard deviation space. That is, the composition of an investor's optimal risky asset portfolio can be separated from his or her risk preferences.

An important concept that derives from MPT is the distinction between diversifiable and non-diversible risk; that is, in 'large' portfolios the contribution of an individual security to total portfolio risk derives from the non-diversifiable risk of that security, measured by the covariance of that security's returns with the existing portfolio. In order that pricing models can be derived it is necessary to say something about both the capital market and the investors who trade in that market.

The capital asset pricing model assumes that all investors maximize the utility of terminal wealth defined over the mean and variance of portfolio returns, and that all investors have unconditional homogeneous expectations of means variances and covariances. The capital market is assumed to be perfect. In the single period analysis, a 'separation theorem' at the aggregate level will arise (manifested by the capital market line) in the presence of a risk-free asset and the capital asset pricing model can be derived by the technique of Lagrangean multipliers.

The linear risk return trade off, with risk measured by the beta factor (which reflects covariance or non-diversifiable risk) is perhaps one of the best known models in the finance field. Its message is simple, the only risk that is 'priced' at equilibrium in the market is that risk which cannot be diversified away. The capital asset pricing model was developed in a relatively restricted theoretical environment. However, it did provide strong empirical implications, that is, that systematic risk and return are linearly related in the capital market. Naturally, the next step was to test the empirical implications of the model.

A fairly sophisticated test methodology was developed within the literature of CAPM tests. The main emphasis in the early research designs was on the reduction of the biases associated with the use of estimated betas rather than 'true' betas in the cross section tests. This was achieved by a portfolio grouping technique (Black, Jensen and Scholes, 1972) that effectively reduced to an instrumental variable estimator. Later studies focused more upon the efficiency dimension as the portfolio grouping technique led to a considerable loss of information. (Campbell, Lo and MacKinlay, 1997, provide a more detailed overview of these testing methodologies.)

The majority of the early tests tended to support the implication of linearity between risk and return. However, the empirical results were more consistent with Black's (1972) 'zero beta' model, where the return on a zero beta portfolio replaced the rate of return on a risk-free security. Since Black's model made no predictions regarding the rate of return on a zero beta portfolio (the minimum variance efficient portfolio which is uncorrelated with the market portfolio), it is difficult to see how this form of the model can be rejected empirically. One considerable advantage of Black's model over CAPM is that it does not have the undesirable implication that all investors hold the market portfolio.

The relaxation of the underlying assumptions of the capital asset pricing model became something of a 'cottage industry' in the late 60s and 70s. In the previous section we noted the very important contribution made to the asset pricing literature by Merton's (1973b) intertemporal model, in which among other things, a multi-fund separation theorem was developed. Subsequent authors have built upon Merton's original framework, for example in some cases endogenizing the multi-period pricing process. That is, rather than imposing a particular price process upon the modelling structure, the process arises as a result of the model itself (see Stapleton and Subrahmanyan, 1983). Consumption based asset pricing models have also been used as a basis for developing intertemporal asset pricing models (see Campbell, Lo and MacKinlay, 1997). The perfect capital markets assumption has been relaxed in a number of papers, perhaps the best known being Brennan (1970), where heterogeneous differential personal taxes are introduced, and Mayers (1972) where non-marketable (that is effectively infinite transactions costs) assets were introduced into the overall pricing structure. The inclusion of human capital into the asset pricing structure has been achieved in a number of papers (for example, Jagannathan and Wang, 1996).

The homogeneous beliefs assumption was relaxed in an early paper by Lintner (1969), while the impact of non-symmetrical return distributions on the resultant pricing model was investigated both analytically and empirically in Kraus and Litzenberger (1976). Other heterogeneities across investors have been analysed in, for example, Grossman and Zhou (1996).

The development of the pricing area occurred with the ready articulation between theoretical and empirical work. The empirical work was carried out with the recognition that variables were subject to measurement error and proxies often had to be employed in particular instances. Indeed some papers, for example, Black, Jensen and Scholes (1972) and Miller and Scholes (1972), specifically discussed and investigated features of the research design from this perspective. Of particular concern was the identification of the market portfolio, the value weighted portfolio of all capital assets. It was originally accepted that proxies for the market portfolio had to be used and that this was just another example of a general problem encountered throughout the social sciences. However, Roll (1977a) demonstrated the critical importance of exactly identifying the market portfolio in order that meaningful tests of the CAPM could be affected. Since an exact identification of the market portfolio was not feasible, the inference was that the CAPM could not be tested directly. On the one hand the 'Roll' critique relates to tests rather than the theory of CAPM; on the other hand, given the strong positivist tradition in which the CAPM was developed, the critique has very far-reaching ramifications which transcend the mere testing issues. For example, to what extent should concerns about the ultimate testability of the model figure at the theoretical development stage? Ryan (1982) argued that the debate which ensued from the Roll critique was largely fuelled by differences in perception within the positivist tradition between those who held to weak-form and those who held to strong-form varieties of realism in the literature.

Two distinct approaches to the Roll critique can be discerned in the literature. One was to develop testing designs which reflect the nature of or attempt to overcome the Roll critique, the other is to focus attention upon other asset pricing models which appear to offer more promise for testing (due perhaps to their lower reliance upon the identification of the market portfolio). We will start with the modified research designs.

The earlier post-Roll tests focused upon the joint hypothesis involved in tests of the capital asset pricing model (for example, Foster, 1977). The tests were, it was argued, based upon a joint hypothesis of, first, the CAPM and, second, the market portfolio proxy chosen providing an adequate construct for the true market portfolio. The rationale for these designs was that better proxies for the market portfolio should be used. As the earlier studies had used stock market equity indices as proxies, the suggestion of this approach was that other assets, such as bonds, should be reflected in the market portfolio proxies.

The drawback of this approach was that the supposedly better identification was still not an exact identification. An interesting variant of this approach was a study which carried out a sensitivity analysis of the research design in the light of the Roll critique (Stambaugh, 1983). Stambaugh found that the empirical results were more sensitive to the assets included in the cross-sectional tests than the composition of the market portfolio proxy. Gibbons and Ferson (1985) developed a research design in which the dynamics of asset returns predicted by the CAPM could be tested independently from identifying the market portfolio. Their results were not consistent with the implications deriving from the capital asset pricing model; results presented in Ferson, Kendal and Stambaugh (1987) are consistent with a capital asset pricing model specification with time varying risk premia.

Fama and French (1992) find that when size is controlled for, there is no empirical support for a relationship between average return and beta. Inevitably this controversial result stimulated further empirical and theoretical research. For example, Kothari, Shanken and Sloan (1995) focused upon the estimation of betas and found that when betas were estimated using annual data, there was some empirical support for a beta–return relationship. From a theoretical perspective, Roll and Ross (1994) establish that market portfolio proxies exist which generate betas unrelated to average returns in cross-section. Such market portfolio proxies plot within a parabola which is tangential to the efficient frontier at the global minimum variance portfolio and which is very close to the efficient frontier in other regions. That is, the use of proxies which are very close to being mean-variance efficient (which, of course, the market portfolio can be in a CAPM world) can lead to an absence of a relationship between the beta estimated against that proxy and average returns. Fama and French (1996) present a three-factor model with factors related to the market, size and book/market value variables; they demonstrate the consistency of this model with Merton's (1973b) intertemporal model and the arbitrage pricing model described below.

The other approach subsequent to the Roll critique has been to focus upon alternative asset pricing models; by far and away the most popular has been the arbitrage pricing model developed by Ross (1976). This approach to asset pricing is now the dominant one in the finance literature. By proposing a multifactor return generating process in frictionless markets Ross demonstrated via the mechanism of arbitrage portfolios (in which zero changes in wealth and systematic risk occur) that a linear relationship will exist between expected asset returns and the factor sensitivities if there are no arbitrage opportunities available in the market. The original derivation assumed large asset economies; since that time, however, a number of refinements to the model have been developed in, for example, Chen and Ingersoll (1983), Connor (1984) and Huberman (1982). Shanken (1992a) provides a sound overview of the status of the arbitrage pricing model. The arbitrage pricing model will relate back to the more general stochastic discount factor structure referred to earlier when the stochastic discount factor is linearly related to a set of common shocks in the market (Campbell, 2000).

One of the major advantages of the arbitrage pricing model is that it does not require the identification of the market portfolio which is, of course, the impediment to the testing of the capital asset pricing model. However, as Roll and Ross (1980) point out it still retains the intuition underlying the capital asset pricing model; namely, there is a distinction between systematic and unsystematic risk and that only systematic risk (that is, factor sensitivity risk) is priced.

Given the apparent testability of the arbitrage pricing model, the next stage was to construct effective tests. The most important early test was that carried out by Roll and Ross (1980) in which five factors were isolated from the return generating process, of which three were found to be priced. A number of tests followed which employed variants of the Roll and Ross procedure (for example, Chen [1983]; Chen, Roll and Ross [1986] also tested a model in which the factors were identified in terms of variables such as inflation and yield spreads). Problems in the research design were pointed out by Dhrymes, Friend and Gultekin, 1984. These mainly concerned problems of testing for the significance of priced factors when such factors are not unambiguously identifiable and the sensitivity of the results to research design, such as size of the asset subsets that were factor analysed. The original Dhrymes, Friend and Gultekin paper drew a response and defence from Roll and Ross (1984).

However, the waters were muddied still further by doubts as to whether the arbitrage pricing model is, indeed, testable (Shanken, 1982). This latter position drew a response, this time from Dybvig and Ross (1985) in which they disputed the original Shanken position; they went on to develop the relationship between CAPM and arbitrage pricing theory and demonstrated the testability of the latter on subsets of the asset universe. Shanken's (1985) rejoinder extends the debate to what he terms 'equilibrium arbitrage pricing theory' and that the relationship between factors and a preference-based aggregate is necessary for empirical studies of asset pricing. Estimation issues have been further developed in a number of ways. For example, Shanken (1992b) demonstrates that, in cross-section, risk premia may be estimated by a two-stage procedure, while Connor and Korajczyk (1988) and Mei (1993) use principal-components based approaches. More recently Connor and Korajczyk (1993) have developed asymptotic tests for determining the number of factors underpinning the model while MacKinlay (1995) uses tests based upon squared Sharpe ratios to distinguish between asset pricing models.

It is, perhaps, fair to conclude that the field of asset pricing, in both the theoretical and empirical domains, has advanced considerably and with a considerable amount of controversy on the way. Throughout, the development of this literature has closely paralleled our description of the development of a discipline discussed in the last section of the previous chapter.

Option pricing

Option pricing models had been developed prior to the 1970s (for example, Boness, 1964); however, these models were incomplete in that a number of important features were omitted from their modelling structures. The significant developments in the pricing of options under conditions of uncertainty were achieved by Black and Scholes (1973) and Merton (1973a) using continuous time mathematical procedures. The uses to which the option pricing model can be put far transcends the derivatives area alone. For example, the equity of a geared company can be viewed as a call option on the underlying assets of the firm with an exercise price equal to the redemption value of the debt capital. As a consequence, capital structure phenomena can be investigated within an option theoretic structure.

The breakthrough that was achieved by Black and Scholes (1973) and Merton (1973a) was to recognize that a continuously risk-free position could be formed via an investment in the underlying asset and an option written on that asset. Since the position was risk free, it should earn the risk-free rate of return to avoid arbitrage opportunities. By imposing this no arbitrage condition, a partial differential equation was obtained which, originally, was solved via the heat diffusion equation. However, no assumptions are made regarding risk preferences in the setting up of the hedge portfolio; thus, if a solution can be found for one set of preferences, this solution must hold for other risk preferences. The solution is particularly tractable if risk neutrality is assumed and this insight has spawned a considerable literature in the 'risk neutral valuation' area with considerable applications (see, for example, Cox, Ingersoll and Ross, 1985).

An alternative option pricing model was developed in discrete time using the same principles as those applied in the Black–Scholes model (see, for example, Cox, Ross and Rubinstein, 1979). In fact, this model is an example of a more general pricing theorem – martingale pricing (see Harrison and Pliska, 1979; Longstaff, 1995). The resultant model can be related to the Black–Scholes model as a limiting case. The model can also be extended to a 'lattice' framework, which is particularly appropriate for pricing in more complex option situations (see, for example, Boyle, 1988). Indeed, numerical methods are often necessary since closed form pricing solutions are not always available; Hull (2000) provides a useful discussion of numerical methods.

The Black–Scholes model was developed within a rigidly defined structure by making assumptions about the market and stochastic processes that are followed by the underlying assets. Not unsurprisingly, given the capital asset pricing literature previously discussed, the theoretical impacts of relaxing the underlying assumptions were investigated as part of the overall research process. In essence, in the development of option pricing models assumptions have to be made regarding the stochastic process and distribution followed by the underlying asset price, the market price of factor risks and the interest rate process. The Black–Scholes model, *inter alia*, assumed that the underlying process followed was Geometric Brownian Motion and that interest rates were constant. Stochastic interest rate models have been developed by Merton (1973b) and Amin and Jarrow (1992). Option pricing models which incorporate jumps into the underlying stochastic process have been derived in a wide range of papers including Merton (1973b) and Bates (1991). Since there is a considerable wealth of empirical evidence that indicates that financial time series are heteroscedastic, much attention has been focused upon developing option pricing models in which the Black–Scholes assumption of constant volatility is relaxed. An early example of such models is the Cox and Ross (1976) constant elasticity of variance model. Hull and White (1987) and Heston (1993), among others, have developed stochastic volatility models. A number of option pricing models have been generated which relax combinations of the above assumptions. For example, models with both stochastic volatilities and stochastic interest rates have been derived by Amin and Ng (1993) and Scott (1997); Bates (1996) and Scott (1997) present jump diffusion/stochastic volatility models. The Black–Scholes model assumed that the underlying stock did not pay a dividend during the option's life; this has implications for the early exercise of the option and consequent impacts on pricing. Roll (1977b) and Whaley (1981) developed pricing models for American option's on dividend paying stocks.

A very large literature has developed on the pricing of interest rate derivatives. The pricing of these derivative securities often necessitates the modelling of the behaviour of the whole yield curve and the incorporation of differing volatilities at differing parts of the yield curve. Ho and Lee (1986) derived the first no arbitrage based model for pricing interest rate derivatives. However, this model had a number of restrictive features (for example, it assumes that all spot and forward rates have the same standard deviations). Hull and White (1990) developed a model which extended the original Ho and Lee (1986) model in a number of directions, incorporating mean reversion into the interest rate process, for example. Heath, Jarrow and Morton (1992) proposed an important interest rate derivative pricing model in which the initial yield curve is taken as given and the evolution of the forward rate structure modelled. A major contribution of the Heath, Jarrow and Morton (1992) model was to demonstrate the restrictions on the parameters of the forward rate process that are necessary to satisfy the no arbitrage condition.

A number of option products have been developed which have pay-off functions that are somewhat more complicated than standard puts and calls. Such option types are referred to as exotic options and examples include barrier options, where the pay-off is dependent upon whether the underlying price passes a particular barrier during a particular period of time, and Asian options, where pay-offs depend upon the average underlying asset price. Pricing models have been developed for these and other types of exotic options; for example, Broadie, Glasserman and Kou (1998) for path dependent options and Kemna and Vorst (1990) for Asian options.

In the capital asset pricing literature we highlighted the articulation between theory development and empirical testing. The empirical testing of option pricing models tended, in the early stages, to be hampered by a lack of good quality data to use in the empirical tests. For example, option and underlying asset prices were never perfectly cosynchronous, with the result that any empirical conclusions were subject to errors-in-the-variables problems. With the advent of databases which contained data of a good quality and which overcame these early problems, the empirical testing in this area has become more robust. One of the early studies by MacBeth and Merville (1979) analysed stock option prices and found evidence indicative of over/ (under)pricing for out/(in) the money options. Rubinstein (1985) found similar results in the first subperiod of his data-set, but found the opposite situation in his second subperiod. In general, the extant empirical evidence suggests that the Black–Scholes model is characterized by pricing biases both in terms of the extent to which the option is in or out of the money and the maturity of the option; the biases are particularly strong for deep out of the money options. Bakshi, Cao and Chen (1997) empirically assess a number of extensions to the Black–Scholes model, both in terms of pricing errors and hedging performance, and conclude that models which incorporate stochastic volatilities and jumps outperform the benchmark Black–Scholes model. Bates (1996) provides an excellent overview and discussion of the empirical work that has been conducted in the option pricing area.

One area of the empirical options literature that has generated a considerable amount of recent interest is that of volatility smiles (see Dumas, Fleming and Whaley, 1998; Xu and Taylor, 1994). Since the variables in the Black–Scholes model are all observable other than the volatility, given the observed option price, the model can be inverted to provide an estimate of volatility – termed the 'implied volatility'. A volatility smile represents the relationship between the implied volatility of an option and its degree of 'moneyness'. This relationship is often U-shaped in that implied volatility is lowest for at the money options increasing as the option moves further into or out of the money. The existence of a smile indicates, for example, that the distribution of the underlying asset return may not be lognormal, as assumed in the Black–Scholes model. Bakshi, Cao and Chen (1997) find that the U-shaped smile still persists to a degree even when a number of the Black–Scholes assumptions are relaxed. Another related area of the empirical literature that is assuming increasing interest is that where the whole distribution (not just the volatility) of the underlying asset is recovered from option prices (see, for example, Jackwerth and Rubinstein, 1996).

The option pricing literature represented a significant theoretical advance in the understanding of the pricing (and associated phenomena) of assets that can be viewed as contingent claims. While the theoretical developments were profound, the models were still subjected to rigorous empirical testing.

Semi-strong form capital market efficiency

The third example that we consider in this chapter concerns the semi-strong form efficiency of capital markets. That is, whether prices 'fully reflect' in some sense publicly available information. This literature differs in its genesis to the asset pricing and options literature in that it did not evolve from a rigorously defined theoretical structure. Its origins lay mainly in the empirical domain, although a loosely defined a priori structure always underpinned the tests; that is, the concept of a semi-strong market being one in which prices speedily and unbiasedly react to publicly available information. The sufficient conditions for semi-strong form efficiency were also well known (Fama, 1970).

The seminal paper in the area is that of Fama (1970) where he surveys the extant empirical evidence at that time in support of market efficiency (the paper discussed weak and strong form efficiency as well as the semi-strong form). Fama (1991) updates this earlier paper and uses the term 'events studies' for semi-strong form efficiency studies. Among the papers discussed in the earlier paper there were two which defined the research design for most of the subsequent tests of semi-strong form efficiency (with, of course, some minor modifications). Fama *et al.* (1969) and Ball and Brown (1968) used the residuals from the market model around particular events to study the firm specific price reactions to those events (stock splits in the case of the former, earnings announcements in the case of the latter). The evidence was broadly supportive of semi-strong form efficiency in that prices reacted speedily and unbiasedly to new information. A significant number of subsequent studies have found similar evidence to support semi-strong form efficiency. The original events study methodology has been extended in terms of the return generating processes used and the statistics used for establishing significance (see, for example, Brown and Warner, 1985; Campbell, Lo and MacKinlay, 1997).

While much of the earlier work was empirically based, considerable efforts have been made on the theoretical front in the modelling of the relationship between stock prices and information. An early paper in the area was by Grossman (1976) where the fully revealing properties of prices were analysed and discussed. Of more direct importance to semi-strong form efficiency was the work of Verrecchia (1978), for example, in which further testable hypotheses were developed from a theoretical structure. More recently, behavioural models have been developed to provide insights into the articulation between information and prices. In Daniel, Hirshleifer and Subrahmanyam (1998), for example, investors are modelled as being overconfident with regard to their private information signals. An excellent discussion of the articulation between prices and information is to be found in O'Hara (1998). Even the definition of an efficient market has undergone some analysis, originating in Leroy's (1976) paper where he pointed out that the original 'fully reflects' definition was tautological; numerous subsequent definitions have been developed, for example, Rubinstein (1976) and Jensen (1978).

Although a considerable amount of empirical evidence was amassed in support of the semi-strong form of the efficient markets hypothesis, a number of studies (for example in the accounting area where the 'post-announcement drift' is a well-documented phenomenon) have found evidence that is not consistent with the Efficient Markets Hypothesis (EMH) in the semi-strong form. The early studies were summarized and analysed in Ball (1978), who pointed out that inherent research design problems (such as mis-specification of the pricing process and thin trading) could have led to the anomalous results. Watts (1978) incorporated the suggestions for changes in research design in Ball's paper but still found evidence inconsistent with the efficient markets hypothesis when quarterly earnings announcements were studied. Foster, Olsen and Shevlin (1984) found some evidence of size effects (see below) in the anomalous price responses.

When Basu (1977) reported that profitable investment strategies could be devised by going long in low price/earnings (P/E) stocks and short in high P/E stocks it seemed that another example of semi-strong form inefficiency had been discovered (as P/E ratios are publicly available information). However, Reinganum (1981) demonstrated that this anomaly was a manifestation of what has now become known as the 'size effect'; that is, smaller market capitalization firms have higher risk adjusted returns than larger market capitalization firms. An early theoretical rationale for the size effect was provided in a paper by Banz (1981) where an equilibrium asset pricing model in which a size variable figure in the equilibrium structure of returns was developed and empirically tested.

Further tests of the size effect (Keim, 1983) revealed a strong degree of seasonality in that the major part of the size effect arose in early January. (Other seasonal effects have been found, such as the day of the week effect [French, 1980] and monthly effects [Ariel, 1987]). An equilibrium asset pricing model of the Banz type clearly could not rationalize this seasonality. As the semi-strong form of the efficient markets hypothesis and the size effect are both strongly driven by empirical considerations, it was natural that a number of researchers such as Roll (1981) and Blume and Stambaugh (1983) should attempt to rationalize the size effect in terms of the features of the research design – in both cases as examples of measurement problems. An alternative rationale would be in terms of 'data snooping' (Lo and MacKinlay, 1990) where spurious patterns are found in past data-sets. A priori rationalizations have also been advanced, such as the tax-selling hypothesis (Roll, 1983) and the small firm distress factor premium (Fama and French, 1996). To date, though, a wholly satisfactory explanation for the size effect has not been forthcoming. The identification of size effects has also had an impact upon the research design considerations in events studies (Dimson and Marsh, 1986) and in tests of asset pricing models (Reinganum, 1981).

DeBondt and Thaler (1985) provided empirical evidence to support the notion that in the long term stock prices overreact to economic news, in the sense that poorly performing stocks in one period experienced higher returns in a subsequent period (with the reverse happening for strongly performing stocks). They advanced a behavioural rationale for this phenomenon – investors were poor 'Bayesians', in the sense that they overweighted sample information relative to priors. Some support for this hypothesis was provided in a number of other studies (for example, Chopra, Lakonishok and Ritter, 1992). However, Ball, Kothari and Shanken (1995) demonstrate that the overreaction detected is reduced when the research design is modified (in particular, the portfolio formation procedures) and that any overreaction is concentrated in stocks which have very low stock prices. Fama and French (1996) provide an explanation for this long-term overreaction in terms of a three-factor pricing model. However, their model is unable to explain the short-term return persistence that is reported in Jegadeesh and Titman (1993). A number of papers have been generated to provide rationales for this latter phenomenon (as well as the long-term overreaction); see, for example, Daniel, Hirshleifer and Subrahmanyam (1998) for a behavioural rationale based upon investor overconfidence and Hong and Stein (1999) for a model with heterogeneous investors characterized by differing rationality bounds. Fama (1998) provides an excellent assessment of the contribution of behavioural finance to an understanding of financial market phenomena and anomalies. Again, there has been much focus upon various features of the research design and Fama (1998) argues that the long-term reaction results are sensitive to various features of the methodologies employed.

An alternative approach to the events study methodology is to estimate the speeds of adjustment of prices towards their intrinsic values (Brisley and Theobald, 1996; Damodaran, 1993). Within a partial adjustment with noise structure it is possible to ascertain whether, over particular differencing intervals, prices overreact or underreact through time and, indeed, whether the price processes are explosive.

The efficiency or otherwise of the markets was given a further twist by the work of Summers (1986) in which he argues that slow mean reversion in price processes as a result of, for example, 'fads' would not be detectable using conventional random walk tests. This paper has spawned a number of papers which have attempted to test this proposition (for example, Fama and French, 1996; Poterba and Summers, 1988).

Summary

The finance field has developed considerably as an academic discipline over the last 40 years or so. In many respects it has represented a paradigm case for the model of discipline development described in the first chapter. There is a clear perception within the literature of a distinction between theoretical and empirical work and numerous sophisticated attempts to link the theoretical terms embedded within financial models with empirical observations. Developments within the literature have stemmed from the employment of relatively rigorous theoretical structures employing assumptions of rationality, perfect markets and full information, together with equally rigorous empirical testing with high-quality financial data. In the three examples described above, the articulation between theory and observation was apparent, particularly in the case of the asset pricing literature. Furthermore, the issues of theory development, experimental design and testing provide numerous illustrations of the problems discussed in Chapter 1.

Traditions of research in management accounting

In this chapter we will explore the traditions of research in management accounting, describing, in particular, the transition from normative to positive theory in the economic-based mainstream, and then some of the alternative traditions that have emerged in the area, specifically, behavioural accounting, contingency theory and interpretive and critical approaches. In addition, we will discuss some of the recent developments in the more practice-oriented research which has produced innovative techniques and systems.

In the late 1970s and early 1980s there was a growing awareness of a gap between the theory and practice of management accounting. At that time management accounting researchers were developing sophisticated mathematical models which practitioners considered too abstract and unrelated to their needs. To set the scene for more recent developments, we will explore the nature of this gap; but first we must consider what is meant by management accounting.

What is management accounting?

In its simplest terms, the conventional view is that management accounting comprises that branch of accounting which seeks to meet the needs of managers. It could be said that management accounting was first practised when managers began to receive information about their businesses. However, general use of the term 'management accounting' is comparatively new.

In the first half of the twentieth century the primary focus of accounting within businesses was on the determination of costs, with particular emphasis on product costing and the control of direct labour, direct materials and overheads. Most of the innovators were cost accounting practitioners. The major concern of cost accounting included the double entry recording systems for cost control and the identification of unit costs (that is, the cost of each product or departmental unit). In particular, systems were developed to identify the 'full' cost of producing each unit of output. Such concerns led to various methods of cost identification and allocation, and to an emphasis on absorption costing.

In the second half of the last century there was an increasing awareness that accounting information within the business should be appropriate to the needs of users – especially managers. This led to an emphasis on accounting information for managerial decision making. Management accounting developed as it became recognized that accounting information could be useful for both planning and control. This represented a fundamental shift away from cost accounting with its emphasis on obtaining an accurate or precise measure of costs, and towards management accounting with its emphasis on recognizing the appropriate (or relevant) cost for particular decisions.

This change in the nature of the internal accounting function was explicitly recognized by professional accounting bodies. For example, the Institute of Cost and Work Accountants changed the name of its journal from *Cost Accounting* to *Management Accounting* in 1965 and its own name to the Institute of Cost and Management Accountants in 1972. In the USA, the National Association of Cost Accountants had changed its name to the National Association of Accountants in 1958.

The management accounting literature expanded rapidly in the 1960s as researchers first developed, and then refined, new techniques for providing accounting information to managers. However, these techniques were developed on an ad hoc basis, and there was no explicit statement of any underlying theory guiding this research. Nevertheless, it is possible to identify some of the assumptions that were implicit in management accounting research, and this will be attempted in later sections of this chapter.

Traditionally the subject matter of accounting has been divided into sections, such as financial accounting and management accounting, for purposes of teaching, research and professional examinations. Undoubtedly, these sections overlap in practice and the boundaries are rather arbitrary. Nevertheless, academic textbooks portray management accounting as a coherent set of techniques which can be used to provide information for managers to assist their decision making. As is mentioned below, over the years there has been a considerable degree of consensus among academic textbook writers concerning the content of management accounting.

An early definition, which has been frequently used over the years, is that management accounting is 'The process of identifying, measuring and communicating economic information to permit informed judgements and decisions by the users of the information' (American Accounting Association, 1966). More recently, the Chartered Institute of Management Accountants (CIMA) included a similar but extended definition in its Official Terminology (see CIMA, 1996), while Drury (1996 – the best selling management accounting textbook in the UK) provides a more concise definition: 'Management accounting is concerned with the provision of information to people within the organization to help them make better decisions' (ibid.: 4). A similar definition, but one which explicitly widens the relevant information set, is contained in the recent European edition of Horngren's textbook (probably the best selling management accounting text worldwide). This points out that 'Management accounting measures and reports financial as well as other types of information that are primarily intended to assist managers in fulfilling the goals of the organisation'

(Horngren *et al.*, 1999: 5, emphasis added). Thus, although management accounting has traditionally been portrayed as providing financial (or economic) information, it is now recognized that other types of information may also be relevant for management decision-making.

As mentioned above, the management accounting literature expanded rapidly in the 1960s, but by the late 1970s and early 1980s researchers were beginning to identify a gap between 'theory and practice' (see Scapens, 1984), as many of the textbook techniques appeared to be little used in practice. The recognition of this gap affected management accounting research in two ways. First, there was increasing interest in studies that explored the nature of management accounting practice. Second, changes took place in the methodology of management accounting research. As we describe below, much of the material contained in current textbooks is derived from research that took place in the 1950s and 1960s. In general, this research was normative in character and based primarily on neoclassical economics. The subsequent research, which remained within the neoclassical economics tradition, developed a more positive stance, seeking explanations of the observed practices of management accountants. But, in addition, alternative approaches to management accounting research began to emerge.

In the following section of this chapter, we will first describe the economic-based normative research in management accounting, from which much of the material in current textbooks is derived, and then trace the change of emphasis that led to more positive (economic) theories of management accounting. Together these economic-based approaches could be regarded as the mainstream of management accounting research. Later, we describe a number of alternative approaches that have been used in management accounting research, including the behavioural, organizational, interpretive and critical. Finally, we will look at some of the recent developments in the more practically oriented management accounting research.

Mainstream (economic-based) management accounting research

The impetus for the development of management accounting as an academic subject in the 1950s and early 1960s came from the recognition that accounting information should be appropriate to the decision needs of users. In particular, it was recognized that a single concept of cost could not be appropriate for all purposes. This was in contrast to the earlier cost accounting that was more concerned with identifying the 'true' cost of producing each unit of output.

The phrase 'different cost for different purposes' became fundamental to the management accounting literature, especially for short-term decision-making. This phrase is taken from the US economist, J. M. Clarke, who in 1923 took a close look at cost accounting and argued that there can be no unique concept of cost. Similar ideas were developed in the UK during the 1930s, especially at the London School of Economics, by economists and accountants trained in economics (Baxter, 1938;

Coase, 1937). The fundamental notion of their approach was that relevant costs should be identified in the context of the particular decision at hand. A neoclassical economic framework was widely used by accounting researchers to analyse decision-making contexts, and this framework had a significant impact on the emergence of management accounting techniques in the academic literature.

Most management accounting textbooks identify the relevant costs for each decision within a neoclassical economic framework, based on the assumption that decision makers are profit maximizers. For this purpose, the profit-maximizing objective is pursued through marginal economic analysis, and this gives rise to the concept of incremental cash flows. However, profit maximization may not be a good description of individual decision-making practices and accordingly some dissent has been expressed about this objective (Anthony, 1960). Nevertheless, the neoclassical economic framework with its profit-maximizing objective forms an essential underpinning of management accounting's conventional wisdom. Most of the quantitative techniques developed in the 1960s were based on this 'information for decisions' approach.

The major attraction of an economic framework, with its profit maximizing objective, was that it permitted the formal analysis of management accounting problems. This provided a considerable measure of academic respectability for the study of management accounting. But it also meant that on occasions mathematical elegance took precedence over practical usefulness. The various planning and decision models described in current textbooks were developed using this framework, principally during the 1960s. Mathematical techniques which were being published at that time in the field of operational research also prompted a number of developments in the management accounting literature: for example, cost–volume–profit analysis, cost estimation models, mathematical programming of output decisions, learning curves, inventory control models and variance investigation models.

Although the link is not direct, the information for decisions approach and the idea of different cost for different purposes also had an impact on the subject of control in the management accounting literature. The conventional wisdom of management accounting puts responsibility accounting at the centre of the management control system. Such a system is used to monitor the outcome of individual decision-making. The link between decision-making and control can be seen in the distinction which is drawn between controllable and non-controllable variances and the notions of ex post budgets and opportunity cost variances (Demski, 1967).

The term 'conditional truth' has been used to depict the general theme of the early management accounting literature and to distinguish it from the 'absolute truth' theme of cost accounting (Horngren, 1975). The conditional truth theme provides a good description because management accounting's conventional wisdom recognizes that different costs are needed for different purposes, or in other words, that accounting information should be determined by the needs of users. Consequently, in developing management accounting concepts and techniques, researchers had to identify the information needs of managers. In general this meant constructing decision models that describe how decisions should be made. Once a decision model is postulated the conditional truth approach implies that the appropriate management accounting information can be determined by deductive reasoning, that is, 'truth' can be attained.

The neoclassical economic framework played an essential role in structuring the decision models used by researchers in the development of management accounting's conventional wisdom. It is not suggested that economics was the only influence, other disciplines such as management science, organization theory and behavioural science were undoubtedly present, but economics and especially the marginal principles of neoclassical economics were the dominant influence.

The neoclassical economic framework entails a number of assumptions. The decision-maker is assumed to have available, at no cost and with no uncertainty, all the information required to structure completely any decision problem and to arrive at a profit-maximizing solution using the principles of marginal analysis (Scapens and Arnold, 1986). In the decision models used by management accounting researchers in the 1960s, profit maximization was expressed in terms of the profits accruing to the owners of the business. This implies a further assumption: the decision-maker is either the owner or shares the owner's goals. Where decision-makers are not the owners, management accounting's conventional wisdom relies on techniques of responsibility accounting to achieve goal congruence. In the early days of management accounting research the way in which such techniques achieved goal congruence was unclear. However, more recently, behavioural science has been used to provide a theoretical link.

Another implied assumption of the decision models underlying management accounting's conventional wisdom is that individual decision-makers can be isolated from other decision-makers within the organization. In other words, decision-makers are identified as individuals, and group decision-making is not considered. This is because group decisions are only a trivial extension of individual decision-making within the neoclassical economic framework. All decision-makers are assumed to be profit maximizers and complete and perfect information assumptions provide a common information set. Thus, every decision-maker within this framework will arrive at the same set of decisions and so any one of them can analysed independently.

The complete and perfect information assumptions permit a high degree of analytical sophistication. Decision-makers are assumed to have the knowledge to use any mathematical techniques and costless information processing places no limits on the complexity of the information system. Once such a decision is analysed the appropriate accounting information can be determined. The normative nature of this approach comes across quite clearly in most textbooks. Management accounting is presented as a collection of methods and techniques, which *ought* to be used in practice.

The basic methodological approach involves deductive reasoning from the assumptions of neoclassical economics. These assumptions were initially accepted as self-evident truths in the early development of management accounting decision models. However, once researchers began to question these assumptions in an attempt to extend their models, there came about a change in emphasis in management accounting research, as we shall describe below.

Developments and extensions of management accounting models

In the early 1970s researchers began refining and extending the neoclassical economic framework which had been developed for management accounting research in the 1960s (see Scapens, 1984). The application of statistical decision theory probably had the most profound effect on the direction of research, principally because it enabled researchers to analyse management accounting problems under conditions of uncertainty. The framework used in the 1960s relied on the assumption that the decision-maker has available, at no cost and with no uncertainty, all the information needed to completely specify the decision problem and to arrive at the profit-maximizing solution. The application of statistical decision theory allowed the researchers to recognize the uncertainty of the decision outcomes. However, these researchers continued to accept (at least implicitly) the assumption of costless information.

Under conditions of certainty the decision-maker has available all the information he or she needs, at no cost. The questions to be answered concern the use of this information in arriving at decisions, that is, the decision model to be used. But when uncertainty is introduced into the analysis, questions concerning the cost and value information also become important. The provision of information can reduce uncertainty, but as information is a costly good its production should be evaluated in terms of its cost and benefit.

In the conditional truth approach, which was typical of management accounting's conventional wisdom, all the necessary information was assumed to be available. When uncertainty was first introduced into the analysis, this assumption was not challenged, and decision models became more and more complex as researchers attempted to construct more 'realistic' models, that is, models which completely specify the decision problem. Information economics, however, provided other researchers with a means of analysing the provision of information (Demski and Feltham, 1976). This represented a departure from the conditional truth approach, and its replacement by a 'costly truth' approach. In this alternative, information production costs are considered in constructing decision models, and the provision of information is itself problematic.

The researchers who developed complex models during the early 1970s, in areas such as cost-variance investigations and cost–volume–profit analysis, did not explicitly discuss information costs or the implementation difficulties associated with their models, and for this reason they can be rightly criticized. Nevertheless, their work demonstrated the limitations of certainty models and the complex nature of the uncertainty in business decision-making. In addition, they highlighted the need to include information costs in decision models. As such, they made a useful contribution at that time. However, the value of current research, which continues to ignore implementation problems and information costs, has to be questioned.

An important contribution which was derived from applying information economics to management accounting was that it caused researchers to identify separately information system choice and information system design (Demski, 1972). Previously, researchers focused exclusively on design issues and this had resulted in a succession of new and increasingly complex techniques. Most management accounting textbooks today still concentrate on design, rather than system choice. There is little explicit discussion of the costs and benefits associated with individual techniques. Nor is any great emphasis given to the rationality of selecting simple methods, when more complex alternatives cannot be justified on a cost-benefit basis.

Although information economics was able to clarify the role of information, it failed to yield general implications concerning the production of information, that is, the management accounting techniques to be used. For example, Demski and Feltham (1976: 249) reached the conclusion that 'whether one cost assessment alternative is preferred to another is an inherently contextual question'. In other words, the most appropriate accounting techniques always depend on the situation at hand and, in particular, on the costs and benefits of the information.

This is the costly truth approach. It implies that truth can be obtained, that is, a preferred accounting system does exist. But truth varies from one situation to another, according to the cost and benefit of the information. Truth in this sense is the 'ideal' accounting system – the system that ought to be used given all the relevant circumstances. Viewed in this way, the information economics approach did not fundamentally change the neoclassical economic framework that underpinned management accounting's conventional wisdom.

A change of emphasis

The application of information economics, however, did have an important impact on management accounting research. Information economics encouraged a number of researchers to examine, using empirical studies and simulation models, the relative advantages of simple and complex techniques (Jacobs, 1978; Magee, 1976). The conclusion that simple techniques can be optimal, given the costs and benefits of information provision, means that practitioners should not necessarily be criticized for failing to use more sophisticated models. An apparent consequence of this conclusion was that by the 1980s researchers had changed the emphasis of their work, and had become primarily concerned with explaining the reasons for observed management accounting practices.

An example will illustrate this change of emphasis. In 1938 Baxter suggested that the allocation of overheads in practice may be an approximate allowance for opportunity costs, but he argued that accountants should not rely on this approximation (Baxter, 1938: 273). He and his colleagues at the London School of Economics refined the concept of opportunity cost, and it became a central element of management accounting's conventional wisdom. In 1979 Zimmerman made a similar observation, without reference to Baxter's earlier paper. However, he attempted to explain the use of such an approximation as a rational choice in a principal–agent framework. He argued that as overheads are frequently allocated in practice, it would be reasonable to infer that the perceived cost of obtaining more accurate measures of the 'difficult-to-observe' opportunity costs are likely to exceed the expected loss caused by using overhead allocations as an approximation.

Other researchers using multiperson, principal–agent models demonstrated that conditions exist in which the simple techniques of management accounting observed in practice can be shown to be optimal (Baiman, 1982). However, few empirical tests were carried out, as the analytical work was not expressed in a form that could be easily subjected to empirical testing. Nevertheless, these approaches did offer explanations of existing practice, and challenged the belief that management accounting's conventional wisdom was not being more widely used simply because of the time lag between theory and practice. This is not to suggest that such models completely explained management accounting practice, but they did reflect a change in the emphasis in management accounting research, and encouraged researchers to develop theories that encompassed existing practices, rather than criticizing practitioners for failing to implement the conventional wisdom. As such, this represented a change of emphasis from normative to positive management accounting research.

Positive accounting research

Normative theories have a long history in accounting research; they have been used in both financial accounting and management accounting. But during the 1970s and 1980s accounting researchers became increasingly interested in positive theories. Whereas normative theories are concerned with prescription (what ought to happen), positive theories are concerned with explanation and prediction (what does/will happen). Positive theories, being grounded in empirical data, appeared to offer accounting researchers the prospect of avoiding the value judgements and theoretical speculation of the normative models. The tradition of positive theory in economics became a major force in accounting research, particularly in the 1980s. The research methods of positive economics first entered accounting research through financial economics and finance theory and, subsequently, influenced both financial accounting and management accounting research, especially in the USA. (See Chapter 5 for research on financial accounting.) Given the economic underpinnings of management accounting's conventional wisdom, it is not surprising that positive economics was influential in the development of positive theories of management accounting.

As discussed earlier, the conventional wisdom of management accounting assumed certainty, costless information and a single owner or decision-maker. During the 1970s researchers first relaxed the certainty assumption and then the assumption of costless information. Subsequently, agency theory researchers went further and separated the decision-maker from the owner. These developments, however, did not challenge the underlying economic basis of management accounting – the owner and decision-maker were still both assumed to be rational economic persons intent on maximizing their personal utilities, and markets were assumed to be available for managerial skills and information. The recognition that information is a costly good led researchers to view the firm as a series of contracts, freely negotiated between rational economic actors (see Jensen, 1983) and, although information asymmetries can arise, they do not affect the functioning of the market mechanism. Information is treated like any other good – it has value, which its owners can extract.

Although the objective of agency theory was to explain the behaviour of individuals as economic agents, such models also provided prescriptions for managerial action (based on the underlying theoretical assumptions). Nevertheless, agency models were regarded as satisfactory, only if at the same time as being prescriptive, they also accorded with the observed behaviour of decision-makers (Baiman, 1982). Thus, agency theory research had a distinctly positive character. But we must be careful. There is a vast range of work which can be described as agency theory research – from sophisticated mathematical modelling to empirical studies and behavioural experiments – each giving different weights to the normative and positive elements. In this context, Jensen, (1983: 334) distinguished between 'principal–agent' model building and the 'positive theory of agency', the former being primarily normative and the latter decidedly positive. Nevertheless, we can reasonably conclude that, to a greater or lesser extent, agency theory research is concerned with explaining observed accounting practices. This concern represents a shift in the methodology of management accounting research.

The methodological basis of positive accounting theory, such as the positive theory of agency, generally proceeds as follows (Jensen, 1983; see also Watts and Zimmerman, 1986): decision-makers choose particular courses of action based on their desires, needs, preferences, etc, and these choices are informed by their understanding of how the world works. Positive researchers cannot assist in the choice of a decision model, but they can help the decision-maker to understand how the relevant variables interact, that is, how the world works. Thus, it is argued, positive theories are concerned with the way in which variables interact in the real world, and are quite separate from the normative dimensions that are the province of the individual decision-makers. However, in order to determine the relevant variables for positive research, it is necessary for researchers to begin with assumptions about the form of the decision model used by the decision-maker (Christenson, 1982).

In management accounting, and particularly agency theory research, it is normally assumed that the decision-maker is a utility maximizer and that his or her actions are set within a system of competitive markets. As we discuss below, these are the core terms of neoclassical research economics. Such assumptions are not formulated as hypotheses to be subjected to positive (that is empirical) testing, they are conditions of the decision-maker which are taken for granted within the research. In view of the importance of neoclassical theory in management accounting research we will now provide a brief review of its nature and origins.

Neoclassical economics

Neoclassical economics emerged in the second part of the nineteenth century, and its essential characteristics changed little during the last century. It was translated into mathematics and its rougher edges were removed, but its core remained unchanged.

However, as we will discuss later, neoclassical theory has come under increasing attack from both inside and outside the economics profession in recent years.

Classical economists (such as Smith and Ricardo) grounded their economics in a theory of value based on the notion of production surplus. Neoclassical economists shifted the emphasis from value to utility, and from production to demand. It can be argued that this shift of emphasis was a response to the political implications of classical economics, and that neoclassical theory attempted to take economics out of the political arena by avoiding questions of income distribution (for example, see Tinker, Marino and Neimark, 1982). But despite such attempts to depoliticize economics, some writers have suggested that neoclassicism borders on an ideology (Wiles, 1983) or a political philosophy (Eichner, 1983). Thus, as argued by Tinker, Marino and Neimark, (1982: 191), it is impossible to divorce economics from political and social processes.

At the heart of neoclassical theory is the notion of economic rationality, whereby each individual maximizes self-interest, usually conceptualized as utility. Economic allocation is determined by relative, or marginal utilities. A requirement of equilibrium in all markets ensures that market prices reflect marginal utilities and thereby secure an optimal allocation of economic resources. In the case of firms, the availability of market prices allows economists to talk of profit maximization, although producers are also assumed to be utility maximizers.

Neoclassical economics has been called the 'marginal revolution' (see Kristol, 1981: 208), the distinctive features of which are: (1) the interpretation of prices as marginal valuations, and (2) the concept of opportunity costs. The notion of economic rationality embedded in neoclassical economics provides the starting point for a rigorous mathematical analysis of economic problems. Over the decades of the twentieth century, as mathematical techniques were developed and used to refine the elegance of economic models, the neoclassical core remained largely unchanged, and it is now deeply entrenched in modern economic theory. The following quote aptly summarizes this neoclassical core:

> Modern economic theory is based upon two specific assumptions about human behaviour and its social settings. One is the idea of 'utility maximization' as the motivational foundation for action, the other is a theory of markets as the structural location where transactions take place. The assumptions converge in the thesis that individuals and firms seek to maximize their utilities (preferences, wants) in different markets, at the best price, and that this is the engine that drives all behaviour and exchange. It is the foundation for the idea of the comprehensive equilibrium. The 'reform' of neoclassical theory has to begin with these two postulates of utility and markets.
>
> (Bell, 1981: 70)

These two postulates have been the subject of much debate (see Bell and Kristol, 1981). There is now a considerable body of empirical evidence, much of it derived from cognitive psychology, which suggests that the individual does not possess the degree of rationality required to undertake the marginal analysis needed for utility maximization. Consequently, a number of economists, including Simon (1959; 1979), have proposed alternative approaches for studying economic behaviour. Simon's postulate of bounded rationality led him to satisfying rather than maximizing behaviour, and this has been incorporated into the writings of a number of other economists, including the works of Cyert and March (1963) and Williamson (1985)

The second postulate of neoclassical economics, namely the centrality of market-based transactions, has also been the subject of debate. Neoclassical theory assumes that the market mechanism (the invisible hand) automatically equates prices and marginal utilities, thereby achieving an efficient allocation of resources. However, issues such as externalities, public goods, and imperfect information have led some economists to examine market failures and to study alternative forms of resource allocation, such as administered behaviour in hierarchies, and to the study of transaction cost economics – see, for example, Chandler (1977), Simon (1957) and Williamson (1975).

Despite the criticisms of neoclassical theory, it has provided the underpinnings for much of the prescriptive element of management accounting's conventional wisdom. Furthermore, the core elements of neoclassical economics are embedded in the positive theory of management accounting. But given the origins of neoclassical theory, it is important to recognize that it involves a political philosophy and as such cannot be regarded as a politically neutral representation of economic processes. Finally, in view of the criticisms mentioned above, we have to be aware of its limitations in management accounting research.

Limitations of positive management accounting research

Despite the criticism, neoclassical theory has remained both the core of modern microeconomics and the basis of much management accounting research. The empirical validity of the objections to utility maximization and the market mechanism are not generally denied by neoclassical economists. The response to such criticism is normally expressed in methodological terms. It is argued that the realism of a theory's assumptions is irrelevant; what is important is the theory's ability to predict economic phenomena (Friedman, 1953). In other words, although neoclassical economics may not explain the behaviour of individual economic agents, it can predict certain types of aggregate behaviour. For example, it is claimed that the neoclassical theory of the firm can help to answer questions such as 'how will the price of cotton textiles be affected by an increase in wage rates?' but it cannot answer such questions as 'what will be the price of cotton textiles?' or 'what will the X Corporation charge? and it is of doubtful validity in answering questions such as 'how will the X Corporation change its price when wage rates are increased?' (Machlup, 1967: 8).

Such methodological arguments recognize that neoclassical economics does not explain 'individual' behaviour; rather, it provides a calculus that, at a certain level of generality, can predict particular classes of economic phenomena. In other words, it is an abstract theoretical model that can be used to generate predictions, or hypotheses for empirical testing. The testing of such hypotheses provides empirical evidence about the hypothesized relationships, but it does not confirm the underlying model. The model is merely an instrument for generating hypotheses or predictions; it is not an empirical explanation of the predicted behaviour. As discussed in Chapter 1, the power of such instrumental models lies in their predictions, not in their explanations.

Over the years, neoclassical economics has been quite successful in predicting economic behaviour at the market level, but has been far less successful in predicting individual behaviour (see Cohen and Cyert, 1975: 51). In management accounting, however, we are normally concerned with the behaviour of individual firms, and of individuals within firms. Unfortunately, it is at this level of analysis that economists generally admit the limitations of neoclassical theory; and in particular, the limitations of the neoclassical theory of the firm.

It can be argued that the neoclassical theory of the firm is not a theory of the firm at all, but rather a theory of markets in which the firm is treated as a black box (see, for instance, Jensen, 1983: 325). Recent developments in the economics of organizations attempt to overcome this limitation of neoclassical theory (Walker, 1996). For instance, the view of the firm as a nexus of contracts offers the possibility of getting inside the black box of the firm. However, such developments continue to rely on the core assumptions of neoclassical economics and are subject to the same methodological underpinnings.

As discussed earlier, in agency theory the decision-maker is still assumed to be a utility maximizer operating within competitive markets. Again it is not the realism of these assumptions that is important, but their ability to generate predictions about behaviour within firms. Thus, following Machlup, we could say that although such theories may not explain the behaviour of individual economic agents, they may be useful in predicting general patterns of behaviour across many individuals and firms. For example, agency theory may not tell us how an individual agent will react to, say, a budget-based reward contract, but it might predict in general terms the circumstances in which we can expect to see budget-based contracts being used. Thus, the usefulness of agency theory is likely to be in predicting the prevalence of a particular accounting system or a particular reward structure across many firms. But agency theory will not explain why a particular individual acts in a certain way, or why a particular firm has a certain type of accounting system.

To summarize, neoclassical theory was developed by economists to predict general patterns of economic behaviour. It was not intended to be an explanation of how individuals do or should behave, except in a world which conforms to the general laws assumed by neoclassical theory. It was certainly not conceived as a basis for designing management accounting systems, although management accounting researchers used it to construct their decision models. Furthermore, economists appear to accept that neoclassical theory cannot be used to explain or even predict individual economic behaviour. It is useful only in predicting general trends in aggregate economic phenomena.

In management accounting research, positive theories informed by neoclassical economics may be useful for predicting general trends, but they will not be helpful in explaining individual behaviour; nor are they likely to be useful as guides to individual managers or firms about their own economic behaviour. Nevertheless, this type of management accounting research remains the mainstream for North American researchers and continues to be published in the principal US journals. Shields (1997), for example, in a study of research in management accounting by North Americans in the 1990s, found that economics is the dominant theoretical framework and that the most popular research methods draw on principal–agent models and production cost economics (Ibid.: 8). Thus, although as we have argued such research has methodological limitations, it is still the dominant approach within the majority of US schools of accounting. There are a number of reasons for this, not least being the need for accounting scholars to maintain credibility within universities dominated by scientists and technologists.

There are, however, alternative traditions and approaches to research in management accounting, many of which have been quite successful in illuminating issues in both theory and practice. It is to these alternative traditions that we now turn. As we will see, some of these traditions, which initially emerged as alternative approaches, are now part of the mainstream.

Alternative traditions in management accounting research

The preceding section discussed the mainstream tradition in management accounting research and its neoclassical underpinnings. However, the criticisms of neoclassical economics encouraged a number of management accounting researchers to develop alternative research approaches. The popularity of these alternatives has expanded rapidly over the last 30 years.

The search for alternatives began in a significant way with researchers looking at the behavioural effects of budgeting. These researchers were unhappy with the prevailing economic assumptions about human behaviour, and they studied how individuals react when presented with various types of accounting information. Behavioural accounting per se began in the 1960s and continues in various forms today. As this research focused on the individual decision-maker some researchers looked to behavioural science and psychology, especially during the 1970s. However, during that decade other researchers began to explore the organizational dimensions of management accounting and they turned to organizational theory to guide their research.

These two alternative approaches considerably widened the disciplinary basis of management accounting research, and it was subsequently widened even further when other researchers began drawing on social theory. These researchers introduced ideas from the work of various social theorists, such as Habermas, Foucault and Giddens. In this section we will describe the development of the alternative traditions in management accounting research and examine their methodological underpinnings. We will start with behavioural accounting, then move on to contingency theory and finish with the various social theories currently used in management accounting research.

Behavioural accounting research

The early behavioural accounting researchers began by questioning the behavioural assumptions of management accounting and examining the impact of accounting systems, and especially techniques of budgetary control, on individual behaviour. Argyris (1952) was one of the first writers to examine the 'impact of budgets on people'. He documented cases in which budgets were used to pressurize both workers and managers (and especially front-line supervisors) and he argued that the result was a general feeling of hostility and conflict between line managers and accountants. Such findings were to lead to an interest in behavioural accounting research, which became increasingly concerned with the impact of budgets on both individual and organizational performance.

A considerable amount of behavioural accounting research was undertaken in the 1960s and early 1970s, although not only by accounting researchers. Its objective was to demonstrate how the design and use of budgets can have an impact on the behaviour of organizational participants, their levels of job satisfaction and, most importantly, their individual performance and the performance of the organization as a whole. The research attempted to identify the important variables in the design and use of budgets that could be manipulated to improve organizational performance.

Other studies drew on behavioural decision theory and cognitive psychology to understand how information is processed in human decision-making. This area of human information processing (HIP) emerged alongside behavioural accounting, but it had a somewhat different focus. It explored how the individual responds to the various 'cues', makes probabilistic judgements and uses heuristics (or rules of thumb). This largely North American research was based on large-scale laboratory experiments, but as MBA students and even undergraduate students were often used as subjects in the research, concerns were expressed about its relevance to accountants and managers.

Although behavioural accounting research began with researchers asking how budgets affect people, by the end of the 1960s researchers were beginning to look at how people affect budgets. For example, Schiff and Lewin (1970) turned around Argyris's original focus and examined 'The impact of people on budgets' and Hofstede (1968) studied *The Game of Budgetary Control*. Such writers had recognized that people should not be looked at as passive objects, which are influenced by budgetary and other management systems, but as individuals who actively influence the way in which budgets operate.

This led to an increasing interest in how budgets work within organizations. Researchers started to explore budgeting, and management control more generally, in its organizational context. Such researchers turned to organization theory for ideas and in the 1970s contingency theory became a feature of management accounting research. Subsequently, other writers called for studies of accounting in its wider social context (for example, Burchell *et al.*, 1980), and for the introduction of various social theories into management accounting research – as will be described later.

Despite this widening of the focus of alternative management accounting research, behavioural accounting research has continued over recent years. There is now a section of the American Accounting Association devoted to 'Accounting, Behavior and Organizations', which publishes its own journal, *Behavioral Research in Accounting*. In addition, behavioural accounting research has also appeared in such mainstream journals as the *Accounting Review* and *Journal of Accounting Research*. In fact, it is probably fair to say that behavioural accounting research is no longer an alternative approach – it is now part of the mainstream. However, recently much of the focus of this research has been on auditors' judgements, and management accounting does not seem to be a significant focus of current behavioural accounting research.

Before moving on to describe the work which introduced organization theory into accounting research, it will be useful to look in a little more detail at the nature of the early behavioural accounting research and its methodological underpinnings. As mentioned above, the aim of the research was to identify the variables in the budgetary process which can influence human behaviour; for example, the tightness of the budget, the extent of participation, leadership style and so on. Knowledge of these variables, it was thought, would facilitate the design of budgetary systems, and ensure that performance was maximized and organizational objectives achieved. The research aimed to make human behaviour more predictable and, hence, make the individual human actor more controllable.

A feature of this research was its interest in the dysfunctional consequences of accounting. The word 'dysfunctional' was normally taken to mean harmful to the objectives of the organization. Behavioural accounting researchers attempted to locate such behaviour and to identify the variables that could be manipulated to limit dysfunctional consequences. An implied assumption of the research was that the function of the accounting system is to achieve organizational objectives, as set by senior management. Any behaviour that does not serve this function was regarded as dysfunctional. Thus, the research was grounded in what might be called a managerialist view of accounting, and it sought to understand the variables that influence human behaviour so that controls could be devised to ensure that organizational goals are achieved.

Although behavioural accounting research had normative objectives, that is, designing improved control systems, it adopted a largely empiricist methodology. Human behaviour was seen to be something that can, through observation and measurement, be categorized and generalized. For example, behaviours of students doing simple tasks in experimental conditions were assumed to reflect underlying behaviours that would apply to managers and other organizational participants in their everyday life. Furthermore, it was assumed that separate elements of behaviour can be isolated and studied, and then the various elements combined to provide theories of, for instance, budgetary behaviour.

This empiricist methodology explains why behavioural accounting research has been assimilated into the mainstream. As an alternative approach behavioural accounting research raised new questions and provided an alternative focus for accounting research, but it did not represent a significant shift in methodology. This shift was to come much later. What behavioural accounting research did achieve, however, was to open up the areas which were studied by accounting researchers and to extend the discipline base of the research to include behavioural science and psychology. In the next section we will discuss the research that exploited ideas from organization theory and later from social theory. However, it was only with the advent of research inspired by work in social theory that there was any significant methodological shift away from mainstream accounting research.

Organization theory and management accounting

In an important article, Otley (1984) surveyed the interrelationship between organization theory and management accounting. He observed that organization theory is not a coherent body of work, but is highly fragmented. His survey revealed that many elements of organization theory have been used by management accounting researchers, for instance, contingency theory, systems theory, and organizational and behavioural decision theory. Despite the fragmentation of organization theory, the work of these management accounting researchers appears to have shared a common goal; namely, the explanation of management accounting practices. However, as Otley pointed out, much of the work was 'armchair theorizing', that is, theorizing based on concepts derived from a reading of the organization theory literature, rather than being more directly grounded in empirical data (Otley, 1984: 138). Nevertheless, the focus of management accounting research based on organization theory was similar to the focus of the economic-based positive management accounting research described earlier. Both types of research were seeking to explain management accounting practice.

Otley concluded his survey with a number of recommendations for further research. Among other things, he called for more qualitative and interpretive research, and especially case studies. Later in this chapter we will describe interpretive research and in a later chapter we will discuss case study research. Here, we will take a closer look at the research based on organization theory that has attempted to develop empirically based theories of management accounting practice.

Such research seeks to identify relationships between particular environmental, organizational, behavioural and accounting variables. The researchers normally use cross-sectional studies in which measures of the relevant variables are obtained by mail or interview-based questionnaires and statistical analysis is applied to the data in order to identify significant relationships. Contingency theory research provides a good illustration of this type of work. Organization theory researchers have for some years been studying the relationship between environmental and organizational variables. This research has its origins in the pioneering studies of Woodward (1958) and Burns and Stalker (1961).

Over the years, organizational researchers have examined the impact of environmental factors such as technology, uncertainty and complexity on organizational design variables such as structure, decentralization, task complexity and so on. Accounting researchers added additional variables into such studies. They have attempted to identify relationships between the environmental variables and accounting variables, and also between organizational design variables and accounting variables. The accounting variables include the accounting techniques or procedures used; for example, some studies have looked at the use of particular types of planning models or budgeting techniques, whereas others have looked at the complexity of organizational information systems, participation in the budgeting process and the style of performance evaluation. Such studies attempted to determine general relationships, that is, relationships which are replicated across a large number of organizations. The object of the studies is to produce generalizations about the relationships between accounting practices and environmental and organizational variables (see Otley, 1980).

Other researchers have adopted somewhat similar techniques to examine further aspects of accounting practices. For example, there is a branch of the literature that examined supervisory styles (for example, Hirst, 1981). Such research is concerned with relationships between organizational and environmental variables and managers' use of accounting information, as well as the impact of different managerial uses of accounting information on the behaviour of subordinates. This research began with the behavioural research mentioned above, which examined management styles. For instance, some managers may be very constrained in their use of budgets, whereas others may use budgets quite flexibly (Hopwood, 1972). The early research was extended to identify generalizable relationships between management styles and such variables as budget performance, dysfunctional behaviour, job-related tension and role conflict. Other researchers have adopted similar approaches in studying the role of information feedback including, for example, its impact on job performance (Daft and Macintosh, 1978). Studies have compared the performance of subordinates who receive regular information about their attainment of, say, budget targets and others who receive the information only at the end of the accounting period. Once again the intention of the research is to derive generalizable relationships.

It is assumed that a knowledge of generalizable relationships will enable managers to design accounting systems which are compatible with the characteristics of their organization. However, such studies are subject to the same methodological limitations as we discussed in relation to economics-based positive management accounting research. They can predict general trends, but they cannot explain the processes through which management accounting systems evolve in particular organizations. The methodology relies on statistically significant correlations and does not exclude the possibility of exceptions. This creates a problem for the accounting systems designer – should his or her system be one of the exceptions? To answer such a question we need to know considerably more about how management accounting systems evolve. Cross-sectional studies can only identify the relationships between given variables at a particular point in time; they cannot explain how these relationships came about. Explanations of this nature require longitudinal studies that look at relationships over long periods of time. However, longitudinal and process studies of management accounting are now beginning to emerge, as will be discussed below.

Cross-sectional studies have been particularly popular in the USA and Australia, although a number of such studies have been undertaken in the UK and other parts of Europe. However, recently research in Europe has been moving in rather different directions. In his survey of organization theory and management accounting, Otley identified a number of cross-sectional studies in the USA, and a lesser number in Europe. He pointed out that, historically, organization theory in Europe has had a different emphasis to US organization theory. In particular, he referred to Kassem's (1977) comparison of American and European styles in organization theory. The US style tends to adopt a micro, or behavioural/psychological approach, to be functional and consensual, and to utilize laboratory experiments, surveys and observations of individual behaviour. The European approach, however, tends to be more macro or sociological, to be structural and grounded in organizational conflict and to utilize case studies of organizational processes and their interaction with the environment. The legacy for management accounting research has been a preference for behavioural, psychological and human information processing studies in the USA, whereas organizational and sociological studies are preferred in the UK and some other parts of Europe.

Whereas, cross-sectional studies in the USA have tended to focus on individual behaviour, studies in Europe have been more concerned with organizational and social factors. For instance, the research on human information processing in the USA has had only a limited impact in Europe, where a number of management accounting researchers have drawn on the legacy of European organizational theory to conduct sociological and organizational studies of management accounting. A good illustration of such work is the study of management control in the National Coal Board in the UK (see Berry *et al.*, 1985). This study attempted to explore management accounting in its broad organizational and social context.

Researchers interested in such organizational and sociological studies of management accounting have begun to explore a variety of methodological approaches, and have drawn on the work of a wide range of social theorists, including Habermas, Foucault and Giddens. Although these researchers can be described as 'post-positivist' in their outlook, they cover a wide spectrum of methodological and philosophical positions – as we see in the next section.

Social theory

As the above discussion indicates, contingency theory is similar to behavioural accounting in the sense that, although it extended the discipline base of management accounting research, it did not represent a shift in methodology. Thus, the continuing work in the area cannot be labelled an alternative tradition – it is now firmly in the mainstream. We have to look at the introduction of social theory to see work that can currently be categorized as alternative research. However, it may itself become part of the mainstream in the future. It is already acknowledged by a sizeable group of management accounting researchers, but it is still not sufficiently widely accepted for the term 'alternative' to have become inappropriate.

Over the years the journal most closely associated with alternative accounting research has been *Accounting, Organizations and Society*. But more recently new journals have joined the field, for example *Critical Perspectives in Accounting* and *Accounting, Auditing and Accountability Journal*. These journals publish such work in all areas of accounting, and not just management accounting. In addition, some journals specializing in particular areas, such as *Management Accounting Research* and *Financial Accountability and Management*, also encourage papers that could be classified as alternative accounting research.

Accounting, Organizations and Society first appeared in 1976, and its early volumes contained behavioural accounting research, as well as research drawing on organization theory. It was not until the 1980s that social theory began to appear in the journal. Its editor, Anthony Hopwood (together with colleagues), wrote a seminal paper in 1980 calling on accounting researchers to incorporate insights from the social sciences and especially the work of critical social theorists into their research (Burchell *et al.*, 1980).

In contrast to the introduction of behavioural and organisation theory, which led to well defined programmes of research – that is, behavioural accounting research and contingency theory – the introduction of social theory has generated a number of different research programmes. Each of these programmes has tended to become associated with a group of accounting researchers who draw on a specific branch of social theory, or more particularly a specific social theorist. Furthermore, there have been disagreements and disputes between these groups. However, as was discussed in Chapter 2 these research programmes can be divided into two broad categories – interpretive and critical research.

Interpretive approaches

The starting point for interpretive (and also for critical) research is the belief that social practices, including management accounting, are not natural phenomena; they are socially constructed. Consequently, they can be changed by the social actors themselves. This means that we should not be looking for universal laws and generalizations (as in the natural sciences), but for the rules, both explicit and implicit, which structure social behaviour. These rules, however, are themselves the outcome of social behaviour. In other words, social structures are recursive in that they are both a condition and a consequence of social action.

Thus, to study social practices it is necessary to look to the relationship between day-to-day social action and the dimensions of social structure. This will involve locating structures in their wider social context and examining how they have evolved through time. For example, we might explore how accounting is conditioned by the socio-economic system, how it provides a set of rules which structure certain types of organizational behaviour, and how these rules themselves emerge out of the social practices of organizational participants.

More specifically, we might start by recognizing that accounting provides a set of meanings or a language which is drawn upon in organizations, but which is itself an outcome of organizational activities. In so far as accounting focuses on the attainment of economic efficiency, it could be described as the language of capitalism. As such, it provides organizational participants with a system of relevance (or a set of meanings) that they can use to make sense of their organizational activities. It is also used to legitimize particular forms of organizational activities and as a source of power for particular groups within the organization.

To study accounting from this perspective requires detailed studies of accounting practices. It is necessary to locate current practices in their historical, as well as their economic, social and organizational contexts. For this purpose, researchers adopt a holistic orientation in which accounting is studied as part of a unified social system and a picture is built up of the system's wholeness. Such studies do not provide the type of predictive theory that is sought by positive researchers, as they are based on the belief that accounting practices are socially constructed and can be changed by the social actors themselves. Nevertheless, we can still construct theories to help us understand the nature of the social structures that shape social practices.

Such research enables us to interpret (that is, understand) management accounting as a social practice. A deeper and richer understanding of the social context of his or her work should enable the management accounting practitioner to cope better with the day-to-day demands of the job. Currently, a number of management accounting researchers, who are examining processes of accounting and organizational change, are drawing on a range of 'institutional' perspectives, from both organizational theory and alternative economic approaches, to inform their research (for example, see Scott, 1995; Hodgson, 1988). These approaches provide a theoretical framework for understanding how management accounting practices are both the medium and the outcome of social structures – that is, institutions (see Burns and Scapens, 2000).

However, critical theorists argue that by illuminating the various structures that underlie the social practices of modern society, the possibility is created for social change, and researchers should go beyond simply interpreting accounting practices. Whereas interpretive research is concerned with understanding the world, socially based critical research is concerned with creating the conditions in which social change is made possible.

Critical theory

Critical theorists explore and amplify the conditions of social life. In a management accounting context, this could involve explaining why accounting practices are so closely tied to the search for economic efficiency and why control is perceived as a technical activity rather than a social process. Also, it should enable us to recognize more clearly that the self-interested nature of organizational participants is as much a consequence of the existing modes of organizational control as a condition giving rise to the need for control.

As mentioned above, one of the criticisms of the interpretive approach is that while it is concerned with understanding social processes, it does not incorporate a programme for social change. This cannot be said of the labour process perspective, which although grounded in the writings of Marx, is associated with the later work of Braverman (1974). Both Marx and Braverman were less concerned with epistemological issues and more concerned with radically reshaping society. They start from the position that individual actions are conditioned by social structures and, in particular, that in a capitalist society work and employment relations are shaped to serve the interests of the capitalist class. Labour process researchers, consequently, seek to reveal how work and employment have evolved to serve class interests.

Some of the team that originally undertook the National Coal Board (NCB) study (mentioned earlier, in the section on organizational theory) revisited it from a labour process perspective. They had argued elsewhere that a labour process perspective can highlight how management accounting contributes to the subordination of labour, legitimates sectional interests, and furthers the aims of capital. In their reinterpretation of the NCB study, Hopper *et al.* (1986) pointed to the importance of class relationships for understanding accounting and financial control within the labour process.

The labour process perspective regards social action as primarily determined by social structures that are dominated by and serve the interests of the capitalist class. However, the relationship between action and structure has been a subject of considerable debate in the sociological literature. On the one hand, there are those who see action as all important, and argue that structure is the result of social action and, on the other hand, those who see social structure as the prime determinant of action. However, in developing his structuration theory, Giddens (1984) argued that structure is both the medium and the outcome of social action. In other words, although social actors draw on social structures in their ongoing social activity, they thereby reproduce those structures and this process of reproduction always carries the potential for change. Macintosh and Scapens (1990) used Giddens's structuration theory as framework for researching the social and political dimensions of management accounting.

However, the most influential social theorist in recent accounting research is probably the French social philosopher Foucault, who derived much of his inspiration from the German nihilist Friedrich Nietzsche. Foucault's work was primarily concerned with prisons, mental illness and sexuality and, although he never wrote about accounting, a relatively large number of alternative accounting researchers have adopted Foucault's ideas and/or methods. Foucault's work is not without its critics, but he has been described as 'the thinker who welded philosophy and history and in so doing developed a dazzling critique of modern civilisation' (Merquior, 1985: 16). In his critiques of contemporary social phenomena Foucault developed two epistemological techniques, which he called *archaeology* and *genealogy*.

For Foucault 'truth' is not the product of the beliefs and intentions of individuals, it exists only within the context of and is constituted by discursive practices (that is, the complex web of concepts, terms, etc. used to describe, discuss and theorize a particular social phenomena) of a particular historical period. His *archaeological* analysis examines discourses in terms of the systems of thought that existed at a specific period of time. However, it cannot account for the transition from one system of discourse to another. *Genealogy* is needed to surmount this difficulty by 'connecting them [the systems of discourse] to changes in the non-discursive practice of social power structures' (Audi, 1995). From this Foucault argues that it is possible to understand the development of modern society in terms of the power–knowledge relationship.

Various accounting researchers have used Foucault's methods to rewrite accounting history. Whereas mainstream accounting historians study accounting history in terms of the progressive development of modern techniques and practices, a Foucauldian analysis challenges the very notion of historical progress. Hopwood and his colleagues have come to be closely associated with the introduction of Foucault into accounting research. Hopwood (1987) discussed the archaeology of accounting systems, and questioned the traditional notion of historical progress, showing how 'accounting had become what is was not'. Aspects of both management accounting and financial accounting have been the subject of Foucauldian analyses. But perhaps the best example of a Foucauldian analysis in management accounting is Miller and O'Leary's (1987) discussion of the 'governable person'. They showed how standard costing and budgeting in the early decades of the last century were part of the complex social and organizational management practices that developed to regulate individual action in the name of economic efficiency.

Before completing this discussion two further social theorists need to be mentioned: Habermas who has attracted the interest of accounting researchers for some time, and Latour who has been introduced into accounting research relatively recently. Whereas Habermas is a social theorist in the sense of theorizing about society, Latour is a sociologist of knowledge who has studied the development of ideas in science.

Habermas's work developed out of the ideas of the Frankfurt School which had in the 1930s attempted to develop the writings of Marx, and which was re-established after the Second World War. Habermas was to become the most prominent of this later generation. His writings and those of other members of the Frankfurt School, such as Gramsci and Lukács, came to be termed 'critical theory', because their work attempted to provide a critique of the prevailing social order to assist the class struggle. However, in recent accounting research the word 'critical' has come to be applied to any approach which is sceptical about the nature of observation and accepts that there can be no value-neutral social facts and which seeks to provide a politically informed critique of the existing social order. In management accounting research, the ideas of Habermas have became associated with a group of accounting researchers who worked under Tony Lowe at the University of Sheffield in the 1980s and early 1990s (for example, see Laughlin, 1987).

The focus of Latour's work, however, is rather different (for example, see Latour, 1987). He is interested in understanding the way in which science and technology are produced, and argues that technology is not part of a pre-existing order waiting to be discovered, rather it emerges as a result of an elaborate process of 'fabrication'. Such ideas have only relatively recently been introduced into management accounting research. For this purpose technology is very broadly defined, to include artefacts (for example, budget documents), processes or uses of technology (for example, producing and making a budget) and the knowledge of people who design or operate a technology (for example, the knowledge which relates costs and specific activities). Preston, Cooper and Coombs (1992) used this broad definition to apply Latour's ideas to a study of the introduction of management budgeting in UK hospitals. The notion of fabrication has become a focus of researchers studying the application of accounting procedures to new areas, especially in the public sector.

The impact of social theory on management accounting research

The introduction of social theory has been a major development in management accounting research and has undoubtedly significantly extended our understanding of its broader organizational and social context. Drawing on the social theorists described above, this research has re-evaluated the history of accounting, revealed its interested nature, challenged the claims to an inherent accounting rationality and neutrality, and provided alternative insights into the functions of accounting.

While recognizing these considerable achievements, in the mid-1990s some concerns were raised about the role of, and the relationship between, social theory and accounting research (see Humphrey and Scapens, 1996). The early accounting research which drew on social theory tended to proceed by outlining the work of a particular social theorist and then providing illustrations, frequently in the form of case studies, of how the theory could be used in a specific accounting context. While this was necessary as researchers explored individual social theories in a management accounting context, it has nevertheless left a legacy of papers that use a selected social theory to illustrate accounting in practice, with little reflection on the theory itself. The social theory or theorist is often used to give authority for or legitimacy to the accounting research, but there is sometimes little interaction between the theory and the accounting research. However, it is now regarded as more important for researchers to use social theory to address management accounting questions and issues, rather than to use accounting cases to illustrate the application of some new social theory.

Although the earlier discussion indicated that there are differences between the various groups who use social theories in management accounting research, there are also important similarities. Accounting is seen as socially constructed, and not independent of the organizational, social and political actors. Furthermore, although, as indicated in Chapter 2, these researchers can be placed at different points on an ontological continuum, there is a generally accepted view in much of this research that social activity is the result of a complex interplay between social structures, social action and individual agency.

Practice-oriented research

Although it could be argued that all management accounting research is in some sense concerned with what management accountants do, and as such is relevant to management accounting practitioners, there has been a particular stream of research in recent years which has focused on issues of direct interest to practitioners. This research has been primarily concerned with the development and application of new techniques of cost management, non-financial performance measurement, strategic management accounting and so on. Such research is frequently reported in journals that are more likely to be read by practitioners, for example, the *Journal of Cost Management* and other professional journals. However, some of the research has also appeared in academic journals.

As mentioned at the beginning of this chapter, much of the early research in management accounting was regarded by practitioners as too abstract and unrelated to their needs, and this led in the 1980s to the recognition of a gap between theory and practice. In the UK, this was clearly illustrated at a management accounting research conference held in December 1980 (see Cooper, Scapens and Arnold, 1983: 1–2). This was to be the first of a series of such conferences at which management accounting researchers, together with a small number of practitioners, met to discuss research. Although a number of management accounting topics were discussed at these conferences, the conclusion emerged that there was an urgent need for research to describe the nature of management accounting in practice. It was generally believed that the conventional wisdom of management accounting textbooks was not widely used in practice. However, at that time, the belief was based on anecdotal evidence, occasional visits to companies and a few published surveys of the use of particular management accounting techniques. There was clearly a need to study the nature of management accounting in practice.

At first researchers used questionnaire and interview studies in order to obtain a general picture of management accounting practice. Questionnaires were sent to companies asking respondents to indicate the extent to which particular management accounting techniques were used. In addition, some researchers visited companies and discussed the use of particular techniques with senior managers. But it was soon realized that such approaches can give only a very superficial view of management accounting practice and can lead to serious misunderstandings about the use of management accounting techniques in individual organizations. As a result, some management accounting researchers began to use more intensive fieldwork and/or case studies, which seemed to offer richer descriptions of management accounting practice. Some of these researchers looked to the work undertaken in Scandinavia, especially Sweden, where there had been a long tradition of case study research in accounting, particularly in the public sector.

The importance of fieldwork and case studies was also recognized in the USA, notably by Kaplan (1984; 1986). But it was Kaplan's subsequent work with Johnson (Johnson and Kaplan, 1987) which had a major impact on both management accounting research and practice, not only in the USA, but also worldwide. Their claim that management accounting had lost its relevance, and was failing to meet the needs of managers in modern businesses, prompted much concern in the management accountancy profession. Subsequently, new management accounting techniques, such as activity-based costing, balanced scorecards and strategic management accounting were developed, largely by practitioners within their own organizations. The role of the researchers has tended to be one of reporting the techniques through case studies of innovative practices, and then refining the practices for more general use (see Kaplan, 1998). In this refining process it is possible to discern some elements of the normative approach of management accounting's conventional wisdom. For example, the techniques tend to be presented as the way in which senior management can obtain the information it needs for decision-making and control – which takes us back to the definition of management accounting at the beginning of this chapter.

But in addition to the development of new techniques, more recent research has attempted to assess the validity of Johnson and Kaplan's criticisms of management accounting practice. Some of this research has used longitudinal case studies and other forms of fieldwork to understand the ways in which (if any) management accounting practices are changing. It examines how traditional and new management accounting techniques and systems are used in practice, the problems and issues of introducing new practices, and the interaction between management accounting and other forms of organizational control. Such research draws on a wide range of theoretical frameworks from economics to organization theory and social theory discussed earlier. As such, it reflects a more pluralistic approach (as called for at the end of Chapter 2), with different theories and research methods, and even different methodologies, being used to address management accounting issues. Thus, rather than seeing different research methods and methodologies as competing, and as basically incommensurable, they are being used to provide a variety of insights into a range of management accounting research questions. Such research has the potential to broaden the scope of management accounting from a narrow microeconomic approach, to a broader more business-oriented approach (Scapens, 1999).

Summary

In this chapter we have traced the development of a number of the major research traditions within management accounting. We noted that management accounting emerged as the techniques embodied within cost accounting were extended to meet the information needs of managers. Initially, the research was based upon concepts of economic rationality and behaviour, which provided ample opportunity for the development of the techniques and tools that are now a central feature of most management accounting textbooks. However, following the recognition of a gap between theory and practice, there was a change of emphasis as researchers attempted to explain observed management accounting practices. Within the mainstream, this research was influenced by microeconomics, especially neoclassical economics, and the subsequent developments in information economics and agency theory.

But in addition to this mainstream research, there are a number of alternative research traditions in management accounting. We described how behavioural, organizational and social theories were introduced into management accounting research. The first two, behavioural and organizational theories, although extending the discipline base of the subject, did not represent a major methodological shift, and as a result they have themselves become part of the mainstream. However, with social theory, a number of different, and sometimes competing approaches, were introduced.

Overall, there has been a considerable diversity in management accounting research in recent years, and the subject is quite different from finance which, as described in the previous chapter, has the coherence of a single intellectual discipline. Although the diversity in management accounting research may be seen as enriching the subject, there are dangers. For example, the lack of a central core, or paradigm, can lead to disagreements over the nature of the subject and the implications of the research. To some extent, this has already happened in management accounting research with, for instance, mainstream management accounting researchers dismissing the work of critical theorists, and vice versa. But if significant progress is to be made, there needs to be a recognition that a range of research approaches are valid, and that together they can provide richer insights into the subject.

In the next chapter we will turn our attention to financial accounting which, as a practical craft, has its roots in antiquity. Accounting historians tell us that the techniques of financial accounting formed one of the oldest academic disciplines and even though it may be disputed, some believe that accounting is the oldest profession.

Traditions of research in financial accounting

Vivien Beattie

Over the years, financial accounting research has gone though a number of distinct phases. In this chapter, we will describe these phases and relate them to developments in accounting practice. We will begin by outlining the development of financial accounting practice over the past two centuries and locating the accompanying changes in accounting theories.

In the second section we will describe some important historical developments in accounting practice and identify issues which were considered important by accounting practitioners.

In subsequent sections we will describe the principal areas of, and approaches to, financial accounting research, and assess their methodological bases. Research areas can be driven either by the use of particular methods or particular theories or by the focus on a particular topic. In this chapter, the section headings reflect a pragmatic approach to the identification of research areas – they should not be regarded as necessarily mutually exclusive. We will begin with the a priori research which was the basis of the income determination model. We will then move on to decision-usefulness research, empirical research, positive accounting theory, the return of the measurement perspective, the interdisciplinary perspectives on accounting project (including critical accounting) and international accounting research.

The nature and origins of financial accounting

Financial accounting is usually considered to be the process whereby the economic activities of an organization are measured, summarized and communicated to entities outside the organization. It is generally associated with financial reporting to the owners of a business. But it also encompasses such activities as the reporting to club members on the financial activities of their club, the reporting to citizens on the financial activities of their community's local government, and the financial reporting of a social service (such as a hospital) to local interest groups. Nevertheless, most financial accounting research has been concerned with the reporting of business activities. This is largely because financial accounting gained much of its practical importance as a result of the need to make businesses accountable to their owners and creditors.

Financial accounting gained its importance as a practical activity long before accounting researchers came on to the scene. Consequently, accounting practices were shaped by accounting practitioners and the government agencies which took an interest in the protection of share-owners and creditors.

However, in more recent years, especially in the USA, academic accounting researchers have had an impact on the development of financial accounting. Today, financial accounting is a technical craft directly influenced by various government agencies and the professional bodies which represent the practitioner and the academic accounting communities. However, the influence which these agencies and bodies exert on accounting practice is conditioned by various environmental factors, that is, the economic, social and political contexts in which they operate. Indeed, it was environmental factors which led to the emergence of financial accounting in the first place, and later to the emergence of the accounting profession. This section briefly traces the development of financial accounting in the UK and the USA, and the next section will explore the relationship between accounting theory and practice. (The focus is on these two countries because, historically, they have been most influential in the development of both practice and research.) Whereas financial accounting emerged earlier in the UK than in the USA, it was researchers in the USA who were influential in subsequent developments, due partly to the early establishment of accounting as a university subject in that country.

Although the literature on accounting extends back many centuries, it was the changes in manufacturing industry brought about by the Industrial Revolution which were responsible for much development of financial accounting in the UK. The rapid increase in the scale of business activity brought about a major demand for bank credit and significantly increased the proportion of business transacted in a corporate form. The English Corporation Acts of the mid-nineteenth century imposed financial reporting and auditing obligations on companies, but without specifying how these obligations were to be discharged. It was natural, therefore, that the estate accounting model, which had evolved from feudal manorial obligations, should form the basis of the reporting obligations of companies. This model assumed the permanency of capital and held the steward accountable for the revenue and expenditure of the estate. Thus, financial accounting emerged with a proprietorial stewardship orientation. Furthermore, the historical cost principle was carried over from the bookkeeping practices of the manorial accounts. In addition, the conservatism principle, common in the estate tradition, where stewards had a self-interest in understatement, was retained and reinforced by legislation and by auditor self-interest.

During this period, the USA remained a predominantly agrarian economy, but by the late nineteenth and early twentieth centuries the complexity of business had increased and the USA caught up with the UK in terms of industrial development. Holding companies emerged and active markets for shares soon developed. The latter led to calls, endorsed by the New York Stock Exchange, for greater public disclosure to mitigate speculative trading. Professional associations of accounting practitioners were formed in England in the 1870s and, in the USA, the forerunner to the American Institute of Certified Public Accountants (the American Institute of Accountants) was formed in 1887. In the early twentieth century university education in accounting was embryonic in the USA and non-existent in the UK. Consequently, there was little accounting research. The developments in accounting thought which did take place were the results of work done by accounting practitioners.

The development of practice and the relationship with accounting theory

In the early stages of its development, accounting theory arose out of accounting practice. It was only later that accounting researchers began to develop theories which contained prescriptions for practitioners. For the time being, we will restrict ourselves to identifying the role of accounting theory in relation to the development of practice. The nature of the theories and the methodological basis of the research will be described in later sections

As already mentioned, accounting practice developed along with the growth of business activity in the nineteenth and early twentieth centuries. Professional accounting bodies were established in both the USA and the UK, and government legislation had a significant impact. However, the economic problems of the 1920s and 1930s led to increased governmental involvement in the development of accounting practices during those decades. In the USA following the First World War, the alleged abuses of corporate funds led to the 1929 stock market crash which was followed by the depression of the 1930s. The 1933 and 1934 Securities Laws institutionalized the corporate audit and in 1934 the Securities and Exchange Commission (SEC), a government agency, was set up with the authority to determine the accounting and auditing practices of public companies. Thus, significantly, control over accounting practices was taken out of the hands of the accounting profession in the USA. The SEC did, however, rely heavily on accounting practitioners, and especially their professional bodies, for guidance.

Members of the American Institute of Accountants (AIA) soon realized that they would have to take action or lose their role in the development of accounting practices. During the period 1932–34 the AIA, in collaboration with the New York Stock Exchange, formulated five principles of accounting to be followed by companies on the stock exchange. The formation of the SEC reinforced the perceived need for 'uniform' accounting principles. However, the profession could only point to 'generally accepted accounting practice' as the source for such principles.

The initiative was taken up by academics, who were by then firmly established in the US universities. Publications by writers such as Paton and Littleton during the 1920s and 1930s led to the development of a coherent income determination model, derived largely from the then existing accounting practices. This model, which recognized income as the surplus arising from the periodic matching of revenues and expenses, switched attention away from the balance sheet and to the income statement as the primary financial statement. Following the stock market crash, a model which emphasized earning power rather than balance sheet values seemed particularly appropriate.

In the UK, it was the Royal Mail case of 1930 which prompted a major revision of what was considered good accounting practice. Until that time, accounting was viewed largely as a matter of private concern between the shareholders and their directors, although there were some regulations aimed at protecting the interests of creditors. This view was reflected in the provisions of the 1929 Companies Act. However, the corporate sector of the economy was changing rapidly. Following the First World War, economic growth, accompanied by a merger wave, saw the emergence of many large corporate entities. In such instances, the shareholder control view of accounting was no longer appropriate, as there was increasing divorce of ownership from control. The Royal Mail case exposed the manipulation of secret reserves to give an appearance of profitability at a time of unsuccessful trading. Consequently, shareholders had great difficulty in obtaining reliable information about their investments.

Paton and Littleton's income determination model incorporated the proprietorial orientation of the existing practice, as well as the historical cost, realization, accruals and matching principles. It provided the intellectual framework for the development of accounting in the USA for the following 30 years, a framework grounded firmly in existing practices. The model was gradually refined and extended to encompass new business developments. Between 1939 and 1959 a committee of the AIA, the Committee on Accounting Procedure (CAP) issued 51 non-mandatory Accounting Research Bulletins. However, during the late 1950s accounting academics became increasingly aware of methodological issues and this led to a concern to establish a rigorous theoretical framework for the development of accounting theory. The work of these academics will be described later in the section dealing with a priori research.

Meanwhile, in the UK the Second World War had caused a shift in social attitudes in favour of state action on matters of public interest. The Royal Mail case focused attention on financial reporting issues, especially those of holding companies. The war delayed subsequent action, but following a lengthy period of debate, in 1945 the Cohen Report indicated the government's intention to intervene to a greater degree in corporate reporting matters. This was followed by the 1948 Companies Act, which set out detailed financial reporting requirements.

However, by the 1960s the limitations of the income determination model developed in previous decades had become apparent. In the USA, the CAP had been replaced by the Accounting Principles Board (APB) in 1959. The intention behind the establishment of the APB was to resolve accounting controversies by investing heavily in research, which would provide a conceptual base for its 'opinions'. A series of 31 Opinions and four Statements on Issues such as goodwill, pensions, business combinations and segmental reporting did emerge, but there was little consensus regarding them. One reason for the lack of consensus lay in the fact that, in the absence of a coherent theoretical framework, accounting issues were being determined through the pressures exerted by special interest groups, such as company managements, government agencies and the financial community.

Furthermore, during the 1960s abuses of accounting principles, particularly with respect to goodwill and group accounting, were being publicized by the press. In 1971, in response to this publicity, the American Institute of Certified Public Accountants (AICPA), the successor to the AIA, appointed two study groups – one to look at the establishment of accounting principles and one to look at the objectives of financial statements. The former resulted in the replacement of the APB by the Financial Accounting Standards Board (FASB) in 1973. The latter resulted in the Trueblood Report titled *Objectives of Financial Statements*, also in 1973.

At about the same time, pressure for reform in the UK came to a head with several public 'accounting scandals', notably the GEC/AEI takeover in 1969. Against the background of intense political pressure the professional accounting bodies set up the Accounting Standards Steering Committee (ASSC, later renamed the Accounting Standards Committee, ASC) in 1970. The early UK standards were similar to those issued in the USA. In 1975 the ASSC published *The Corporate Report*, a study which, like the Trueblood Report, explicitly considered the objectives of financial reporting.

At that time accounting researchers were also interested in the objectives of financial statements. It became generally accepted that the primary objective of financial accounting should be to aid users in making their decisions. Investors and creditors continued to be seen as the main users in the USA, while in the UK *The Corporate Report* acknowledged wider reporting responsibilities, identifying also employees, the government, customers, suppliers, and the general public as legitimate user groups. Consequently, accounting researchers adopted a decision-usefulness approach, and the earlier income determination model was replaced by a user decision-making model. This move was consistent with the conclusions of various studies of income measurement, that is, that there is no 'ideal' income measure, but rather different measures of income are required for different users in different decision-making settings. By the mid-1970s, the decision-usefulness approach was firmly established in both the USA and the UK.

In the USA, the 1970s saw an increasing interest in the use of empirical research methods, especially in capital markets research. As the decade progressed these methods were applied to financial accounting issues. Such research methods typify the mainstream US financial accounting research tradition of the 1980s, with its emphasis on what came to be known as 'positive accounting research'. This research evolved from interest in the late 1960s and early 1970s in the economic consequences of financial reporting practices. In the 1980s it was extended, using agency-theoretic arguments to explain management's choice of accounting policies and to provide a theory of regulation (see Watts and Zimmerman, 1978; 1986).

In the UK, the 1970s saw extensive growth in the academic accounting community. However, research in the UK did not follow the US direction, for theoretical work on income theory continued to be central to the UK research effort. The standard-setting programme of the ASC provided a stimulus for research with a focus on income measurement issues. Another significant difference between accounting research in the USA and the UK was the interest in the UK in the disclosure of information to employees, trade unions and other social interest groups. This arose, in part, because of the existence of a powerful labour movement in the 1970s and a concern with issues of industrial democracy. Some of this research was conducted within the user needs framework, while other work was performed in specific contexts, such as redundancies and proposed factory closures. This concern with wider social issues led some UK researchers to begin exploring accounting regulation as a social process. This contrasts with the economic orientation of studies of accounting regulation in the USA. Thus, there continues to be a diversity of interests among accounting researchers in the USA and UK.

At the practical level, however, there did seem to be some similarity of interests. Practitioners in both countries were particularly concerned with accounting standards and there appeared to be a shared desire for a conceptual framework to provide a rigorous foundation for the logical development of accounting standards. Although many researchers appeared to believe that it would not be possible to find a framework that met the decision needs of all the various interest groups, it was widely recognized that the desire for a conceptual framework arises out of the need for accounting standard setters to deal with the lobbying and pressures imposed on them by the representatives of these various interest groups. A literature began to emerge during the late 1960s dealing with the political nature of the standard setting process, including the incentives of the interested parties and the role of technical accounting considerations versus economic consequence arguments in standard setting. In addition, in the early 1970s, writers started to explore the economic and social consequences of accounting standards (Zeff, 1978). Clearly, these two themes are linked, for it is generally a belief in the existence of economic consequences that gives rise to lobbying behaviour.

During the 1990s, there have been two major developments affecting practice, driven largely by developments in information technology – the globalization and growth of world markets, especially capital markets, and the rise in the importance of intangible assets as the major drivers of corporate value. This environmental change, which has resulted in the 'New Economy', is frequently referred to as the 'Information Revolution' (analogous to the earlier Industrial Revolution). It has impacted upon accounting practice in two ways. First, since investors now wish to invest worldwide, the existence of national accounting rules is seen as a barrier to greater investment that also increases the cost of capital for companies. There is a major effort under way, spearheaded by the International Accounting Standards Board (IASB), to gain worldwide acceptance for a single set of standards. In 2000, a comprehensive core set of standards was conditionally approved by the International Organization of Securities Commission (IOSCO) for use in cross-border listings and also in that year the European Union (EU) said that European listed companies will be required to adopt International Accounting Standards (IASs) by 2005.

Second, there is a concern that the traditional accounting model, with its focus on historical, financial information and adherence to strict recognition and measurement rules, is increasingly inadequate to serve users' needs. There is considerable discussion about a more comprehensive model of business reporting that captures more non-financial, forward-looking and soft information about strategy, risk and intangibles (for example, AICPA, 1994; FASB, 2001; ICAEW, 1999; ICAS, 1999; Lev 2000; 2001; for a review see Beattie, 2000).

A further influence upon research from the world of practice has been the statements emanating from the SEC during the late 1990s, encapsulated by the now famous speech given by the former Chairman, Arthur Levitt, in 1998 called 'The numbers game'. In this, he expresses grave concern regarding the manipulation of accounting numbers and hence the quality of earnings and of financial reporting generally (Levitt, 1998). Since financial reports are the joint product of decisions made by both company management and the external auditors, both parties come under fire. This has given further motivation to studies into earnings management and disclosure choices.

A priori research

As described above, financial accounting research developed in the 1920s and 1930s in the USA, where accounting was already established as a university subject. However, there was a smaller but significant research effort conducted in the UK mainly at the London School of Economics by economists and accountants trained in economics. In those early days of financial accounting research, accountants were interested in distilling theoretical principles from existing practices, whereas economists were interested in deriving measurements of 'true income'. Whittington (1986) described the former as an empirical inductive approach and the latter as a deductive approach. These different approaches began to converge after the Second World War, leading to the research of the 1960s which was described by Nelson (1973) as the 'golden age' of a priori research in financial accounting .

The empirical inductive approach of the early accounting researchers involved first of all surveying and synthesizing accounting practices, and then attempting to generalize about the principles underlying observed practices. According to Whittington (1986: 7), these researchers produced inductive theories based on rationalizations of the prevailing practices. They culminated in the American Accounting Association's *Accounting Principles Underlying Corporate Financial Statements* published in 1936. The most thoroughly worked out general principles were based on the historical cost method and incorporated such ideas as the realization principle and the matching concept, and notions of materiality, conservatism and going concern. As Whittington notes, the empirical inductive approach does not purport to be solely positive (a statement of what is), but can also be used in a normative context (as a statement of what ought to be). The implicit normative assumption is that specific accounting methods should conform to the general principles that are believed to underlie current practice.

While accounting researchers were attempting to derive the general principles of current accounting practice, economists such as Canning (1929) in the USA and Edwards (1939) in the UK were using economic analysis to criticize basic accounting methods. Such researchers used microeconomic theory as a benchmark for evaluating accounting methods. They 'deduced' an ideal income measure from the basic postulates (assumptions and laws) of neoclassical economics. Canning, for example, used the income measure proposed by the economist Irving Fisher (1906). He admitted that Fisher's ideal measure of income was impracticable, but suggested a number of surrogates that he considered to be practicable. He used these surrogates as the basis for his critique of existing accounting practice. Other economists in the period attempted to build similar income determination models. The primary objective of their research was to determine a measure of 'true income' or, if that was impracticable, to derive a practical surrogate for 'true income'.

Following the Second World War this line of research was followed enthusiastically by accounting researchers, and also by some economists, especially in North America. This culminated in the golden age of accounting theory in the 1960s. Many notable pieces of research were published at that time, including works by Bedford (1965), Chambers (1966), Edwards and Bell (1961), Ijiri (1967), Mattessich (1964) and Sterling (1970). These works followed the deductive methodology used by the economists in the 1920s and 1930s, but attempted to meet the requirements and constraints of existing accounting practices. In other words, attempts were made to derive measures of income which, on the one hand, conformed to economic theory, while, on the other hand, also satisfied the requirement of existing accounting practices.

In a comment on Nelson's characterization of the 1960s as the golden age of financial accounting research, Gaffikin (1988) described the methodological basis of such work as hypothetico-deductivism. He described the research process as one in which a priori assumptions are used to deduce an income determination model which can then be used as a basis for comparing existing practice or for making prescriptions about accounting issues, such as the nature and content of accounting standards. He argued that the a priori assumptions of these researchers were a mixture of empirical observations of accounting practice and the postulates of economic theory, such as economic rationality, the nature of shareholder decision making and the role of market prices. The resulting income determination models were claimed to be practical bases for determining true income. However, these models were not themselves subjected to detailed empirical testing, although casual empirical observation had formed the basis of the a priori assumptions.

The 1960s saw major debates over the relative attractions of replacement cost-based measures of income and selling price-based measures. Edwards and Bell's model was one of the few which suggested that it may be necessary to use different income determination models for different purposes. This realization that financial reporting is concerned with providing information to various decision-makers led to a change in research direction in the 1970s and to the era of decision-usefulness (or user needs) research.

Decision-usefulness research

As described earlier, the late 1960s and early 1970s saw accounting standard setting becoming a major issue in the USA and the UK. This required standard setters to make choices between different accounting methods and prompted accounting researchers to consider ways of selecting among the alternative income determination models which had been developed by a priori accounting researchers. Various writers suggested that accounting choices should be based on a consideration of the needs of the users of financial statements. Although many of the a priori researchers had appealed to user needs in order to justify their models, their appeals generally took the form of post hoc justifications, rather than providing the starting point for their analysis.

Writers who favoured a decision-usefulness approach argued that the starting point for financial accounting research should be a consideration of the objectives of financial statements. It was anticipated that this would require an identification of the users of financial statements, a specification of their decision-making processes and an analysis of their information needs. As already mentioned, such concerns led to the publication by professional accounting bodies of the Trueblood Report in the USA and *The Corporate Report* in the UK. Both of these reports pointed to a wide range of financial statement users, with *The Corporate Report* being the more wide-ranging. This recognition of the range of users (now often referred to as stakeholder groups) meant that consideration should be given to the various users' needs in formulating accounting standards. Nevertheless, both the accounting standard setters and financial accounting researchers tended to focus on the needs of the shareholders, and of investors in general. At the pragmatic level, it was argued that financial statements are addressed to shareholders.

This focus on the needs of shareholders and investors led to the use of a predictive ability criterion in financial accounting research at that time. Much of this research was based on a neoclassical economic model in which investment decisions are determined by the net present value of future cash flows (that is, dividends). The first best solution for investors would be to receive forecasts of future cash flows. However, it was generally accepted that managers would be reluctant to publish their own management forecasts and hence investors would be forced to rely on financial statements as a predictor of future cash flows. Thus, the financial statements with the greatest predictive ability would best meet the information needs of shareholders, and choices between alternative accounting methods could be based on an assessment of their effects on predictive ability. Some researchers used hypothetico-deductive methodology to deduce, from neoclassical economic analysis, the predictive abilities of accounting alternatives. Others designed empirical studies to test the predictive abilities of different accounting methods. The decision-usefulness approach succeeded in moving accounting research away from the search for 'true income' and towards a consideration of the utility of accounting methods to the various user groups. It also encouraged empirical research in the area. However, it did not succeed in providing the logical basis for accounting choices which its advocates had hoped for. No simple basis for accounting standard setting could be derived from the analysis of users' needs, although there is a legacy of this approach in the continuing professional interest in conceptual frameworks (for example, in the UK, the Accounting Standard Board's *Statement of Principles* – APB, 1999). But as Puxty and Laughlin (1983b) pointed out, the provision of information to meet the needs of particular user groups will not necessarily lead to greater general welfare, as seems to have been believed by the advocates of the decision-usefulness approach. This approach, which displaced the stewardship perspective, did not prove to be a research panacea. In recent years, the stewardship (or accountability) perspective has been given renewed prominence, albeit subsidiary to, and subsumed within, the decision-usefulness perspective.

Moreover, the failure to find logical choice criteria led subsequent researchers to study the actual process of accounting standard setting and to evaluate the economic consequences of the alternative choices. It is now generally accepted that the process of choice is essentially a political one. We will describe research adopting this political perspective later in this chapter, and in the mean time we will look at empirical research in financial accounting.

Empirical research in financial accounting

The decision-usefulness approach stimulated two principal types of empirical study. First, behavioural accounting research (BAR), which explored the production and use of financial information. Although initially lacking any theoretical framework, BAR gradually focused on the decision processes and decision outcomes of *individual* users, drawing upon the discipline of psychology for its concepts, models, and methods. Second, market-based accounting research (MBAR), which focused on the impact of investors' decisions on market security prices, drawing upon the discipline of finance for both its theories (especially the capital asset pricing model and the efficient market hypothesis) and methods (typically event studies similar to those discussed in chapter 3). These two types of empirical study have expanded and developed such that they now address many issues that lie outside the decision-usefulness approach.

Behavioural accounting research comprises a large and somewhat disjointed body of literature. It covers four distinct methods of undertaking research: surveys, field studies, laboratory experiments and field experiments. Surveys explore the attitudes and opinions of interested parties (preparers, users and auditors) and many seek to establish users' declared information needs. Other studies draw explicitly upon human information processing (HIP) theory, seeking to generate (in financial settings) insights into information search and selection strategies (predecisional behaviour), probabilistic judgements and the influence of cognitive style. In particular, we now know that decision-makers have bounded rationality and that they depart consistently from normative models of decision-making, due to the use of simplifying heuristics, which introduce biases. An implication is that, in structured tasks, models should be used rather that humans.

Financial BAR has, until recently, been a relatively small field in comparison with managerial BAR and auditing BAR (Arnold and Sutton, 1997, especially ch. 7). This was due to criticisms that the individual was irrelevant in market settings, that many such studies were undertheorized, and that important decision attributes were ignored (Berg, Dickhaut and McCabe, 1995; Maines, 1995). Since the 1990s, however, there has been a resurgence in experimental research due to the growing body of evidence indicating capital market inefficiencies and the method's comparative advantage at both disentangling variables that are confounded in natural settings and revealing underlying processes to permit strong causal inferences to be drawn (Libby, Bloomfield and Nelson, 2001).

Market-based accounting research arose from a group of studies that examined the predictive ability of accounting information. The purpose of these predictive ability studies was to examine the usefulness of financial reports in predicting the variables of interest to decision-makers, for example, future cash flows. However, because of the difficulty of determining future cash flows, these studies generally examined the relationship between accounting information and current share prices (taken to represent the market evaluation of future cash flows). Similar early studies examined the usefulness of accounting information in predicting corporate failure and credit ratings of corporate debt.

It was the capital market studies of the relationship between accounting information and share prices that became the most popular during the 1970s. A major breakthrough for these studies came when Ball and Brown (1968) pioneered the share price residual approach to measuring stock market reaction. This seminal work, which has been particularly influential and widely quoted, began a major industry in stock market reaction (or information content) studies. The principal objective of these studies was to determine the way in which the stock market, through share prices, reacts to different types of accounting information. The major focus of attention was accounting earnings, although the incremental information content of other accounting signals has also been examined. These other signals include interim reports, balance sheet values and information disclosed in the notes to the accounts. Initial price-earnings studies, based on monthly returns data, were supplemented by studies using intra-day returns, as the quality of data available improved. Trading volume, in addition to prices, was also studied.

These stock market reaction studies had a significant impact on standard-setting practice in the USA. For example, the efficient markets hypothesis leads to the proposition that all available information is impounded in the share price. Thus, whether a particular piece of information is presented in the body of the financial statements or in the footnotes should not matter, as in both cases the information content will be impounded in the share price. The implication for accounting standard-setters is that they should de-emphasize the 'bottom line' of the income statement, and make the issue of disclosure more important than the form of the financial statements. As noted above, however, there is a growing body of evidence that is inconsistent with semi-strong form market efficiency, in particular, market anomalies, evidence that past returns have predictive power and evidence of post-earnings announcement drift (where share prices react fully to earnings news but only with a considerable lag).

More recently, non-BAR empirical research has focused on five (overlapping) main areas: methodological issues, fundamental analysis and valuation research, tests of market efficiency, value relevance and corporate disclosure. A great deal of this work continues to be of a capital markets nature. Methodological issues include earnings response coefficients (ERCs), properties of analysts' forecasts and models of discretionary accruals. Earnings response coefficients arise from the study of the earnings–price relation, rather than the traditional price–earnings relation, the slope coefficient on earnings being interpreted as an estimate of the ERC. Research into analysts' forecasts examines the properties of consensus forecasts and also the properties of individual analysts' forecasts. Several discretionary accruals models have been developed, of which the Jones (1991) model and the modified-Jones model (Dechow, Sloan and Sweeney, 1995) are most commonly used. Earnings management studies that use these models now focus more on the incentives that managers have to influence share prices in an inefficient market than on the contracting and political cost arguments of positive accounting theory (positive accounting research is discussed in the following section).

The growth of interest in fundamental analysis and valuation, which aids our understanding of the determinants of value, is a natural outcome of the mounting evidence of market inefficiencies. The residual income valuation model developed by Ohlson (1995) (see below) is widely used in empirical studies of this type. The phrase 'quality of earnings' is now used to refer to the extent to which reported earnings reflect operating fundamentals.

Tests of market efficiency include event studies (both short-window and long-horizon studies) and cross-sectional tests of return predictability. For an excellent recent review covering these three areas, see Kothari (2001).

The association between accounting numbers and equity market values (information content studies) has received renewed interest during the 1990s, under the label 'value relevance'. There is often a suggestion in the literature that such studies can help standard-setters by indicating the 'usefulness' of various accounting numbers. An interesting finding is that the relation between returns and earnings has declined over time, although the value relevance of book values has increased (for example, Francis and Schipper, 1999; Lev and Zarowin, 1999). This finding is used by some to argue that the relevance of the traditional accounting model is in decline and to justify the need for new (additional) forms of business reporting. The focus has been on non-financial information relating to intangible assets (for example, Amir and Lev, 1996; Barth *et al.*, 1998; Hughes, 2000; Ittner and Larcker, 1998). The topic of value relevance in the context of standard-setting is reviewed by Holthausen and Watts (2001), with an alternative perspective being provided by Barth, Beaver and Landsman (2001).

Finally, corporate disclosure, in particular its determinants and consequences, has grown in importance as a research area. This topic includes studies of discretionary choices within mandated disclosures and voluntary disclosure. A difficulty in conducting research into voluntary disclosure is the need for metrics to measure salient attributes, such as amount or quality. Until recently, the AIMR produced subjective analysts' rankings of disclosure quality in the USA, and these continue to be widely used (for example, Lang and Lundholm, 1993, who examine the determinants of disclosure quality and Healy, Hutton and Palepu, 1999, who examine the association between increases in disclosure ratings and stock performance and intermediation changes). The alternative is to use a researcher-constructed measure (for example, Botosan, 1997, who examines the impact of disclosure amount on the cost of equity capital). One type of quantitative voluntary disclosure which has been the subject of considerable recent research is management earnings forecasts (for example, Frankel, McNichols and Wilson, 1995).

The usefulness of narrative disclosures, in the form of the management discussion and analysis (MD&A) (similar to the Operating and Financial Review – OFR – in the UK) has received particular attention (for example, Barron, Kile and O'Keefe, 1999; Clarkson, Kao and Richardson, 1999). In addition to their usefulness, the manipulation of narrative disclosures has been examined, as has the manipulation of financial graphs in corporate reports (for example, Beattie and Jones, 2000). Empirical research in the area of corporate disclosure has been the subject of recent reviews by Healy and Palepu (2001) and Core (2001). .

Various factors contributed to the popularity of empirical research in accounting during the past three decades, including: (1) the development of computer technology, (2) the establishment of large security price databases, and (3) the increasing number of accounting faculties, especially in the USA, with an economics and/or quantitative background and little or no accounting experience. The *Journal of Accounting Research,* which has become a world leader in empirical accounting research, commenced publication in 1963 and in discussing its origins Davidson (1984) commented: 'the previous decade had seen substantial advances in the development of statistical techniques and quantitative analysis ... a more scientific approach to accounting research was clearly on the horizon' (ibid.: 282).

Implicit in this quote is the view that the then current a priori approach to accounting research was in some sense 'unscientific'. However, as Gaffikin (1988) demonstrates, both a priori and empirical research are based on a hypothetico-deductive methodology. The a priori theorists and the empiricists differed only in the emphasis they placed on the testing of hypotheses. The a priori researchers conducted no formal testing of their deductively derived conclusions, but they relied on empirical observations in formulating their assumptions. The empirical researchers, however, formally tested their hypotheses, but they derived these hypotheses from accounting and economic models which contained a priori assumptions.

Positive accounting theory

The expression 'positive accounting theory' as it is understood in North America, and especially at the universities of Chicago and Rochester, represents a particularly extreme form of empiricism in accounting research and a reaction to the excessive a priori theorizing in financial accounting in previous decades. Advocates of positive theory distance themselves as far as possible from the normative methodology of the a priori theorists. As discussed in Chapter 4, positive theories, being grounded in empirical data, appeared to offer accounting researchers the prospect of avoiding the value judgements and theoretical speculations of normative models. Positive theory is concerned with explanation and prediction, whereas normative theory is concerned with prescription. The advocates of positive accounting theory such as Watts and

Zimmerman (1986), argue that 'scientific' research can only be concerned with 'what is' questions, it cannot be used to answer 'what ought' questions. For example, positive accounting research can be used to predict stock market reactions to accounting information, but cannot prescribe how income ought to be measured in financial statements.

As discussed at length in Chapter 4, neoclassical economics and especially agency theory have had a significant role in the development of positive accounting theory. The neoclassical economic model is extended by explicitly recognizing the costs and benefits of information and the need to motivate managers to pursue the interests of the shareholders rather than their own interests. Despite positive accounting researchers' proclaimed aversion to theoretical speculation in the design of their empirical studies, neoclassical economics and agency theory are taken for granted. They are used as instrumental theoretical frameworks which are not themselves subjected to empirical tests, although their predictions are tested against empirical data. For example, positive accounting research relies to a considerable extent on finance theories such as the capital asset pricing model and the efficient markets hypothesis.

Positive accounting research, and in particular the research based on agency theory, has stimulated numerous studies into the role of financial accounting in contractual relationships between managers and shareholders. In this research, managers are considered to be the agents of the shareholders and in a contractual relationship in which incentives, based on the financial statements, are used to motivate the agent's decision-making. These studies rely on the assumption that managers and shareholders are rational economic persons pursuing their own self-interests. The purpose of the analysis is to examine the implications of such self-interested behaviour.

There are several distinct strands to this research area, each of which concerns managers' (and auditors') choices with respect to financial information: accounting method choices/changes, earnings management and voluntary disclosure. Early empirical accounting choice studies examined the agency costs associated with management compensation contracts, debt contracts, and the contracting costs associated with the political process. The hypothesis tested was that managers selected accounting methods opportunistically to enhance their own wealth (the 'opportunism hypothesis'). In a meta-analysis of extant studies, Christie (1990: 15) concludes that 'the posterior probability that the theory taken as a whole has explanatory power is close to one'. The overall explanatory power of these models was, however, typically low. More recent positive accounting research has viewed accounting method choice as part of the company's overall efficient organizational technology, that is, that which maximizes the value of the firm (the 'efficiency hypothesis') (Watts and Zimmerman, 1990). Empirical studies attempt to assess the relative influence of these two hypotheses (for example, Christie and Zimmerman, 1994).

Early research into earnings management (or income smoothing) implicitly assumed that the market accepted reported accounting numbers at face value, without attempting to 'undo' discretionary accounting choices. Positive accounting theory rationales suggest that earnings management occurs because contracts are written in terms of accounting numbers. In this area, the study of discretionary accruals, rather than accounting changes, has now come to the forefront (see section immediately above).

Finally, the early atheoretical disclosure index studies, which related the level of a company's disclosure to various company-specific characteristics such as size, listing status and industry, have been superseded. Formal analytical models of voluntary disclosure are now being developed (for example, Verrechia, 1983; Wagenhofer, 1990). These models are simplified structures that allow the main economic forces governing the issue at stake to be focused upon. They underpin the empirical research into corporate disclosure discussed in the section immediately above. In addition, a grounded theory approach has been used to model the *management* of financial disclosure (Gibbins, Richardson and Waterhouse, 1990; 1992).

The assumption of managerial self-interest is also a feature of the research into the standard-setting process which has been undertaken by positive accounting theorists. Watts and Zimmerman (1978), in particular, have argued that the lobbying behaviour of corporate management is based on their managerial self-interest. In other words, managers attempt to secure through political lobbying the accounting standards which best meet their own self-interests and only indirectly the interests of their companies and shareholders. Such arguments raise serious doubts about the feasibility of a conceptual framework for accounting standards. Watts and Zimmerman contend that accounting standard setting is a political, and not a technical process, arguing that: 'The predominant function of accounting theories is now to provide excuses which satisfy the demand created by the political process; consequently accounting theories have become increasingly normative' (Watts and Zimmerman, 1979: 301).

Watts and Zimmerman believe that a priori accounting theories simply provide a 'supply of excuses' or rationalizations which are used by the various interest groups involved in the political process. Empirical studies of accounting standard-setting and the role of political lobbying have been undertaken from this perspective.

Positive accounting theory explains the regulation of accounting (such as government legislation and the emergence of standard-setting bodies) in terms of the public good characteristics of financial statements. It is argued that the production of financial statements can confer social value on the economy as a whole. The market mechanism is used as an ideal or benchmark for evaluating other institutional arrangements in the belief that market efficiency is a necessary condition for social welfare.

Positive accounting researchers study the political nature of the standard-setting process through an examination of the lobbying behaviour of corporate managements. The analysis is based on the assumption that managerial self-interest is a key factor in determining lobbying behaviour. The political process of standard-setting involves the working out of the relative interests of the different managerial groups and their corporate shareholders. It is the 'power' of the various groups in the political process that determines accounting standards. As part of this research, studies have been undertaken of the economic consequences of accounting standards, in particular, studies of the effects on managers, shareholders and corporate profitability. Other interest groups are not considered.

Positive accounting theory has been subjected to a number of critiques, especially during the 1980s: Christenson (1982); Lowe, Puxty and Laughlin, (1983); Tinker, Marino and Neimark, (1982); Sterling (1990); and Whittington (1986). All these critiques have pointed to the impossibility of divorcing empirical testing from theoretical analysis. For example, the design of any empirical test requires theoretical constructs and the development of positive theory will inevitably contain theoretical assumptions. As mentioned above, much positive accounting research is based on the assumptions of neoclassical economics and agency theory. Such research, and especially the work emanating from Chicago and Rochester, relies on an implicit belief in the effectiveness of the free market system. Watts and Zimmerman have been widely challenged by other writers. As their work is heavily dependent upon the logical positivist tradition, much of the criticism levied against them is fairly levelled against that tradition. It is a different argument whether their work is sound within the methodological framework in which they quite explicitly operate.

Return of the measurement perspective

A priori research adopts a measurement perspective for accounting information, whereas BAR, MBAR, and positive accounting theory adopt an information perspective. An important recent trend in financial accounting research has been the coming together of, arguably, the best of each of these perspectives. The interest in recognition, measurement and valuation issues, which received scant attention for 20 years, has re-emerged, albeit in a different form, that is, analytical rather than normative.

In particular, Ohlson (1995) develops a residual income valuation model that shows how the clean surplus relation (defined as the change in book value of owners' equity plus dividends equals earnings) can be used to generate predictions about the relation between market prices, book value and earnings. The concept of residual income can be traced back to Edwards and Bell (1961), among others. Empirical studies based on this analytical research are now being undertaken (see above section on capital markets research).

One external factor responsible for this renewed interest in measurement issues has been the growth in the use of derivative instruments by companies. The traditional financial reporting model fails to adequately reflect the risky nature of such assets, and as a consequence the advantages of fair value accounting and probabilistic disclosures are being reassessed (for example, Barth and Landsman, 1995).

Increasing environmental awareness has also resulted in a new measurement issue coming to the forefront of research – voluntary environmental disclosures and the role of the accountant in measuring environmental impact and providing related attestation services.

Interdisciplinary perspectives on accounting and critical accounting research

A number of writers have become concerned to examine the social processes surrounding accounting and some have questioned whether an analysis of accounting standards based on the private interests of managers and shareholders (as in positive accounting theory) is an appropriate basis for analysing the effects on social welfare (for example, Cooper and Sherer, 1994; Puxty and Laughlin, 1983a). This emphasis on private interests implies an acceptance of the existing social order, as the social value of financial statements is equated with the value to the shareholding and managerial classes. Such concerns have led to calls for researchers to study the social nature of accounting and, in particular, to examine the role of financial reporting in its economic, social, and political contexts.

In positive accounting theory it is the relative power of the interested managerial and shareholder groups which determines the accounting standards that are set. However, this represents only one dimension of the concept of power, the dimension which treats power as the ability to achieve a particular outcome when an issue is contested. A second dimension of power concerns the determination of the particular issues which are considered, that is, the accounting alternatives which are put on the agenda for accounting standard-setters. Groups that can dictate the issues on the agenda are in a very powerful position in the standard-setting process. A third dimension of power concerns the ability to define the terms in which issues are contested and the basis on which the debate takes place. For instance, in assessing accounting standards, certain types of argument are regarded as legitimate. At the present time, the debate on accounting standards is expressed largely in technical economic terms which will favour economic interests over others interests.

Consideration of these second and third dimensions of power raises questions about the established social order. Furthermore, it suggests that studies of the standard-setting process require social analysis rather than quantitative economic analysis. Many accounting researchers feel uncomfortable about such 'radical' studies because they involve questioning the social position of accountants and accounting standard-setting. As many accounting research projects, especially in North America, are funded by the accounting profession, it may be difficult to obtain funding for projects which question the position (the very powerful position) of that profession.

In addition, radical studies often entail different views of the nature of accounting and the role of research. Indeed, it can be said that researchers undertaking such studies hold quite different 'world views' compared with the researchers undertaking more traditional accounting research. Chua (1986) identified three world views which underlie the different approaches to accounting research. The traditional approaches combine empiricism based on realism and positivism with a belief in the existing social order which is assumed to have resulted from goal-oriented, rational, utility-maximizing behaviour. With this set of fundamental beliefs, the role of accounting is one of technical control of economic processes. Accounting research is viewed as a means of enhancing this control, and especially the control exercised by the shareholding and managerial classes. An alternative, 'interpretive' world view combines a quite different set of beliefs about the nature of society. In this case, subjectivism and relativism together with the view that social order is negotiated through social interaction lead to the use of qualitative, naturalistic research methods. The role of accounting research is seen to be a passive one, and theory is seen to be a vehicle for enhancing mutual understanding and communication between the various groups in society. A more radical, 'critical' world view is characterized by still further different beliefs about society. Researchers who hold these beliefs view conflict as endemic in society due to the unequal distribution of power. The objective of accounting research from this perspective is to highlight these inequalities and to provide a vehicle for social change.

These alternative world views constitute the 'interdisciplinary perspectives on accounting project' which subsumes 'critical accounting'. Although the major developments in this project have occured in management accounting, financial accounting research has also been influenced. Critical accounting can be seen as emerging from, and building upon, earlier research at the individual level (BAR) and at the organizational level, by offering a social perspective on accounting. Critical accounting encompasses a variety of 'ways of seeing' – interpretive sociology, constructionism, Marxist perspectives and, most recently, postmodern/poststructuralism – with this plurality being seen as desirable in the generation of 'composite knowledges' (Roslender, 1996: 542).

One manifestation of this new paradigm in financial accounting is the attempt to extend the analysis of accounting choices beyond the traditional positivist investigations to encompass socio-political factors (for example, Neu, 1992). The role of design and image in the corporate annual report (within which the technical accounting components are embedded) is also being examined (for example, Graves, Flesher and Jordan, 1996; Preston, Wright and Young, 1996).

A natural development of accounting researchers' growing interest in the role of accounting in organizations and society has been studies of the accountancy profession, which seek to apply various general sociological theories of the professions to the specific example of accountancy, often using historical analysis. These studies have explored and articulated key relations in the professional project: Foucauldian power–knowledge relations are elaborated by Hopwood (1987), the professional–state relationship (particularly issues concerning regulation) are investigated by Robson *et al.* (1994), while the relations between the various accountancy bodies are addressed by Walker and Shackleton (1995). In addition, the particular issues of education and training (Power, 1988) and ethics (Parker, 1994) have been explored.

International accounting research

It was stated early on in this chapter that the globalization and growth of world markets, especially capital markets, over the last decade has led accounting practice to become increasingly international in orientation. Traditionally, international accounting research has focused upon comparative country studies which describe and explain accounting diversity in terms of contextual factors such as culture, industrialization, economic development, and legal and political systems (Gernon and Wallace, 1995). Recent research also addresses international capital market issues, the international accounting of multinationals, and (now of major importance) accounting harmonization (frequently referred to as accounting convergence or comparability). The recent availability of international databases of market and financial information (for example, Global Vantage) further encourages growth in this research area.

Summary

In this chapter we have examined the historical development of financial accounting research. From a methodological point of view there are two very strong traditions which have come to dominate the literature. The first, and still by and large the predominant tradition, is strongly positivist. It follows a weak form of realism; namely, that 'theories' are utilitarian entities which have value only in as far as they generate empirical generalizations which can be subjected to real and decisive empirical tests. Value judgements lie outside the domain of such research and the question of what 'is' is rigorously separated from questions about what 'ought' to be. There is no doubt that this tradition has been very productive, at least in terms of the number of research papers generated. In addition, it is arguable that many insights into the relation of financial accounting to various markets have been obtained.

There are signs that this tradition has reached a new level of maturity *vis-à-vis* the information perspective. The value of the measurement perspective (without its a priori overtones) has been re-established and the excessive focus on empirics has been redressed. Accounting research is now a more balanced combination of theory and empirical analysis. The search for universal truths and general laws has given way to the more realistic aim of developing context-dependent theories, based on specific institutional settings.

The second tradition has grown from two sources: (1) a concern with the interpretation of practical reality as it is perceived by accountants, and (2) a tradition of thought which is strongly 'relativist' in orientation. By this we mean that researchers in this tradition believe that what might appear to be objective facts and real issues are predominantly socially constructed. As the debate within this tradition has developed, some have argued for more radical positions culminating in the view that there are no objective rational criteria for choosing between one theory and another, one test and another or one accounting standard and another. This tradition too has reached a new level of maturity, reflected in criticism from within the group that the interdisciplinary perspectives on accounting project has 'lost its way because it is divided on methodological, philosophical and ideological lines' (Roslender and Dillard, 2001).

We draw this section to a close with an observation that we have made before and which we hope is now well exemplified, namely, that accounting and finance encompass very rich and diverse intellectual traditions. In the next section of this book we move on to discuss ways of doing research within these differing traditions.

Part Two

Methods of Research

······ 6

Methods of empirical research

This chapter will introduce a number of the principles and concepts of research design that are employed in empirical research projects in the accounting and finance area. These principles should be incorporated into any research design to ensure, as far as possible, the validity of the results derived. All research projects are conceived in order that some underlying research question may be answered. In a large number of empirical research studies in the accounting and finance areas the research question to be answered involves the testing of a statistical hypothesis or set of hypotheses.

The initial stage in the overall process is the identification of what might be termed the research question. Once identified, the next stage is usually the formulation of the research question as a single scientific hypothesis or set of hypotheses. The ways in which hypotheses may be generated and validated have been described and discussed in general terms in Chapter 1 and specifically in the contexts of finance, management accounting and financial accounting in Chapters 2 to 4. The present chapter is concerned with the next stage of the process, that is, it is concerned with the testing of a statistical hypothesis or set of hypotheses. In particular, we will focus upon the different types of research design available to the empirical researcher in the accounting and finance domains. However, before we are able to describe the available research designs a number of associated concepts will have to be considered, such as variables and measurement error, experiments and internal and external validity. In the final section we will briefly consider the nature of hypotheses and hypothesis testing.

If the researcher has created a 'good' research design, then more valid conclusions and inferences may be drawn from the work. This chapter will discuss the conclusions that can be drawn from research projects as well as what the research design should accomplish. However, the assessment of research work and the conclusions deriving therefrom will be more fully discussed later.

Variables and their measurement

Empirical research is generally concerned with establishing the relationships between variables. That is, for example, how does one variable change as another variable changes? A variable simply represents a property of an event or phenomenon associated with a particular object (for example, the earnings of a firm or its total market value). The variables are characterized by probability distributions and, as such, may be termed 'random variables'. For example, the observed return on a security will be a realization from the return distribution of that security.

The variables considered in empirical work may be dichotomized as dependent or independent variables. The independent variable in an experiment is the variable that is manipulated by the researcher; it is the effect of this variable that is being studied by the experimenter. The dependent variable measures the response to the manipulation of the independent variable. Thus, in an experiment, the researcher is interested in determining the impact of changes in the independent variable upon the dependent variable.

Variables are properties of events or phenomena through a defined measurement system. Measurement itself is difficult to define and is surrounded by a methodology of its own. There must be a theory of measurement which encloses the objectives of the measurement process, states the standards against which measurement will be made and nominates the scalars of the measurement system. Within the double language model discussed in Chapter 1, the measurement system can be defined as the 'correspondence rules' which link observation to theory. For example, we measure temperature (a theoretical property) in order to determine the heat contained within a body (the objective property) relative to a chosen standard or norm (the measurement standard).

An essential element of this process is the agreement of a measurement standard. Usually, where a physical variable is involved, there will be some common agreement as to the denomination of the scalar involved as well as some physical reference. Measurements of length, such as the metre, are a good example in that a standard metre is a denomination of length within the decimal number system (a property of the scalar) against an agreed physical standard. Other standards of measurement such as, for example, the pound sterling or dollar have a standard scalar but there is no agreement relating them to a concept of value now that neither currency is tied to a gold standard. In addition, measurement can be unitary in that it relies on a single measurement standard, or complex in that it relies on a multiplicity of standards (the light year is a complex physical standard in that it relies on a standard measurement of length or distance and a standard measurement of time).

Where a variable can be measured by a system where both the scalar and the referent are standardized we usually refer to it as a quantitative variable. On the other hand, a qualitative variable is one where only the scalar is standardized (potentially only informally).

Some qualitative variables such as sex, race or, more appropriately in financial research, industrial classification are often referred to as 'nominal' variables in that numerical values can only be assigned by constructing binary or dummy variables (for example male = 0, female = 1). Such variable types are employed throughout accounting and finance. Within the quantitative variable set there are differing types of variable corresponding to a level of measurement that can be achieved for that variable. These range from ordinal through interval to ratio. As the name implies, it is possible to rank ordinal variables. Interval level variables may be measured at a level higher than ordinal variables. That is, not only can they be ordered, the distances between categories can be defined. Finally, at the highest measurement level come ratio level variables, which have the incremental characteristic over ordinal and interval variables that the zero point on the measurement scale is uniquely defined.

While the definition of measurement might appear robust it is not always straightforward to measure variables in all disciplines. Often a variable represents some high-level concept which is not necessarily readily amenable to measurement, for example managerial effort in agency theoretic settings. The researcher is then faced with the problem of operationalizing that concept in a meaningful way; this operational process will involve both theoretical and empirical considerations. Many social researchers have to consider the 'construct validity' of the variables that they employ. In finance, the vast majority of variables utilized tend to be relatively easily measured, though the problems associated with the construct validity of market portfolio proxies provide a salutary warning. However, in many areas of accounting research the construct validity can severely limit the inferences that can be drawn from a particular piece of research.

An important concept in the theory of measurement is the notion of measurement error. That is, the numerical value assigned to a particular variable is equal to the 'true' value plus an error term. This may be expressed as

$$M = T + e \tag{6.1}$$

where M is the measured value, T the 'true' value and e the measurement error. Measurement errors may be classified in two types: (a) random measurement errors and (b) non-random or systematic measurement errors. The distinction between the two measurement error types hinges upon the properties of the error term (e) in (6.1). When the expectation of the error term is zero and serially independent, the error type is random (this error type is often referred to as 'white noise' when the distribution is stationary). Effectively, measurement errors randomly fluctuate around the true values (that is $E(M) = E(T)$, where E is the expectation operator). When the error term expectation in (6.1) is non-zero, there is a systematic bias in the measurement of the variable. In this case, $E(M) \neq E(T)$. An example of a random measurement error is the non-synchronous trading problem analysed in Scholes and Williams (1977), Miller, Muthuswamy and Whaley (1994). With consecutive trades and identically and independently distributed non-trading periods, the expected measured return equals the expected true return. Use of transactions prices to estimate mean equilibrium returns will lead to an upward bias in the expected measured return relative to the true return (see Blume and Stambaugh, 1983). Campbell, Lo and MacKinlay (1997) provide an excellent discussion of the impacts of various microstructure phenomena upon observed return series.

Measurement error will impact upon the strength of association between variables. For example, if we are interested in the relationship between our true variable T and another variable X (which will be assumed to be measured without error to simplify the analysis), then the correlation coefficient between T and X, $r(T,X)$, is given by:

$$r(T, X) = Cov(T, X)/\{Var(T) * Var(X)\}^{\frac{1}{2}} \tag{6.2}$$

where Cov and Var are the covariance and variance operators, respectively.

The measured correlation between the observed or measured variables will be:

$$\begin{aligned} r(M, X) &= Cov(M, X)/\{Var(M) * Var(X)\}^{\frac{1}{2}} \\ &= Cov(T + e, X)/\{Var(T + e) * Var(X)\}^{\frac{1}{2}} \\ &= [Cov(T, X) + Cov(e, X)]/\{(Var(T) + Var(e)) * Var(X)\}^{\frac{1}{2}} \\ &= Cov(T, X)/\{(Var(T) + Var(e)) * Var(X)\}^{\frac{1}{2}} \end{aligned} \tag{6.3}$$

assuming that $Cov(e,X) = 0$. Thus, assuming a random error (that is, $Cov(e,X) = 0$) and since $Var(e)$ is strictly positive then

$$r(M, X) < r(T, X) \tag{6.4}$$

that is the measured association will be biased downwards.

When the measurement error is non-random, the $Cov(e,X)$ term may not necessarily equal zero and the directional impact upon the measured correlation is indeterminate. The important point to note, however, is that measurement errors in the variable will impact upon the conclusions regarding the relationships investigated.

With both types of measurement error, the reliability of the measured variable reduces directly with the variance of the measurement error. The reliability of M as a measure of T is defined as the ratio of the variance of the true value to the variance of the measured variable. Defining R as the reliability, we have:

$$R = Var(T)/Var(M) \tag{6.5}$$

or alternatively:

$$R = Var(T)/(Var(T) + Var(e)) = 1/(1 + Var(e)/Var(T)) \tag{6.6}$$

that is, $R \rightarrow 1$ as $Var(e) \rightarrow 0$.

When discussing the error term, e, above, the concept of 'stationarity' was introduced. Stationarity is an important concept, particularly in time series work. A time series is defined as strict sense stationarity when its joint and conditional distribution is invariant with displacements in time. A weaker stationarity concept exists, wherein the above definition is restricted to the first two moments (that is means, variances and serial covariances) rather than for the whole distribution (this is often referred to as covariance or second-order stationarity). Much recent work has been conducted in the development of tests for stationarity (unit root tests) and working with non-stationary random variables (cointegration) (see Maddala and Kim, 1998). The unit root tests entail testing whether b in equation (6.7) is statistically significantly different from one

$$X(t) = bX(t-1) + e(t) \tag{6.7}$$

Where X(t) is the value of variable X in time t and e(t) the random error (disturbance) term in period (t). If b equals one, X(t) will follow a random walk – a non-stationary process. Testing the hypothesis that b = 1 is not straightforward and a number of test statistics are available (see, for example, Dickey and Fuller, 1981; Diebold and Nerlove, 1990)

A non-stationary time series can be transformed into a stationary one by differencing the series (that is, the first difference of X(t) is X(t) – X(t – 1), which is stationary if X(t) follows a random walk). However, by differencing some information may be lost (particularly regarding longer term equilibrium relationships). To overcome this, the concept of cointegration has been introduced (Banerjee *et al.*, 1993; Engle and Granger, 1987). By way of a simple example, assuming that both X(t) and Y(t) follow random walks and that β is non-zero, if the disturbance e(t), in model (8) does not have unit roots,

$$X(t) = \alpha + \beta Y(t) + e(t) \tag{6.8}$$

then X(t) and Y(t) are said to be cointegrated. That is, if there is a long run relationship between X(t) and Y(t) they will not be able to deviate from each other (that is, X(t) $-\alpha - \beta Y(t)$) in a non-stationary fashion.

When carrying out an experiment, it was noted previously that the researcher is interested in studying the impact of the independent variable upon the dependent variable. This may be interpreted loosely as meaning that changes in the independent variable 'cause' the change in the dependent variable. The topic of causality is fraught with problems and has been the subject of much heated philosophical debate.

While the subject of causality has been discussed and analysed for some time (see, for instance, the four canons of causality in Mill, 1874) the situation on causality is far from clear and beyond the scope of this chapter, However, the directional relationships between variables have become important in a number of areas of financial research such as, for example, in the inflation/stock returns literature (see Geske and Roll, 1983, for an early example).

As much empirical work employs time series data it is perhaps worth while pointing to the causal time series arguments advanced by Granger (1969). A simple causal relationship exists between a dependent variable D and an independent variable I, if knowledge of past values of I reduces the variance of forecast errors of D to a level lower than the forecast error variance arising from a knowledge of past values of D, only. Formally, causality from I to D can be imputed if the condition:

$$\begin{aligned} &\mathrm{Var}(D^1(t)) | [D(t-1), D(t-2), ...I(t-1), I(t-2)...] \\ &\quad < \mathrm{Var}(D^1(t)) | [D(t-1), D(t-2), ...] \end{aligned} \tag{6.9}$$

holds where $D^1(t)$ is the time t forecast error in the dependent variable, and the slash(|) is the conditional sign. This concept of causality is persuasive but not without its problems and Zellner (1979) provides a useful discussion of its potential limitations (see also Engle, Hendry and Richard, 1983, for a discussion of the related concept of exogeneity).

Experiments

Poincare (1905: 140) argued that 'experiment is the sole source of truth. It alone can teach us something new, it alone can give us certainty'. The notion of what constitutes an experiment is relatively well defined in the natural sciences. In other disciplines, such as psychology, similar notions of an experiment also exist. The essence of an experiment is control within the research project, that is, in studying the impact of the independent variable upon the dependent variable the experimenter attempts to hold all other variables constant (that is, control them) while manipulating the independent variable. Control is clearly relatively easily achieved in the natural sciences.

For example, if an experimenter wishes to investigate the impact of temperature upon reaction kinetics, then other variables, such as pressure, can be controlled/held constant within the laboratory setting. In psychology, likewise, experiments are still possible. Extraneous variables are potentially less easily controlled than in the natural sciences; however techniques such as randomization can be used as effective controls such that, barring other forms of experimental contamination (such as subject–researcher interactions) the impact of the independent variable may be studied. Direct manipulation of the independent variable can be made by the researcher by varying the level of the independent variable (that is, dosage levels) or by utilizing what is known as the absence–presence dichotomy (that is, treatment or non-treatment).

In empirical studies in the financial field, the direct manipulation of the independent variable(s) by the researcher is not generally possible. This is not to say that controls are impossible but usually that the levels of control which can potentially be achieved are lower. Indeed, much empirical financial research cannot strictly be described as experimental and many of the experimental designs employed are of a quasi-experimental nature. Such experimental designs are widely available and will be discussed below. However, a number of research projects are truly experimental (see Bloomfield and O'Hara, 1999; Copeland and Friedman, 1987; Flood *et al.*, 1999) and it is worth while emphasizing that experimental studies are generally more powerful than non-experimental studies as greater control can be achieved. The likelihood of confounding effects impacting upon the relationships under analysis is higher in non-experimental designs.

Internal validity

Control over extraneous influences in experiments has been discussed in the previous section. The internal validity of an experiment is determined by how much control has been achieved in the study, that is, the greater the control achieved, the higher the internal validity. When a study is described as having a high internal validity this is understood to mean that the changes in the dependent variable have been brought about, in the main, by the independent variable changes, not by other confounding factors. Essentially, the results arise as a result of relationships between variables rather than as a result of the way in which the study was designed. The internal validity of an experiment determines whether valid conclusions can be drawn from a study.

Deficiencies in the design of research studies will lead to studies with low internal validity. For example, if a bias exists in the sample there will be problems in drawing valid conclusions from a study (the external validity of the study, see below, will also be correspondingly low). Survivorship biases can reduce considerably the internal validity of studies (see, for example, Brown, Goetzmann and Ross, 1995). The omission of, or failure to control for, relevant variables in a functional relationship will also lower the internal validity of an experiment/study as will a mis-specification of a functional relationship. Examples of other phenomena which can lead to low internal validity are measurement errors in the variables, regression towards the mean and maturity effects.

In designing a research project, the objective is to maximize the internal validity of the study. By building in sufficient controls to the research design, the likelihood of drawing valid conclusions from the study is enhanced. Available control techniques include, *inter alia*, randomization and matching.

External validiy

To be able to draw valid conclusions from an experimental study is clearly a very important consideration in any research project. Equally important from the viewpoint of building up a systematic body of knowledge is how readily generalizable the results of a particular study are. Without generalization, prediction is not possible. The extent to which the results of a study may be generalized to other settings and samples is termed the external validity of an experiment or study. It should be apparent that an experiment which has a low internal validity will likewise have a low external validity. In designing a research study, the researcher can choose to optimize in terms of either internal or external validity. It is generally found that optimizing in one dimension will tend to reduce the validity in the other dimension. Different researchers will have different priorities as between the two types of validity. In general terms, however, it might be argued that in fundamental research internal validity is of prime importance, while in applied work the external validity is more important.

The problems which can threaten the external validity of a study may be grouped into three broad categories. The first category relates to the population validity, that is, how justifiable is a researcher in drawing inferences from a particular study of a given population. Inevitably, the researcher will work with a sample of observations rather than the whole population. There are, however, two distinct types of population. The target population is the population to which the results of the particular study are to be generalized. However, a researcher is often constrained as regards the population from which samples may be drawn. For example, not all company data of a particular classification may be available as a result of the particular computerized database used. A second type of population exists, that is, the experimentally accessible population. The external validity of an experiment is seriously threatened when biases or other limitations exist in the accessible population.

The second type of problem which can constrain the external validity is the time validity of the study. The time validity of a study is concerned with the extent to which results of a particular study at a point in time can be generalized to other periods of time. When structural changes in the relationships between variables occur, the time validity of such studies will be low.

The final type of validity restriction is environmental validity or the facility with which the results can be generalized across experimental settings. For financial research, international generalizability is one potential problem, although this may also be classified under the population validity hearing. Environmental validity has a more ready interpretation in non-financial disciplines such as psychology and sociology. In these areas, environmental validity is concerned with, for example, the generalizability of results from a laboratory setting to other experimental settings. Phenomena such as the Hawthorne effect (see Bracht and Glass, 1968) and other experimenter effects can reduce the external validity of experiments.

One particular constraint upon the external validity of financial research derives from the extensive use of computerized databases in certain research areas. In particular, as a large number of studies use the same database, a 'data-snooping' bias can arise (see Lo and MacKinlay, 1990). Given the passage of time and the intensive use of such databases, it is possible to discover what are apparently significant relationships but which are, in fact, spurious and arise purely as a result of over working the data.

Quasi-experimental research designs

It is via the design of an experiment that a researcher can establish the level of internal validity; it goes without saying that the researcher will design the experiment in order that the internal validity is maximized (subject to the external validity considerations discussed in the previous section). The research design of a study is the plan which is adopted to answer the research question. The research designs available depend, in the first instance, on whether the study can be considered to be an experiment or not. It has already been pointed out that the majority of empirical financial studies cannot be strictly regarded as experiments (although some true experimental designs have been employed – see, for example, Bloomfield and O'Hara, 1999). There are a number of research designs which can be employed in non-experimental (or quasi-experimental) research settings. The four types of quasi-experimental research designs to be discussed in this section will be:

(1) pre-test/post-test designs
(2) interrupted time series designs
(3) correlational designs
(4) *ex post facto* designs.

A significant number of empirical studies in financial research employ correlational research designs; however, the other research designs also find applications in empirical finance research.

In describing the research designs it will be convenient to use a design notation similar to that originally used by Campbell and Stanley (1963). Observations on variables will be denoted by an 'O' and a numerical subscript will be used to order the observations, that is, O_1 is an observation occurring before O_2. An 'X' will be used to denote the impact of an event or change in an independent variable. Again, a subscript will be used to order the events.

Pre-test/post-test design

In this design observations or measurements of the dependent variable are taken prior to and subsequent to the event under study. The simplest pre-test/post-test design may be represented as:

$$O_1 \ X \ O_2 \tag{6.10}$$

The pre-test/post-test research design is a particularly simple one. The underlying rationale when employed is that the event or change in independent variable, X, brings about the change in the dependent variable (that is, $O_1...O_2$). This, however, tends to be one of the drawbacks associated with the use of this research design. The controls built into the design are not necessarily sufficient to ensure that the event has brought about the change. Internal validity may be correspondingly low. Other phenomena may have occurred between the two measurements, O_1 and O_2, or alternatively a history or maturation effect may have occurred.

The design may be improved upon by carrying out the experiment on a multigroup basis; in particular, by matching the group under study with a group which has not been subjected to the event (the control group). That is, in the ideal case all subjects will be identical save for the independent variable effect or event. This type of design may be represented as:

$$
\begin{array}{ll}
O_1 \ X \ O_2 & \text{Study group} \\
O_1 \ X_0 \ O_2 & \text{Control group}
\end{array}
\tag{6.11}
$$

where X_0 signifies the absence of the event. While this multigroup structure is an improvement upon the single group design, its success does depend upon the extent to which matching has been achieved (matching is, in fact, a less powerful control mechanism than randomization). Perfect matching is never likely to be achieved; however, matches should be made on the basis of the most important extraneous influences. In the financial research area, for example, control variables would include industrial classification and company size. The multi-group version of the pre-test/ post-test design may also be subject to the problem of statistical regression towards the mean.

Interrupted time series design

This type of design differs from the pre-test/post-test design in that observations are taken on a series of the dependent variables both previous to and subsequent to the application of the independent variable or event occurrence. In general terms, the interrupted time series can be represented notationally as

$$O_1O_2...O_{n-1}O_nXO_{n+1}...O_m \qquad (6.12)$$

There is no formal requirement that the number of observations prior to and subsequent to the treatment need to be equal although a number of texts do suggest this. The number of observations available is more important. Given that time series models such as the Box and Jenkins (1970) type can often be employed, it is important that a large number of observations should be available. To apply the autoregressive integrated moving average (ARIMA) models it is necessary to have at least 50 observations.

Interrupted time series designs have the advantage in comparison with simple pre-test/post-test designs that trends in the data may be detected and eliminated as confounding effects upon the dependent variable. For example, consider an experiment which investigates the impact of the independent variable I upon the dependent variable D. In a simple pre-test/post-test design, the observations upon D pre and post application of I may be of the form in Figure 6.1.

Confronted with the observations in Figure 6.1 a researcher could conclude that the independent variable has an impact upon the dependent variable. However, if trends are present in the dependent variable such as depicted in Figure 6.2 it is not necessarily valid to conclude that the independent variable has had an impact upon the dependent variable.

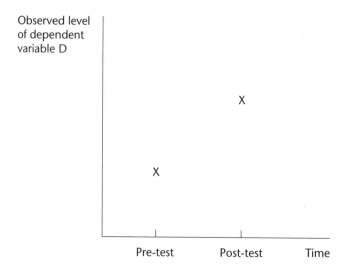

FIGURE 6.1 Plot of dependent variable D against time

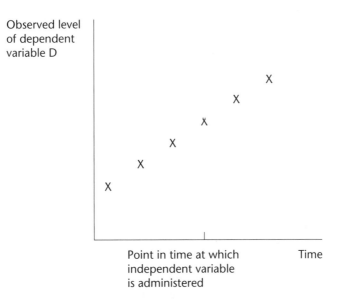

Observed level of dependent variable D

X

X

X

X

X

X

Point in time at which independent variable is administered

Time

FIGURE 6.2 Plot of time series of observations of the dependent variable

In order that a researcher can detect the impact of the independent variable upon the dependent variable the time series needs to have any trend removed or the properties of the moving averages of the time series studied. Time series are generally more complicated than that depicted in Figure 6.2; for example, the series may randomly fluctuate around its trend. However, powerful statistical tools are available for detecting and isolating other components of time series such as seasonals and other cycles (see Maddala, 1992). It is of critical importance for the internal validity of a study that these phenomena be controlled for in the research design (Caporaso [1973] discusses various types of time series in the context of research designs).

A limitation of the interrupted time series design is that the researcher can never be sure that some other variable is not impacting upon the dependent variable contemporaneously with the independent variable, for example a history effect may be present. This may be overcome by adopting a multiple time series design where observations are taken upon the dependent variable of both the study and the control groups. This design may be represented as:

$$O_1O_2...O_{n-1}O_nXO_{n+1}...O_m \quad \text{Study group}$$
$$O_1O_2...O_{n-1}O_nX_0X_0O_{n+1}...O_m \quad \text{Control group} \tag{6.13}$$

Again the success of this particular research design will depend upon how well matched the characteristics of the study and control group are.

Correlation designs

This design type is perhaps the most familiar to the student and researcher in accounting and finance. Many of the theoretical models developed in accounting and finance predict that correlations should exist between variables. At the simple correlation level there is no implication of causality; all that is implied is that the variables under study covary. The correlation research design is very simply represented in the design notation employed in this chapter as (starkly):

$$O \tag{6.14}$$

where O signifies that observations are taken on two or more variables. The correlation between the variables may then be estimated using either the parametric Pearson product moment correlation coefficient or the non-parametric Spearman rank correlation coefficient. Note that a distinction between dependent and independent variables is not necessary with this type of design. The correlations between the variables can be measured at one point in time across a set of subjects.

This type of design is termed 'cross-sectional'. When observations on the variables are taken at differing points in time the correlational design is described as 'time series'. The latter type of experimental design has advantages over cross-sectional designs in that some (not necessarily conclusive) evidence may be gleaned in the causal relationship between the variables; that is, if leads in one variable are correlated with lags in another variable, there is a potential causal relationship running from the latter to the former. The correlations between two variables have been discussed to this point. Where the researcher wishes to investigate interrelationships between more than two variables, factor analysis can be used (see Tabachink and Fidell, 2001).

The major problem associated with simple correlation designs is that spurious correlations can arise between variables as a result of both variables being correlated with a third variable. Where the underlying theoretical structure predicts a causal relationship between the variables, designs employing regression techniques should be used. Where the causal relationship is between the dependent variable and one independent variable, simple regression techniques are employed, but when the relationship is between a dependent variable and more than one independent variable multiple regression techniques should be employed.

Thus, if the dependent variable, D, is predicted to be dependent upon a set of independent variables, $I_1, I_2 \ldots I_k$, the relationship can be represented linearly as

$$D = b_0 + b_1 I_1 + b_2 I_2 \ldots b_k I_k + u \tag{6.15}$$

Where b_0, b_1, $b_2 \ldots b_k$ are the coefficients of the model which are estimated from the data and u the disturbance term. Ordinary least squares (OLS) provide a popular and simple estimator. When problems occur with the disturbance term (such as heteroscedasticity and autocorrelation) generalized least squares (GLS) estimators are more appropriate (efficient). The generalized methods of moments (GMM) estimator has become increasingly popular in a number of empirical studies. The relationship between the variables has been represented in linear form. Many non-linear relationships can be expressed in linear form by transforming the variables; however, techniques (such as maximum likelihood) are also available for estimating non-linear relationships. Maddala (1992) provides a useful introduction to the estimators mentioned in this paragraph.

A significant problem with this type of design is the omission of relevant variables from the relationship. Where relevant variables are not included in the model, the coefficient estimators will be biased unless the omitted variables are orthogonal to the variables included in the model. Instrumental variable estimators provide one approach to overcoming this particular problem by providing consistent estimators.

Ex post facto designs

Ex post facto designs arise when the variables under study are not under the direct control of the researcher, but have to be chosen after the event of interest has occurred. This type of design can be represented notationally as:

$$X_1 O_1 \tag{6.16}$$

Matched

$$X_2 O_1 \tag{6.17}$$

Where X_1 and X_2 are the differing treatments or independent variables (either independent variable may be the XO, or absence, variable). The important characteristic of this design is not only its *ex post* nature in terms of observations: the two groups in the experiment are also matched post the event.

The success of this design will naturally depend upon how well matched the two groups are. Failure to match adequately, such that the two groups differ on an important variable or variables will threaten the internal validity of the study. Potentially, some pre-test matching on the dependent variable could be made. Another important problem with the matching process in *ex post facto* studies is the decline in sample size that can occur as subjects are matched. Samples can shrink by factors as large as 10 or 20 when matching is implemented.

Experimental research designs

Experimental research designs are generally more powerful as the researcher can potentially control all extraneous variables and thereby focus directly upon the impact(s) of the independent variable(s) on the dependent variable. In an experimental study, subjects can be assigned by the researcher to different categorizations on the basis of particular characteristics of the independent variable; ideally, the assignment should be at random. There are a number of experimental research designs available to the researcher just as in the case of quasi-experimental research designs. We will focus on just one design type to give the flavour of experimental design as such research designs are less commonly employed in the financial disciplines than their quasi-experimental counterparts (although Glosten, 1999, for example, calls for more experimental type studies in the microstructure area). The two-group after-only research design is the simplest of all the experimental designs. Subjects are (randomly) assigned to two groups on the basis of the levels etc., of the independent variable and then the post test level of the dependent variable is observed. This design can be represented in terms of the notation developed in the previous section as

$$X_1O_1$$
$$X_2O_1$$
(6.18)

This design is similar to the pre-test/post-test design described in the previous section. Note, however, the critical difference is that in this case the researcher assigns subjects to groups *ex ante*, while in the pre-test/post-test design, the researcher works with subjects that have been 'assigned' *ex post*. The major internal validity concern associated with this design is with the assignment of subjects to groups. If there is any bias at this assignment stage, then the internal validity of the experiment will be correspondingly lowered. The basic two-group after-only research design may be extended in a number of directions such as the use of multiple groups, time series and pre-test observations.

Hypotheses and hypothesis testing

When the research problem has been identified, the problem is generally analysed by formulating a hypothesis. A hypothesis may be regarded as a statement of the empirical relationship between a set of variables. In general, this type of hypothesis is referred to as a scientific hypothesis. A statistical hypothesis is a hypothesis about the parameters of a probability distribution. The probability distribution may be of the variables or the coefficients of (correlational) relationships between the dependent and independent variables. When a statistical hypothesis completely defines the probability distribution it is termed a simple hypothesis; all other types are composite hypotheses. Statistical hypotheses are generally investigated by specifying a null hypothesis (usually referred to as H_0) and an alternative hypothesis (often referred to as H_1), which is simply a negation of the null hypothesis. In studying the relationships between variables, the null hypothesis is usually set up as stating that there is no relationship between the variables. Thus, the scientific hypothesis is investigated by testing the statistical null hypothesis.

When conducting tests of the null hypotheses there are two types of error that can occur. The first type of error – termed Type I error – occurs when the null hypothesis is rejected when true. Formally, this may be defined as:

$$\text{Type I error} = \text{Pr (reject } H_0/H_0 \text{ true)}$$
(6.19)

where Pr is the probability and the slash the conditional probability sign.

A second type of error can be committed when the null hypothesis is accepted when, in fact, it is false. This is referred to as a Type II error and is defined as:

$$\text{Type II error} = \text{Pr (accept } H_0/H_0 \text{ false)}$$
(6.20)

One minus the Type II error is referred to as the power of the test. Strictly speaking the use of 'accept H_0' is incorrect since logically the null hypothesis can never be accepted. 'Fails to reject H_0' would be more correct but 'accept H_0' has been used here as its use is more economical.

Type I errors are controlled by the significance levels adopted in the statistical tests employed in the research design. The significance level of a test indicates the probability that the null hypothesis has been falsely rejected. Alternatively, it indicates the probability that the relationship specified in the specific hypothesis has been accepted due to chance. Commonly applied significance levels are the 1 per cent and 5 per cent levels although, increasingly, researchers report the actual probability, or p, value of their tests. The significance level is determined first in most experiments, and then the Type II is minimized by selecting more powerful statistical tests (parametric tests are more powerful than non-parametric tests, for example) and by increasing the sample size.

Throughout this chapter, there have been a number of references to the usage of statistical methods in carrying out empirical research. There are a considerable number of statistical techniques available for use in empirical research and to give a full description of all of these techniques is beyond the scope of the present chapter and indeed of the whole book. However, there are a number of texts which do discuss the statistical methods available. An excellent user-oriented text on econometrics is Maddalla (1992), a widely cited text describing non-parametric tests is Daniel (1978), while Tabachink and Fidell (2001) provides a full discussion of multivariate statistical analysis. Parametric tests are described in a large number of texts – useful texts include DeGroot (1989) and Wonnacott and Wonnacott (1990). The sampling techniques used in an experiment will have impacts upon the overall validity of the work and a fairly concise discussion is provided in Stuart (1984).

Summary

The principles of research method and design have been outlined in this chapter. The whole area of research method and design is very extensive; only those particular areas which are relevant to the empirical accounting and finance researcher have been discussed (more general coverages of the research design process can be obtained from texts such as Campbell and Stanley, 1963; Hinkelman and Kempthorne, 1994; Pukelsheim, 1993).

In conclusion, the three important criteria that need to be considered when evaluating a research design are:

(1) Does the design afford the means of testing the hypotheses formulated from the research question?
(2) Is the internal validity of the design sufficiently high?
(3) Is the external validity satisfactory?

In carrying out empirical tests in the financial area, these three criteria should always be at the forefront of the researcher's mind.

Interpretation of positive research

The research process does not finish with the completion of an empirical study or theoretical analysis. The results of the research are generally written up for wider dissemination, whether it be to the thesis supervisor, book or journal editor or some other peer group. While the style and content may vary, the process is clear; research results are supplied to the 'market'. The market in this case comprises the consumers of such research: other academics, students of the subject, professionals and policy-makers. In this chapter, we will focus upon these consumers and how they might interpret the research reports that are made available to them. In many cases, of course, these consumers will be the producers of further research.

The approach that we adopt will be to highlight the main areas to which attention should be directed for a 'positive' research study to be adequately interpreted. There is clearly no one right way of interpreting research, and the discussion in this chapter should not be regarded as presciptive. However, the chapter does bring together some of the essential features of the overall research process that have been discussed in previous chapters. In particular, in this chapter we will be primarily concerned with 'positive research' of the type discussed in Chapter 1. The interpretation of case study research will be dealt with in the next chapter.

It is often convenient to classify research as either theoretical or empirical. The former is concerned with constructing theoretical models and articulating relationships between them, while the latter is concerned with the empirical testing of models. However, in the overall research process involving observation, modelling, theorizing and empirical testing the distinction between theoretical and empirical research is not always clear as there will be dynamic interactions between the various stages in the process. We will, however, follow the comovement theory/empirics distinction in this chapter and discuss the interpretation of research under two headings: the interpretation of theoretical research, and the interpretation of empirical research.

Interpretation of theoretical research

The philosophy of financial research, together with the research traditions in both accounting and finance have been discussed in previous chapters. What was apparent in those chapters was the important role of the positivist tradition. As part of the necessary abstraction process, a tractable theoretical structure is developed on the basis of a set of assumptions regarding the problem structure. This process then generates a set of predictions which may be rejected by empirical testing. For example, Poincare (1905: 144) observed that 'Every experiment must enable us to make a maximum of predictions having the highest degree of probability'. Furthermore, a new theory should satisfy, at the minimum, two criteria:

(1) It should explain the existing empirical evidence in a coherent and parsimonious fashion.
(2) It should generate additional predictions that can be tested 'out of sample' (see, for example, Fama, 1998).

Some argue that the stronger the assumptions that are made, the stronger the predictions of that model and hence the less ambiguous the resultant tests will be. The debate regarding the realism of assumptions has already been rehearsed in Chapter 1. While the assumptions debate itself may be indeterminate, a number of points can be made regarding the assumptions made in developing theories which are relevant to the interpretation of a theoretical piece of research.

While it may be reasonable to create abstract assumptions in order that a particular problem structure is made more tractable, it is necessary to ensure that the structure is not overly abstracted in the sense that particular and important parts of the overall problem structure are removed. In Miller and Modigliani's (1961) seminal work on dividend policy, they established the important result that dividend policy is irrelevant in ideal markets (that is, ones consisting of rational investors operating in perfect and complete capital markets). However, although this result was very important at the time of its development it was just the starting point in the analysis of dividend policy. In the spirit of Miller and Modigliani's approach, what is required is an analysis of the types of imperfections which might lead to dividend policy becoming relevant in the valuation of the firm. For example, how will the existence of differential taxes on dividends and capital gains impact upon the proposition of dividend irrelevance? How will information asymmetries impact? Relaxing some of the initial assumptions in the Modigliani and Miller analysis will modify the implication of dividend irrelevance since objectives such as optimizing in terms of tax status and signalling will enter the analysis. The important point to note is that some results may be generated by the model as a result of assumptions made which are unsatisfactory given the objectives of the theoretical analysis. In a sense, this is the theoretical counterpart to the concept of internal validity developed in Chapter 6 on research design. It is also related to the notion of 'overabstraction' discussed above. Clearly, if the objective of a piece of theoretical research is to analyse investor diversification for example, then the use of an unembellished capital asset pricing model structure could well prove unsatisfactory since in this scenario all investors will be fully diversified.

When undertaking theoretical analyses it is easy to make a number of unstated but implicit assumptions or conversely a number of redundant assumptions. Implicit assumptions are more common in the verbal, as distinct from mathematical, theoretical structures. However, many mathematical models employed in finance do have implicit assumptions embedded into their modelling structure. For example, many models of asset markets under uncertainty such as stochastic discount factor models rely on the existence of complete markets (of course, a number of theoretical analyses make this assumption explicit). It can often be instructive when evaluating a piece of theoretical work to try and disentangle any implicit assumptions which are present within the modelling scenario. Once discovered, the natural consequence is to consider whether an important part of the problem structure has thereby been removed and how the removal of this assumption would impair the articulation between the remaining assumptions and the implications of the model concerned.

Redundant assumptions tend to be less critical. Overidentification of a theoretical structure will not necessarily remove essential features of the analysis; it may, however, be a warning to the research consumer to consider the rest of the theoretical analysis carefully. In Chapter 1 we discussed the role of Occam's Razor in theoretical analysis. Redundancy in a set of assumptions may not impair the validity of any model deducted from that assumption set but when such redundancy is identified it may be a sign that the logical structure of the model concerned has not been fully thought out.

The internal consistency of a model's structure is of prime importance both in mathematical and verbal reasoning. For example, a model which employs both the assumption of normally distributed equity returns and limited liability is likely to run into trouble when analysing particular types of problem. Clearly, the presence of limited liability as an assumption implies that the distribution of returns generated by the security are likely to be truncated and hence not normally distributed. The two assumptions are, therefore, contradictory and any model based upon them will be inconsistent. Similarly, if an argument for a particular assumption or phenomenon is developed in a framework of uncertainty and is then embedded in a problem structure embracing certainty there are likely to be problems.

Inconsistencies are easier to identify in mathematical models as the problem structure is generally much more transparent. But verbally developed theories are not necessarily immune from inconsistencies. While in mathematical analyses the symbols used will be abstractions, in verbal theories the language used will, itself, be symbolic, and potential inconsistencies can arise between both the usage of the symbols throughout the theoretical analysis and between the symbol or word and the object or reality under analysis. Not only does a problem arise in trying to operationalize higher-level theoretical concepts for empirical testing, there can often be a problem in operationalizing and consistently treating more objective levels of reality throughout a theoretical analysis.

In financial research, as in any academic discipline, great emphasis is placed upon intellectual or rational analysis in theory development. There are, of course, other psychological functions (which might be termed 'extra-rational') and, perhaps, the most important for the prospective researcher is plain intuition or 'nous'. Inevitably, in the process of theorizing, abstractions and linearities have to be introduced which may, in a number of senses, restrict the scope of the analysis. Intuition is not similarly bounded. It is often very useful once the hard rational core of a theoretical study has been internalized to consider, less formally, whether the whole theoretical structure is coherent and appears reasonable. Clearly, counter-intuitive results do occur in theoretical analysis since intuition itself can be faulty, but equally clearly, the existence of such results should, at the very least, be reviewed.

Theoretical analyses inevitably entail abstractions from reality. An important consideration in assessing any piece of theoretical work is to establish or investigate how readily generalizable the results are. In finance, for example, a number of theoretical results are developed in a single period setting, for example the capital asset pricing model. A natural question to ask is whether the results from these analyses are generalizable to multiperiod settings. In the case of the capital asset pricing model the conditions for generalizing to a multiperiod setting have been developed in Fama (1970) and Merton (1973b), for example. Other issues include the ease with which results obtained under conditions of certainty could be extended to settings entailing uncertainty and the generalizability of theoretical results across alternative institutional or international settings.

In general terms, there is a similarity between the previous discussion and the concepts of internal and external validity as applied in empirical studies. The analogy is strongest in the case of external validity and generalizability. While the internal consistency of a theoretical analysis does bear comparison with the internal validity of an empirical analysis, the analogy is not always as strong as might appear at first sight. Theoretical assumptions will inevitably 'force' conclusions in a fashion which would be unacceptable in empirical research designs were they to 'force' empirical results. Nevertheless, the broad analogy between internal and external validity in experimental design and the internal and external validity of theoretical constructs can be a useful rule of thumb when evaluating theoretical research.

The final point in this discussion of theory interpretation relates to the uses to which theoretical analyses and results are put. It is always sound practice to evaluate carefully the relationship or 'correspondence' between theory and practical application. For example, if a model is developed on the assumption that markets are frictionless, then considerable care should be taken if that model is to be used in an environment characterized by transactions costs or regulation. It is tempting to overextend the 'relevance' of theory and to misinterpret its implications. This is most apparent in the use of abstract financial modelling techniques in computer algorithms which are then sold as commercial products. A number of option pricing packages employ the unmodified Black and Scholes's option pricing model which assumes (among other things) frictionless markets, unrestricted short selling and no dividends on the underlying stock. At a simpler level a number of spreadsheet packages employ financial modelling tools whose use is dependent upon a number of very questionable assumptions about the nature of financial markets.

Interpretation of empirical research

The interpretation of empirical research is somewhat easier to discuss in general terms than theoretical research. Theoretical research tends to involve modelling structures which are specific to the particular topic area with the result that it is often difficult to provide a general discussion which is appropriate to the financial research area as a whole. For example, the rationality assumption employed widely in finance and some areas of accounting would be a singularly inappropriate structure for theoretical analysis in the behavioural areas of accounting and finance. Empirical research, by its nature, will often support a number of alternative theoretical explanations and thus permit a more general discussion of how such research may be interpreted.

We have emphasized at various points the very necessary articulation between theory and empirical testing. Without a theoretical structure to guide the researcher he or she risks engaging in little more than crude data-dredging. Theory should provide the empirical researcher with a set of empirical implications (hypotheses) that can be investigated by empirical testing. A primary requirement of any empirical study is the development of hypotheses that are well specified, in the sense that they are unambiguous and testable.

When a particular theory is empirically investigated, the researcher will be confronted with the problems of testing joint hypotheses. It is even argued that joint hypotheses are inevitable in the social sciences as a result of the necessity to operationalize concepts for which there are no ready empirical counterparts. In other words, many empirical studies will be tests of joint hypotheses: the theory under review and the empirical constructs used in generating the empirical implications for testing purposes. The results of the joint tests will be contingent upon these empirical constructs and the unambiguous rejection of the theory concerned becomes impossible. This is a slightly different point to that made by Lakatos (see Chapter 1) in his rebuttal of Popper's falsificationism. Lakatos (1970) argued that any well developed theory will include a number of *ceteris paribus* clauses which will protect the theory from empirical rejection. When interpreting a piece of empirical work it is necessary to consider how particular concepts or variables have been operationalized and how they articulate with the theory and results. A prime case in point was the problem of identifying the market portfolio for tests of the capital asset pricing model. That is, as Roll (1977a) points out, it is necessary to identify exactly the constitution of the market portfolio in order to test satisfactorily the capital asset pricing model.

The preceding paragraph has dealt with one aspect of empirical research control, namely, internal validity. Another important aspect in developing control is in the selection of the sample employed by the researcher. A first consideration is the sample size. Under normal conditions, sampling fluctuations will be reduced as the sample size increases and there are, therefore, advantages in having as large a sample as possible. However, there is a limit, apart from increasing cost. As sample size is increased there is a possibility that new observations will not be from the same distributions as the existing sample constituents. For example, in extending a time series of observations a structural change may occur in the relationship between the variables being investigated. Thus, in evaluating the adequacy of sample size the trade-offs between potential reductions in sampling fluctuations and the increased risk of degrading the representativeness of the sample must be considered.

While sample size is important, an equally important consideration is whether there are any biases inherent in the sample selected. Where a biased sample is used in an empirical study both the internal and external validities will be low. One example of a biased sample would be where the researcher has concentrated upon items with particular characteristics, for example, large firms. Another more subtle bias is termed 'ex post selection' or 'survivorship' bias (see, for example, Brown, Goetzmann and Ross, 1995). In a study which uses observations on firms which have existed for (say) at least 20 years, there is an in-built selection bias in the sense that at the beginning of the period (with a finite chance of bankruptcy) it would not be known *ex ante* which firms would still be in existence at the end of the period. Similar arguments would apply to financial markets such as the emerging markets (see Jorion and Goetzmann, 1999). Tests of the profitability of various trading strategies (in market efficiency studies) and the performance of mutual funds are particularly prone to this type of bias.

It is also necessary, when reviewing a sample, to ensure that the sample selection criterion is adequate, given the objectives of the research being conducted. What we mean here is that it is important to ensure that the sample selection criteria do not 'force', in whatever sense, the results (and thereby reduce the validity of the study). In their classical empirical study, Miller and Modigliani (1966) focused upon the electric utility industry. A number of criticisms of their work were specifically directed at their choice of the electric utility industry as it was argued that a number of their results arose as a direct consequence of this industry choice. Kothari, Shanken and Sloan (1995) argue that studies entailing the use of book–market ratios will lead to the exclusion of failing stocks and potentially drive the pricing results reported in Fama and French (1992).

A crucial step, once the sample has been scrutinized, is to investigate whether the research design is adequate to support the study of the phenomena concerned. The general principles of research design and types of design available were described at some length in Chapter 6. We will not repeat that discussion here. However, it is important to remember that, just as sample selection can 'force' results, so too can the way in which a study has been designed. The results and conclusions of a poorly designed study will be seriously flawed. When particular research designs are always used (such as, for example, in event studies) the scope for design errors is diminished. Even in these types of design, however, elementary mistakes can still be made as, for example, in the case where correct exclusion periods are not employed and the properties of least squares residuals not appreciated.

The interpretation of research is more straightforward when standard research designs are employed to study particular phenomena. The actual research design employed can then be compared with the standard design and any departures from established practice can be considered in depth. Often departures from such standard design practice will be justified by an author of a research paper and the reader should investigate further if this is not the case. However, the application of standard research designs repetitively to the same database can induce additional problems – for example, the problem of data-mining. Essentially, if a particular database is extensively analysed by researchers over a long period of time there is a likelihood that strong, but spurious, relationships may be established within the variable set.

When a study is carried out for which there is no well received research design, interpretation will, of necessity, be more difficult. A prime requirement will be an understanding of the principles discussed in Chapter 6. Sometimes the task is made easier by the researcher describing the motivation and rationale for the innovative research design employed. In such situations, both the execution and interpretation of research is at its most exciting and challenging. In general, innovations in theoretical structures necessitate innovations in empirical research design. The challenge of such innovations is well exemplified in the asset pricing literature which was discussed in Chapter 3. The problems of the general research design for testing the capital asset pricing model were pointed out by Roll (1977a). This led to changes in the testing techniques (see Gibbons, 1982; Stambaugh, 1983). More recent controversial results in the asset pricing literature (Fama and French, 1992) led to analytic reconsiderations (Roll and Ross, 1994) and research design re-evaluations (Ball, Kothari and Shanken, 1995). The Roll critique also led to a greater concentration of empirical research upon other theories of asset pricing. Arbitrage pricing theory, for example, had to be tested using different research designs to those employed in testing the capital asset pricing model and the challenge associated with developing new testing designs was well exemplified by the debate in the literature.

The discussion of the problems of testing asset pricing models again emphasizes the problem of measurement in the social sciences. The Roll critique indicated the problems of identifying the market portfolio and hence measuring its (expected) return. When reviewing any empirical paper, particular attention should be directed towards how well particular variables are measured, that is, the extent of any measurement error. If variables subject to measurement error are included in the regression model, for example, the estimators of the model coefficients will be biased (see below).

To be realistic, measurement problems will almost always occur in empirical financial research. The question to be addressed by the researcher and the reviewer of such research is the extent of that error and the likely direction of the bias induced. Where the directional bias of measurement error is towards rejecting the null hypothesis and the empirical study does not reject that hypothesis, then the impact of such error, although making the overall study less 'tight', will not be fatal to the study as a whole. Where measurement error is a significant feature of a particular research design then the use of some sensitivity analysis is indicated. That is, the researcher should investigate the sensitivity of test results to different measurement techniques. A low sensitivity would clearly provide more support for the results of the research.

Once the internal validity of a research study has been assessed, the next stage in any interpretation is to examine the generalizability of the results, that is, the external validity of the research should be assessed. It should be apparent that if the internal validity of a study is low, then its external validity will accordingly be low. For example, if the sample selection criterion is biased towards some particular type of firm (for example, large firms or firms from a particular industrial classification) then the results may be specific to that type of firm. Similarly, the results could be specific to the time period used in the study. Results and conclusions could differ in periods of high inflation from periods of low inflation. Changes in the fiscal environment, such as changes in tax rates or capital allowance regimes, could impact upon results and hence limit their generalizability. The degree to which the results may be sample specific (whether cross-sectionally or temporally) should be assessed when the generalizability of a study is being considered. The use of 'hold-out' samples, that is where the model is estimated by using one data-set and tested using a subsequent data-set, will provide some insights into the generalizability of the results. Such tests will also mitigate against the tendency to 'overfit' the models in the estimation period.

When subjecting a theoretical model to empirical testing, the model is generally tested as a statistical hypothesis and either rejected or not rejected at a particular level of significance. However, any model is, by definition, an approximation to reality and will not hold as a complete empirical description in every instance. As such, then, this begs the question how useful is a particular model when either rejected or not rejected? That is, if a model is not rejected by the empirical testing, should the model be used and treated as if it perfectly described reality? Alternatively, if the model is rejected, should it be regarded as providing no useful insights into the structure being analysed at all? These types of question are addressed within a Bayesian framework by Pastor (2000) and Pastor and Stambaugh (1999). In Pastor (2000), for example, a Bayesian type framework incorporating prior beliefs in asset pricing models is used to investigate the 'home bias' in international asset allocations.

The statistical techniques and methodology employed in an empirical study will influence the nature of the results and the conclusions that can be inferred. Theories are generally tested via statistical hypotheses which entail the use of particular statistical tests. In any assessment of a research study the statistical methods employed must be carefully scrutinized. Many statistical tests, for example, are based upon the assumption of the normality of the distribution of the underlying variable. The common statistical tests of sample means and variances, such as t-tests and F-tests, have normality assumptions inherent in their structures. Similarly, some estimating techniques such as maximum likelihood often rely upon normality assumptions. The assessment of any piece of work which uses such statistical tools should include a consideration of how appropriate such normality assumptions are. Where the distribution is identified but non-normal, tests based upon that distribution are more appropriate. Where the distribution is not known, distribution free or non-parametric tests should be employed, albeit with some loss of statistical power. For example, a number of financial variables such as accounting ratios, stock returns and exchange rates have been found to be non-normally distributed. In such cases, non-parametric tests such as Mann–Whitney and Kruskal–Wallis have been used either to supplement tests based upon the normality assumption or as 'stand-alone' tests (see, for example, Theobald and Price, 1984).

Many empirical tests involve the use of formal econometric models, particularly where theory predicts that certain independent variables 'explain' the dependent variable. Tests of this type of relationship entail investigating whether the coefficients on the independent variables are statistically different from zero. There are a number of well-known problems associated with this type of analysis (see Maddala, 1992) which should be considered whenever a piece of research using this form of analysis is being assessed or interpreted; Campbell, Lo and MacKinlay (1997)) provides an excellent discussion and presentation of the econometrics associated with various aspects of financial research.

A particular problem in research designs which are not theoretically well founded is what is termed 'under-specification bias'. Whenever a relevant independent variable is omitted from the independent variable set, the resultant model is said to be under-specified. Such under-specification can have a serious impact upon the results of any test, since it will inevitably lead to bias in the estimators of all the coefficients of the independent variables included (unless the omitted variable is orthogonal to the independent variable set). This is clearly an example of failure to control for extraneous variables in the overall design. When interpreting a piece of econometric work some consideration must be given to whether all relevant variables have been included in the model specification. Under-specification bias clearly emphasizes the necessity for working through the theoretical development as thoroughly as possible before proceeding with empirical testing.

We have already mentioned the problem of measurement error. The biases induced by measurement error can be significant and many researchers develop sophisticated estimating techniques to overcome this problem. For example, in the early tests of the capital asset pricing model, considerable emphasis was placed upon reducing the 'errors in the variables' bias caused by using measured betas in cross-sectional tests. While bias reduction is important, there is another dimension to be considered, namely estimator efficiency. The early asset pricing tests virtually ignored this dimension, although later estimators did attempt to incorporate efficiency considerations (see Black and Scholes, 1974; Campbell, Lo and MacKinlay, 1997).

When we were discussing sampling considerations at the start of this section we mentioned that the determination of optimal sample size involved a trade-off between sampling fluctuations and the risk of sample degradation. The same consideration applies when estimating the parameters of a fully specified econometric model. When reviewing empirical research, a careful watch should always be kept for potential structural changes in the relationship between the dependent and independent variables. These changes can occur both cross-sectionally and temporally.

Two phenomena that can impact upon estimator efficiency are autocorrelation and heteroscedasticity. Both relate to the statistical properties of the disturbance term in a formal econometric model. The commonly used ordinary least squares (OLS) estimator will only be efficient *inter alia* if the disturbance term has a constant variance (homoscedasticity) and is not correlated through time or cross-sectionally; if either of these conditions are not fulfilled then a more efficient estimator will exist which makes use of this information. The generalized methods of moments estimator (GMM) is now widely used in the empirical literature to alleviate such problems (see, for example, Campbell, Lo and MacKinlay, 1997).

Summary

In this chapter we have pointed out that the analysis of any piece of research work, whether it be theoretical or empirical, entails two processes. First, the internal consistency (or validity) of the research should be considered; that is, in a theoretical piece of work, are there any contradictions in the analysis or logic employed? In empirical research, the ultimate question to be asked is whether it is reasonable to draw the conclusions arrived at by the researcher given the research design and the controls employed. The second issue concerns the generalizability of the theoretical or empirical results obtained. How specific are the theoretical results to the structure employed (in the sense that would they still pertain in a differing modelling scenario)? How specific are the empirical results to the particular sample frame, for example? The issues of validity and generalizability in case study research will be discussed in the next chapter.

It is perhaps worth while emphasizing, again, the very necessary articulation between theory and empirical testing in positive research. Matching observable 'reality' to theory is, necessarily, a conjectural business but confidence in experimental results and in theories to which they relate increases with the quality of the research design. The concept of 'articulation' referred to in this chapter relates to the quality of the relationship between theory and observation guaranteed by good experimental design. The process of research continues via the articulation between observation, theorizing and empirical testing. The process may be more correctly envisaged as circular rather than linear. That is, there is no necessary ordering strictly from theory to empirical testing; feedbacks into theory from empirical tests are very likely and, in the long run, highly desirable.

• • • • • 8

Methods of case study research

> Case study research is remarkably hard, even though case studies have traditionally been considered to be 'soft' research. Paradoxically, the 'softer' a research technique, the harder it is to do.
>
> (Yin, 1984: 26)

Case studies have become quite common in accounting research, especially in management accounting, although they are relatively rare in finance (but see Miller and O'Leary's, 1997, study of capital budgeting). In accounting research case studies are gaining acceptance as an appropriate research method, and increasing numbers are appearing in the research literature. However, a range of questions need to be raised in connection with case studies in accounting research. For example, what constitutes case study research? How do we evaluate an accounting case study? When are case study methods more appropriate than other research methods? In this chapter we will try to address such questions through a discussion of the methods of case study research.

The chapter will begin by describing different types of case studies that might be used in accounting (and possibly even in finance) research. We will then discuss the potential of case studies in different types of research: distinguishing positive and interpretive research. This will be followed by a review of the issues to be considered in selecting suitable cases. Next we will describe the main steps in conducting a case study and then the issues to be considered in writing up case study research. The chapter will finish with a discussion of the weaknesses and problems of case study research, and of the implications of case studies for accounting research.

The term 'fieldwork' is often used in connection with case study research. In the social sciences fieldwork is usually taken to mean studies of social practices in the field of activity in which they take place. In accounting, this could be a study of a single organization or a number of organizations. A case study, however, usually implies a single unit of analysis. This might be a company or other form of organization, but it could also be a more aggregated unit of analysis. For example, we might undertake a case study of accounting in a particular country. In the literature, the terms case study and fieldwork are both used to refer to studies of accounting in its practical setting. In the remainder of this chapter, we will use the term case study in this way and thereby embrace most of what might also be called fieldwork.

Case studies offer us the possibility of understanding the nature of accounting in practice; both in terms of the techniques, procedures, systems, etc. which are used and the way in which they are used. For instance, we can use case studies to provide descriptions of accounting practice, to explore the application of new procedures, to explain the determinants of existing practice and even to illustrate the exploitative nature of accounting in advanced capitalism. Obviously, these various uses of case studies rely on quite different theoretical and methodological perspectives – as we discussed in Chapter 2. In the next section we will distinguish the different types of case studies that are used in accounting research, and later we will explore some of the issues raised in doing case study research.

Types of accounting case study

As indicated above, case studies provide a research method that can be used in a variety of ways by accounting researchers. The following are some of the different types of accounting case studies.

Descriptive case studies

These are case studies that describe accounting systems, techniques and procedures used in practice. A number of companies may be selected as cases to describe different accounting practices or the similarity of practices in different companies. The research objective of these studies is to provide a description of accounting practice. Such studies may be useful in exploring the use of traditional or more modern accounting techniques and practices. They are often supported by professional accounting bodies because they appear to offer the possibility of determining 'best' practice – sometimes conceived as the most common practice and sometimes as the practice adopted by 'successful' companies. However, such studies beg the crucial questions of what constitutes 'best' practice and 'successful' companies. Nevertheless, such case studies are useful in providing information concerning the nature and form of current accounting practices.

Illustrative case studies

These are case studies that attempt to illustrate new and possibly innovative practices developed by particular companies. Kaplan (1986; 1998) has argued that accounting researchers have a lot to learn from studying the practices of innovative companies. Such case studies provide an illustration of what has been achieved in practice. However, there is an implied assumption that the practices of these 'innovative' companies are, in some sense, superior to the practices of other companies. The case study itself cannot provide a justification for this assumption.

Experimental case studies 实验性

Accounting researchers have frequently developed new accounting procedures and techniques that are intended to be helpful to accounting practitioners. These procedures and techniques are developed from existing theoretical perspectives, using normative reasoning. They are intended to indicate what should be done in practice. However, it can sometimes be difficult to implement the recommendations of the researchers. An experimental case study could be used to examine the difficulties involved in implementing the new proposals and to evaluate the benefits which can be derived.

Exploratory case studies 探索性

These studies can be used to explore the reasons for particular accounting practices. They enable the researcher to generate hypotheses about the reasons for particular practices. These hypotheses can be tested subsequently in larger-scale studies. As such, the case study represents a preliminary investigation, which is intended to generate ideas and hypotheses for rigorous empirical testing at a later stage. The objective of such subsequent research is to produce generalizations about accounting practices. The exploratory case study is a first step in such research.

Explanatory case studies 解释性

Such case studies attempt to explain the reasons for observed accounting practices. The focus of the research is on the specific case. Theory is used in order to understand and explain the specific, rather than to produce generalizations. The theory is useful if it enables the researcher to provide convincing explanations of the observed practices. If available theories do not provide such explanations, it will be necessary to modify existing theory or develop new theory, which can then be used in other case studies. The objective of the research is to generate theories which provide good explanations of the case.

The distinctions between these different types of case studies are not necessarily clear-cut. For example, it may not be clear which practices should be thought of as innovative new developments and the subject matter of illustrative case studies, and which should be regarded as existing procedures and the basis for descriptive case studies. Ultimately, it is the intention of the researcher that determines the classification in each instance. Furthermore, the distinction between exploration and explanation is rather ambiguous. An exploratory study, for instance, may be concerned with generating initial ideas, which will form the basis of an explanation of accounting practices. Despite such ambiguities, the above list gives an indication of the range of uses of case studies and the different emphases which researchers give to their work.

The particular uses made of case study research methods will depend on the nature of the research and the methodology of the researcher. It should be recognized that case studies are a research method, and not a methodology. Furthermore, although case studies can be used for different methodologies, they are better suited to some methodologies than others. In the following section we will discuss different uses of case studies in accounting research.

The potential of case study research

Traditionally, accounting research has utilized a positive empirical methodology, relying to a great extent on the methods and theories of neoclassical economics. Although approaches based on behavioural, organizational and social theories have been developed in recent years, the positive methodological approach still dominates mainstream accounting research. As we have already discussed, within positivism and empiricism the role of research is to derive universal laws or theories about the world. However, it is largely accepted that it may be necessary, especially in the social sciences, to regard such laws and theories as statistical generalizations, that is, statements about the likelihood of particular occurrences in a population. Consequently, exceptions are always possible.

An illustration of a statistical generalization would be a theory that, in general, participation in the setting of budgets leads to greater employee satisfaction, which in turn leads to higher performance. Such a theory has a standard form: in general, if X then Y. However, an observation of X without Y would not refute such a theory, because the relation holds 'in general', but not necessarily in every case. It may also be the case that X would be qualified with a *ceteris paribus* clause of the type 'all things being equal' and in that case, as we explained in Chapter 1, it may be difficult to decide whether a given observation was refuting the theory or the *ceteris paribus* clause. Consequently, such a theory does not provide satisfactory explanations in all cases. For example, it does not explain why in some instances participation in budget-setting does not lead to higher performance.

Such theories deal with aggregates, not specifics. Thus, statistical generalizations do not provide explanations of individual cases. Their objective is to derive general laws and theories, which simplify our understanding of the empirical observations. However, an alternative would be to expand our understanding of the empirical observations by developing theories that explain individual observations in their specific context. Such an alternative is provided by holistic research

The holistic approach is based on the belief that social systems develop a characteristic wholeness or integrity and it is inappropriate to study their individual parts taken out of context. Holistic research methods seek to explain this holistic quality and to locate particular social systems in their practical context. Clearly, there is a role for case studies in such research. Case studies have been used by holistic researchers in a number of areas of the social sciences, from anthropology to sociology, including institutional economics (see O'Hara, 1993; Ramstad, 1986).

In Chapter 2 we described the nature of interpretive accounting research and explained that it seeks to provide deep and rich understandings of the social nature of accounting practices, and attempts to locate these practices in their organizational,

146 METHODS OF RESEARCH

Type of Research	Positive	Interpretive
View of the world	External and objective	Social construction
Types of study	Exploratory	Explanatory
Nature of explanation	Deductive	Pattern
Nature of generalization	Statistical	Theoretical
Role of theory	Hypothesis generation	Understanding
Nature of accounting	Economic decision-making	Object of study

FIGURE 8.1 Differences in case study research

economic and social contexts. Such research adopts a holistic orientation, studying accounting as part of the broader organizational and social systems of which it is part. Consequently, case studies undertaken from an interpretive methodological position are likely to be quite different from case studies undertaken by positive researchers. Some of these differences are discussed below and summarized in Figure 8.1. However, it should be emphasized that the dichotomy shown in Figure 8.1 is used only for purposes of illustration. There are many ways in which case study research methods are used, and a distinction is drawn between positive and interpretive research simply to bring out some of the issues which should be recognized by case study researchers.

View of the world

The starting point for the work for interpretive research is the belief that social systems because of their inherent complexity and recursiveness cannot be treated in the same way as natural phenomena; social systems are socially constructed and, as such, can be changed by the activities of individuals located within a specific social context. The recognition of the importance of human actions is an essential feature of such an approach. In particular, it rejects both methodological individualism where social systems are viewed as a the simple product of individual activity and scientific reductionism which treats the person as a set of variables.

Positive research, however, seeks to identify relationships between variables in a world that is seen to be objective and external to the researcher. It is essentially reductionist – seeking to isolate specific relationships, or sets of relationships, and then constructing explanations by combining these relationships into general theories.

In the terms used in Chapter 2, positive research is at the objective end of the ontological continuum, whereas interpretive research is grounded in a more subjective ontology. Arguably, in the growth of any discipline there is a stage where positive research permits a rapid development of the subject through theory construction and modelling. However, in the closing decades of the twentieth century the limits of that approach started to be recognized and alternatives developed which relied more upon subjective and interpretive research.

Types of case study

Positive researchers are concerned with developing general theories, and they regard case studies as a tool for the generation of ideas and hypotheses, which it is intended will be subjected to empirical testing in large-scale statistical studies at a later stage. Thus, for them, case studies are inevitably exploratory, as the core of their research programme entails the empirical testing of hypotheses.

The purpose of interpretive research, however, is to develop a theoretical framework that is capable of explaining the holistic quality of observed social systems and the practices of human actors. There is clearly potential for explanatory case studies in interpretive research. But in the early stages of such research, exploratory case studies may be conducted to identify the issues to be explored in later studies. Nevertheless, even these exploratory studies will have an explanatory element, and they will be followed by further explanatory case studies.

To understand fully the significance of the differences between exploratory and explanatory case studies it is important to recognize the different modes of explanation that are used in the two types of research.

whole :

Pattern versus deductive modes of explanation

The traditional 'scientific' mode of explanation in the social sciences, especially in economics and accounting, relies on a process of deduction. In the deductive model, a particular occurrence or a relation is explained by deducing it from one or more general laws. Every observation is deemed to belong to an implicit class and its explanation depends on statistical generalizations (covering laws) that link the empirical and theoretical domains. A clear distinction is drawn between the *explanandum* (the thing to be explained) and the *explanans* (which does the explaining). The explanans are always at a more abstract (theoretical) level and more general than the explanandum. For any explanation to be valid, there must be at least one general law from which the empirical observation can be predicted.

However, from an interpretive perspective, generalizations and general laws do not explain, only the specific circumstances of the case can be used to explain. The particular social system being studied and its context provide the basis for an explanation. It is the relations between various parts of the system and the system's own relationship with the larger system of which it is part (that is, its context) which serve to explain the system. This type of explanation is what Abraham Kaplan (1964) termed the 'pattern model of explanation'.

In the pattern model both explanandum and explanans are of the same level of generality, that is, the level of the particular system. No general laws appear in the explanation; it comprises only the various elements that make up the system being explained and its context. This is not to deny that regularities do exist. There may be regularities within the system, or within the larger system of which it is a part. But it does deny the possibility of general laws that transcend all social systems.

Whereas the deductive model of explanation provides predictions of occurrences at the empirical level, based on more abstract general laws or theories, it does not provide explanations of those occurrences. Statistical generalizations do not explain, they only indicate the statistical regularities that may or may not apply in specific cases. The pattern model, however, provides empirical explanations of particular occurrences, but it may not be suitable for making predictions about other occurrences. The explanations provided by the pattern model are intended to help us *understand* the world (or the social systems) in which we live. 'To arrive at some understanding of what is going on is hard enough, without having also to meet the demand that we anticipate what will happen next' (Kaplan, 1964: 351).

In case study research, the deductive model directs the researcher out from the case – from the specific to the general. From such a perspective the value of case studies is limited to exploratory work, such as hypothesis generation and theory development. The 'important work' of hypothesis testing must be carried out in other ways. The pattern model, however, directs case study researchers inward into the particular case. The researcher seeks to identify a pattern in the case and uses theories to explain the observed relations. Where existing theories do not provide convincing explanations, then new theories may have to be developed or existing theories modified.

A researcher who favours the pattern model of explanation will view case studies as an opportunity to understand social practices in a specific set of circumstances. Theories will be used to explain empirical observations, and empirical observations will be used to modify theory. As such there is a two-way interaction between theory and observation. However, researchers who favour a deductive approach view case studies as a means of exploring phenomena in order to generate hypotheses. Such researchers might use case studies to test hypotheses, but this would be a relatively poor test because of the limited number of observations.

Finally, it should be noted that the deductive model of explanation is likely to be appropriate where there are stable relations between variables which can be expressed in the standard form: if X then Y. The pattern model, however, is more likely to be appropriate in dynamic processes in which relations between variables are constantly changing. It has to be admitted that although case studies are useful for the former, they are not necessarily the best research method to use; but for the latter, they are probably the only satisfactory method available.

Generalizing from case studies

Case studies are sometimes referred to as small-sample studies, and authors of accounting case studies frequently apologize that the size of their sample creates difficulties in generalizing their findings. This labelling of case studies as small samples stems from a positive methodology, in which the purpose of the research is to determine the extent of particular occurrences in a given population. The researcher selects a sample from a population and attempts to draw inferences about that population by studying the sample. From such a perspective, a case study is a small sample from which it is difficult to make a statistical generalization about the population from which it was selected. Nevertheless, as indicated above, it is usually accepted that case studies can be useful in generating hypotheses for subsequent testing through large sample studies.

Thus, it is argued that case studies are particularly appropriate in areas where theory is not well developed. Such studies represent an exploratory device that can be used as a precursor to more 'scientific' research. Case studies suggest hypotheses for later testing, and it is then that generalization becomes possible. However, such arguments represent a restricted view of the process of generalization (see Lukka and Kasanen, 1995).

Statistical generalizations are clearly problematic in interpretive research, where the findings of a case study are inherently context specific. However, the objective of such research is to develop theoretically informed understandings that provide explanations of the observed phenomena. The researcher will come to the case with knowledge of existing theories, and these will assist in the pattern modelling process. In analysing the case the researcher will examine whether the observations accord to this existing theory, and if not, the theory will have to be modified. But if the theory does explain the observations, other researchers may want to replicate the study, both in similar conditions and in different contexts. Consequently, theories are developed and modified through case study research, and retained so long as they continue to explain contemporary observations.

Thus, it is more appropriate to apply a logic of replication and extension, rather than sampling logic, to such case study research. This means viewing case studies as a method by which theories are used to explain observations. The theories that provide convincing explanations are retained and used in other case studies, whereas theories that do not explain will be modified or rejected. The objective of individual case studies is to explain the particular circumstances of the case, whereas the objective of a research programme based on these case studies is to generate theories capable of explaining all the observations which have been made. As case studies seek to apply theories in new contexts, the theory is likely to be refined and/or modified, and through this process the theory is generalized. Such a process could be described as theoretical generalization.

In interpretive case study research we look for 'theoretical generalizations', rather than 'statistical generalizations'. The former attempt to generalize theories so that they explain the observations that have been made, the latter, however, are concerned with statements about statistical occurrences in a particular population. Although such statements may enable researchers to make predictions about occurrences, they do not necessarily provide explanations of individual observations.

An alternative form of theoretical generalization occurs when a theory is used to argue that the findings of a particular case study, in a specific context, can be applied in other contexts. The theory is used to identify the connections between the different contexts. Thus, there are two forms of theoretical generalization. In the first, case studies in new or different contexts are used to generalize (that is, extend) the theory to a wider set of contexts. In the second, theory is used to extend the applicability of the case study findings to other contexts.

These differences in theoretical generalizations and the potential confusion between statistical and theoretical generalizations have led some case study researchers to avoid the term 'generalization' altogether. According to Lincoln and Guba (1985) 'the only generalization is: there is no generalization'. Instead, they talk about the 'transferability of the findings from one context to another' and the 'fittingness as to the degree of comparability of different contexts'.

Nevertheless, the distinction between theoretical and statistical generalizations provides us with a means of further elaborating the distinction between exploratory and explanatory case studies. Researchers who adopt a sampling logic and seek to produce statistical generalizations will inevitably regard case studies as no more than an exploratory research method. However, case studies can be explanatory and their real potential will be realized when they are used in conjunction with the logic of replication and extension to produce theoretical generalizations.

The role of theory

As was discussed above, in positive research, theory development occurs through the generation and testing of hypotheses. From such a perspective existing theory will assist case study researchers to identify appropriate hypotheses from the case study and these hypotheses will be tested later through large-scale statistical studies. The development and extension of the theory comes through the process of statistical testing of hypotheses, not through the case studies per se. The case studies are simply a means for generating hypotheses.

However, in interpretive research, theory plays a central role in case study research. It is both the input and output of the research process. In the case study itself, there is an ongoing relationship between theory and observation. Existing theory is used to make sense of case study observations, but through these observations it may be found that the theory needs to be refined, modified or even rejected. As discussed above, this 'generalized' theory will then be used in other case studies, through which it could be further generalized.

Assumptions about the nature of accounting

In positive accounting research the role of accounting is normally not questioned. Accounting is implicitly assumed to be the provision of information to enable users to make economic decisions (see Chapter 4). However, in interpretive research the nature of accounting and its role in organizations and society is open to question – and is often the object of the research. In such research it is important to explore how accounting practices interact with other social practices to constitute the larger social system of which they are part.

Returning to Figure 8.1, we have now seen a number of differences in case study research methods. It must be remembered that the dichotomy described in that figure is illustrative, rather than definitive. It was set up to emphasize that case study research methods can be used in different methodologies. So, in reading case studies it is important to identify the research methodology being used. Case studies are a research method, not a methodology. Furthermore, the role of case studies can be different in different methodologies. As we have seen, in positive research case studies are somewhat secondary to the 'scientific' work of statistical hypothesis testing, whereas in interpretive research case studies are central to the process of theory development. In the remainder of this chapter we will describe the elements of case study research in more detail. Unless specifically stated to the contrary, we will assume that the case studies are explanatory, and being used for interpretive research, and as such explanations are based on the pattern model, generalizations are theoretical and theory is used to understand the nature of accounting practices. (For a more positivistic approach to case studies see Atkinson and Shaffir, 1998.)

Selecting suitable cases

Researchers who approach case studies from a traditional, that is, positive, methodological perspective may fall into what Yin (1984: 39) calls 'the trap of trying to select a "representative" case or set of cases'. Such researchers, being concerned with producing statistical generalizations, will view case studies as a sample which, if correctly selected, may be used to generalize to a larger population. However, as we have already argued, case studies can also rely on theoretical generalizations. Thus, the issues involved in selecting such cases should reflect the needs of theory development, rather than statistical analysis.

Where there is a well-formulated theory and the major research issues are clearly defined it may be possible to select a 'critical case' which directly addresses these issues. In such a case, some critical event or other has occurred and raised the issues of interest to the surface. The objective of such a case study would be to determine whether the theory provides good explanations, or whether alternative explanations need to be developed.

In situations where the researcher wants to extend a theory to cover a wider range of circumstances, it may be appropriate to select an 'extreme case'. Such a case study would indicate the extent to which existing theory can be extended to provide explanations in widely differing circumstances, and identify any areas in which the theory needs to be modified. This line of argument can be extended to situations where there is little available theory. Here an 'exploratory case' could be used to begin the process of theory development. The selection of the particular case for study is relatively unimportant. What is needed is a relevant case that will enable the researcher to begin the process of theory development. Possibly, the case should be 'simple', so that the study can focus on particular key issues – although it may actually be difficult to specify what these should be before the study is undertaken.

Exploratory case studies are also used in positive research, as discussed earlier, and then a representative case would be useful. However, in interpretive research, the exploration is part of the theory development process, and is not necessarily concerned with generating hypotheses (for later statistical testing). The theory will be refined and extended as additional cases are studied by the researcher, or by other researchers, which brings us to the issue of multiple case studies.

In a programme of case study research multiple case studies can be used for two purposes – replication and theory development. A number of similar cases might be selected to replicate the theoretical explanations. Alternatively, dissimilar cases may be selected to extend the theory to a wider set of circumstances. The differences between the individual cases will be determined by the direction in which theoretical extension is desired. The objective of such multiple cases is to develop a rich theoretical framework, capable of explaining a wide range of circumstances.

It is important to recognize the difference between multiple case studies and cross-sectional analysis. In the latter, the analysis and explanation are based on the differences between the various cases. In the former, however, each case should be analysed separately and explanations derived from the particular circumstances of the case, then the theory should be developed to encompass all the cases.

The role of the researcher

In selecting a case study, it is important to consider the role of the researcher *vis-à-vis* the subject(s) of the research. There is a range of possibilities from the complete outsider to an agent of change:

(1) *Outsider*: as an outsider the researcher can maintain a distance from the case, but must rely on available evidence, such as published reports and other secondary sources.

(2) *Visitor*: this is probably the most common perception of the case researcher – someone who visits the case 'site', and interviews the subjects of the research. Here the researcher is not directly involved in the issues being researched, but even the act of talking about these issues could have an impact upon those who are the subject of the research.

(3) *Facilitator*: here the researcher raises issues, gives advice and opens up the options for the subjects of the research. The researcher does not provide solutions, but enables the subjects of the research to identify their problems and helps them to find their own solutions.

(4) *Participant*: in some sociological studies, researchers have taken jobs in the company they are researching – such as on the production line of an automobile company. Working as a participant allows the researcher to obtain insights into the everyday workings of the company. In most instances, the researcher does not disclose the research agenda to those with whom he or she is working. The researcher simply works as a member of the organization, but maintains detailed records of his or her experiences.

(5) *Actor*: in this case, the researcher is directly involved in the organization – possibly introducing a new system or procedure. As such, the researcher is an active participant in the process being researched.

When the researcher is an actor it is very clear that the research process itself has an influence on the case study. But even in the other instances, with the possible exception of the outsider, the researcher cannot be independent of the case. Thus, it is important for such researchers to be aware that case research cannot be a neutral and objective process.

Main steps in a case study

In this section we will describe the main steps in a case study, assuming that a case has been selected for study and access arranged. Although the steps will be listed in what might appear to be a logical sequence, it has to be emphasized that case study research is a complex interactive process that cannot be characterized by a simple linear model. In the course of a case study, the researcher may have to iterate through these steps many times, possibly in different orders and with different interactions between the individual steps. Nevertheless, it is useful to list the various steps so that the main elements of a case study can be discussed.

Preparation

The first step in any research, and particularly in case research, is to specify as clearly as possible the research question(s) to be addressed. This will usually be done by reviewing the existing research literature. The research question will then shape the research design, including the research methods and even the methodology. The question(s) should be sufficiently focused to provide a feasible research plan, given the available resources, especially time. This is particularly important where the research is undertaken for a research degree, as the time frame may be constrained and other resources quite limited. Given a specification of the research question(s), it will then be possible to select the appropriate type of (case) research method, and to decide the extent of the researchers role in the case (see above).

Now, assuming the research question(s) has (have) been specified, and the nature of the case and the involvement of the researcher decided, the available theories relevant to the case should be reviewed in order to draw up a checklist of things to look for in the study. This review of prior theory will determine the way in which the researcher approaches a case. It is sometimes suggested that the researcher should begin a case study totally unencumbered by prior theory. This is quite impossible. Every researcher will be influenced by his or her past experience, previous research, papers read and so on. But as discussed in Chapter 2, the level of prior theorization can differ. Nevertheless, in any case study there will be prior theory, although much of it may be implicit. To make the research meaningful to others, the researcher should make explicit, and as comprehensive as possible, the theory that shapes the case study. As we discuss in a later chapter this can be important for the process of 'rational reconstruction'. In addition to a preparatory review of prior theory, additional theory may be introduced as the case proceeds and new theories are developed. The researcher should be sufficiently flexible to allow such developments to take place.

Collecting evidence

The preparatory review of theory will give an initial indication of the types of evidence that should be looked for in the case study. It may be helpful to consider each research question, possibly each element of each research question, and identify the evidence which is needed in each instance. But in addition, the researcher should be constantly alert for any evidence that appears to be important in explaining the case, and should allow issues and theories to emerge out of the case, rather than being imposed on it. In most cases it will be necessary to use multiple sources of evidence. These could include the following:

(1) *Artefacts*: these are any tangible items, such as formal reports and statements, minutes of meetings, informal records, and personal notes and memos made during meetings.

(2) *Questionnaires*: these can be useful, even in case studies, to obtain evidence from a number of people. They can also be used to gather information in a consistent and comparable way.

(3) *Interviews*: this is the type of evidence most usually associated with case research. Interviews can take different forms, but probably the most important issue to consider is whether they should be structured or unstructured. Structured interviews ensure that similar questions are asked of different people and that comparable information is obtained. But this requires the researcher to have a clear idea of the information that the interviews are expected to generate. Unstructured interviews, however, allow the researcher the flexibility to pursue new issues and ideas as they are raised, and thereby to explore emerging lines of enquiry.

(4) *Observing actions and meetings*: attending meetings can be an important source of evidence for accounting researchers. Clearly, it is better to attend meetings than to rely on the recollections of other who were present. However, in some circumstances it may be difficult to obtain permission to attend important meetings. It is often easier to gain such permission when the researcher is actively involved as, say, a facilitator, participant or actor (see above).

(5) *Assessing (measuring) the outcomes of actions*: where actions have been carried out at the case site, either by the researcher or the subjects being studied, evidence of the outcomes of such actions is likely to be very important. Evidence collected by the researcher is clearly desirable, but it may be necessary to rely on the subjects' own recording systems.

All evidence collected by the researcher should be recorded in an ordered and coherent manner for subsequent analysis and reflection and, where possible, interviews and meetings should be tape-recorded or notes taken at the time. Where neither recording nor note-taking is feasible, the researcher should record in writing (or on tape or word processor) what was said as soon as possible thereafter. Memories can fade quickly. Even where working notes are made at the time, these should be converted into a more formal record as soon as possible. It is sometimes said that this should always be done before the end of the day. Thus, in arranging interviews, etc., it is important, if several are to be held on the same day, that time is allowed for writing notes, etc.

While formally collecting evidence, it is important for the researcher to be aware of informal evidence. For example, when interviewing a manager about the use of an accounting system, clues may be obtained about, say, the relationship between production and accounting staff through casual comments, tone of answers, physical gestures, etc. The researcher should be prepared to follow up such informal clues in any appropriate way; for example, by asking additional questions, interviewing other managers, observing meetings, and so on. Apart from suggesting new issues to explore, informal evidence may also give indications about the credibility of information sources. All such evidence should be noted. For example, where an interview is tape-recorded, if interesting non-verbal signals are obtained, the researcher could append suitable notes at the end of the tape.

All the records, notes and other evidence collected by the researcher should be retained and will comprise the 'field notes' from which the case analysis will be produced. Care should be taken to ensure that the field notes are as comprehensive and coherent as possible. They are the case researcher's database.

Assessing evidence

Researchers who conduct quantitative, empirical research are concerned with the reliability and validity of their evidence (see Chapter 6). Reliability is the extent to which evidence is independent of the person using it, and validity is the extent to which the data are in some sense a 'true' reflection of the real world. But in case research, such notions of reliability and validity are unlikely to be appropriate. Reliability implies an independent, impersonal investigator, and validity implies an objective reality – both of which are likely to be meaningless in interpretive research. As discussed above, the interpretations of the researcher and his or her relation to the subject matter is an essential element of the explanations of the case. Furthermore, such research starts from the belief that reality is socially constructed, and as such it rejects the idea of an external objective reality. Thus, alternatives to criteria of reliability and validity, discussed in Chapter 6, are needed for case research.

Whereas in quantitative research, reliability requires an independent and neutral observer, in case study research it is important to know that the researcher has adopted appropriate and reliable research methods and procedures. This is known as *procedural reliability*. The research should have a good research design which addresses clearly specified research questions, there should be a comprehensive research plan, all evidence should be recorded in a coherent set of field notes and the case analysis should be fully documented. In this way the researcher can demonstrate that the case study findings are reliable, and another person could in principle, at least, examine what has been done. In accounting terms, this might be described as an audit trail.

In Chapter 6 we distinguished between internal and external validity. Whereas internal validity relates to the use of appropriate controls within the study, external validity concerns the extent to which its findings can be generalized to other settings. We discussed the issue of generalizability above and pointed out that the notion of theoretical generalizations is more appropriate for case study research. It was also noted that this could be related to the *transferability* of the study's findings.

In addition, in case study research we replace the traditional criteria of internal validity with the notion of *contextual validity*, which indicates the credibility of the case study evidence and the conclusions that are drawn therefrom. This can entail several different elements.

First, the validity of each piece of evidence should be assessed by comparing it with other kinds of evidence on the same issue. Other subjects might be interviewed, records checked or observations made. This process of collecting multiple sources of evidence on a particular issue is known as triangulation – specifically data triangulation.

Second, the validity of particular sources of evidence should be assessed by collecting other evidence about those sources. If characteristic distortions emerge about a particular source the researcher will be able to assess the validity of evidence from that source. In addition, evidence might be collected using different research methods – for example, using a mixture of questionnaires to collect information from a large number of people, together with a combination of structured and unstructured interviews, and observations of meetings. This could be described as method triangulation.

Third, researchers should also assess the validity of their own interpretations of the evidence. Feeding evidence and interpretation to the subjects of the study can be helpful in confirming the researchers' own interpretations. But this may not always be appropriate, especially where an assurance of confidentiality has been given to individual informants. Sometimes researchers work in teams in order to avoid the bias which an individual researcher might bring to the study. By using a number of researchers, possibly with different academic backgrounds, areas of interest, research experience and so on, it may be possible to arrive at an agreed interpretation of the case, rather than one biased by the personal characteristics of the individual researchers. This could be described as researcher triangulation.

Finally, alternative theories, or even alternative methodologies, could be used to study a specific case. This might open up a diverse range of insights to be considered in interpreting the case. However, whereas an individual researcher might draw on alternative theories – using theory triangulation – it might be more difficult for an individual researcher to adopt alternative methodological positions. However, if different researchers approach the same issues using alternative methodologies, it might be possible for them to at least discuss their respective findings. Some might argue that such an approach would be unfruitful because of the incommensurability of different methodologies. But if a pluralistic attitude is taken and the alternative finding approached in an open-minded way, it may be possible to derive richer understanding through such methodological triangulation.

To summarize, whereas traditionally, empirical and especially quantitative researchers have talked about reliability, validity and generalizability, we should think in terms of procedural reliability, contextual validity and transferability in case study design.

Identifying and explaining patterns

As the case study progresses various themes and patterns should emerge. It is sometimes helpful to prepare diagrams or charts that attempt to link the various themes and issues so that patterns can emerge. In this way missing connections, inconsistencies, etc., can often be identified and avenues identified for further investigation. As more evidence is collected, it may be possible to expand the diagrams and charts, adding new connections and even reinterpreting the evidence collected earlier.

The emerging patterns identified by the researchers will serve both to describe and explain the case. As discussed earlier, we do not need general theories to explain, it is the pattern discovered in the case that does the explaining. Nevertheless, theories still have their place. Patterns observed in the case may be related to patterns discovered in other cases (and captured in prior theories). Consequently, the pattern model developed to explain a case should always be compared with the available theories.

If existing theories conflict with the patterns observed in the case it will be necessary to collect evidence in order to ascertain explanations for these conflicts. In this way, theories can be extended to meet the new circumstances. In principle, the pattern model can be extended indefinitely as new evidence is collected. But in any individual case, the researcher must select boundaries for the study (as discussed below). This inevitability means that *all* explanations are partial and capable of development in the future.

Writing up case study research

The time and effort involved in writing up case study research should not be underestimated. It can be a time-consuming process. A useful rule of thumb in case study research is that it takes one-third of the time to set up the study, one-third to do the fieldwork and one-third to write it up. However, case study research is all about writing – writing is not confined to the final writing-up stage. Planning a case study involves writing proposals, research plans, preparing interview schedules and so on. During the fieldwork there will be considerable writing of notes and possibly reports to be fed back to the subjects of the research and so on. Finally, the writing-up stage involves the production of a detailed case analysis and an interpretation of the case, which together will form the basis of research papers and possibly a dissertation. Thus, case study researchers need to have good language skills as this is the basis of their research method, in the same way that quantitative researchers need numerical skills.

The writing-up stage involves the construction of the *case study* from what is likely to be a mountain of data, field notes, reports, etc., which have been collected during the fieldwork. This is a creative and literary act, and, as such, the case researcher is the author-writer of the case study. In this writing the case study researcher has to produce a convincing text – that is, a text that convinces the reader. But the first stage in convincing a reader is convincing oneself as a researcher. First, the researcher should feel he or she fully understands what is happening in the case. There should be no loose ends or outstanding issues – all issues considered relevant should have been explored and explained. Second, the research must have a high level of procedural reliability, contextual validity and transferability. Finally, and most importantly, the researcher must be convinced that selective plausibility has been avoided. Selective plausibility occurs when evidence is selected simply because it fits the researcher's theory. This can be a very real danger in case study research – the case researcher sees what he or she expects to see. One way to avoid selective plausibility is to look explicitly for evidence which would contradict the researcher's own theory – either prior theory brought to the case study, or the theory emerging in the case study.

Once the researcher has convinced himself or herself, the task of writing a text to convince others can begin. Golden-Biddle and Locke (1993) suggest that convincing texts have authenticity, plausibility and criticality. Case study research can meet these three criteria in a variety of ways, but the following are points to be considered:

(1) *Authenticity* is achieved by demonstrating that the researcher's interpretations are grounded in the case. The text should give the reader a clear sense of the author having been there. This may be achieved by providing rich details of the case and by explaining the extent of the researcher's relationship with the case. For example, details of the people interviewed, meetings attended, etc., should all be provided in sufficient detail for the reader to see how deeply the researcher has become immersed in the case. Authenticity will also be enhanced by the use of quality data and extensive evidence to support the points, issues and argument made by the researcher.

(2) *Plausibility* will be enhanced if the text make sense to the reader and displays a high level of knowledge on the part of the author. The issues raised by the case should be linked to the existing literature and should recognize relationships with other cases and theories, including other disciplines, where relevant. In addition, a coherently written and well-structured case study will increase the plausibility of the text.

(3) The *criticality* of the text relates to the possibilities it provokes. The case may raise new ideas and/or add to theory. Further, it may have implications, both at the level of the case itself and more generally, for example, by drawing out theoretical insights which can be taken to other case studies.

Although these three criteria can be met in a variety of way, a text which has authenticity, plausibility and criticality is likely to be convincing and, as such, a good case study.

Weaknesses and problems of case study research

We hope this chapter has answered some of the traditional prejudices of writers who do not regard case studies as an acceptable method for social scientific research – namely, their claims that case studies lack academic rigour and cannot be generalized. Frequently, such writers conveniently overlook the biases and inherent assumptions of their preferred research method. In case study research it is important to give considerable care and attention to the collection and evaluation of evidence which is used in developing and generalizing theory. Thus, case study research has its own rigour and is capable of generalization. Nevertheless, this is not to suggest that there are no weaknesses or problems in case study research. In this section, we will look at three aspects of case studies that are a common source of difficulty for researchers.

First, there is the difficulty of drawing boundaries around the subject matter of the case. The interpretive perspective emphasizes the importance of locating accounting practices within the context of the wider organizational, economic and social systems of which they are part. But how far should a researcher expand the case in studying interrelations with other and broader systems? A similar problem occurs in the historical dimension as social systems and practices evolve through time. For example, accounting practices in a particular organization will have evolved with the development of the business. How far back in time should the case study researcher probe?

The holistic ideal of studying all aspects of a social system is clearly unattainable and we must be satisfied with approximations. Case study researchers must place some limits on the subject matter. One possibility is to place limits on the area of study, but to make those limits quite explicit. This will permit a detailed study of the area, and allow other researchers to extend the work into other areas. The other possibility is to attempt to study 'everything', but in a more superficial way. To some extent, the work of survey researchers can contribute to the latter, whereas case study methods are essential for the former. As already discussed, the process of theoretical generalization in case study research can expand our understandings of the subject area into the larger social systems, as more case studies are undertaken.

The second difficulty for case study researchers stems from the nature of the social reality which is being researched. If, as argued earlier, social systems are not natural phenomena, they cannot be understood independently of human beings, and the researcher cannot be regarded as a neutral independent observer. The researcher must interpret the social reality and, thus, case studies should represent interpretations of the social reality. There can be no such thing as an 'objective' case study. This emphasizes the problem of researcher bias. As discussed earlier, it may be possible to reduce such bias in the collection and assessment of evidence by using a team of researchers, with different backgrounds, experiences, etc., and by feeding back the researchers' interpretations to the subjects of the study. Nevertheless, it has to be accepted that case study research provides an interpretation of the social system being studied, not an objective representation. But can any social science research method claim to do more?

The final difficulty of case study research, which we want to discuss, is the ethics of the researcher's relationship with his or her subjects. Many accounting case studies require access to organizations and to confidential information. Access may only be secured if confidentiality is assured. In addition, subjects may be much more open in their dealings with the researcher if they are confident that the information disclosed will be treated in confidence. This raises particular problems in writing case reports. For instance, it may be necessary to disguise the identity of the organization studied. While this will limit an appreciation of the context of the study, it may be essential in order to obtain detailed confidential information. Furthermore, in a study of relationships between members of an organization it may be necessary to guarantee the confidentiality of information received *within* the organization. A subject may not be prepared to reveal his or her views, opinions, etc., if the researcher is to feed this information back to others in the organization. Maintaining such confidences within an organization may prevent the researcher from checking the validity of evidence through feedback to the subjects. Other means of checking must then be found, for example, observing the subject's actions, examining documentation and appropriate questioning of other subjects.

For the researcher to maintain good relations with subjects in the study, and to avoid damaging the prospects for other case study researchers, it is essential that all confidences are respected. Thus, a balance must be struck between the need to obtain access to confidential information and the prospects for using that information in a wider arena, either in the study or in publishing the results.

Implications for accounting research

In a book on the methods of field-based research, Burgess (1984) described developments in anthropological fieldwork during the twentieth century, which have clear implications for case study research in accounting. In the early years of the century anthropological fieldwork was based on what Burgess called the 'Veranda Model'. The researchers viewed the natives from the verandas of colonial homes, often with a certain amount of contempt. They frequently relied on the reports of vested interest groups, such as administrators and missionaries, and when they questioned natives they removed them from their day-to-day experiences. The shortcomings of such a research method for understanding the natives' culture and way of life are now well accepted by social science researchers. Let us compare some approaches to accounting fieldwork and case studies that have emerged in recent years.

Accounting researchers are now using case study methods to examine the nature of accounting practices within organizations. How should we evaluate this research if it is based on interviews with vested interest groups (for example, senior executives and accountants), treats managers with contempt (as irrational and unable to understand accounting information) and stresses the centrality of accounting when interviewing production, sales and other functional managers? Such an approach looks very similar to the Veranda Model in anthropological research. Perhaps in accounting, it might be called the 'Senior Management' model. If accounting researchers want to exploit the full potential of case study methods to understand the nature of accounting, they must be prepared to study accounting practices at various levels within the organization and to explore the relationships between the various groups of managers. The implication of the above analogy for accounting research is that case studies should explore the day-to-day accounting practices of 'real' people, and attempt to study the context in which they work.

In comparison with the more traditional forms of accounting research, it is important to recognize that case studies are concerned with explanation, rather than prediction. Case study researchers should avoid the temptation of thinking of their work in terms of statistical generalizations. Researchers who see generalizations only in this sense will either reject case study methods or produce poor quality case studies. Good accounting case study research will be concerned with explanation and theoretical generalization. Such work should provide clear understandings of the subject area studied and help the individuals working in that area or in similar areas to work out their problems on a day-to-day basis. It may also act as a stimulus for sorting out problems that remain below the surface. Case study research methods themselves will not provide the answers to such problems, but should provide the subjects concerned with a deeper and richer understanding of the social context in which they work and make them aware of the problems, and the possibilities for solutions.

An interesting parallel to this view of case studies is given in a comment on management consultancy which was made by a former director of McKinsey and Company. 'In McKinsey's practice we could export ways of thinking about problems but we could not export solutions … because each case took place in a different historical and cultural context' (quoted by Smith, Whipp and Wilmott, 1988: 102). In the same way accounting case studies cannot locate general solutions to the problems faced by managers and accountants, but they can provide a better awareness of the issues that are involved. Case studies provide ways of thinking about problems and, as such, are an important tool of accounting research.

Summary

In this chapter we have explored the potential of case study research in accounting. We identified a number of different types of accounting case study, and in particular distinguished the role of the exploratory case study in positive empirical research and the explanatory case study in interpretive research. Whereas case studies are only an exploratory device in positive research, they have real potential in interpretive accounting research, where they can provide detailed explanations of contemporary accounting practice. Such case studies can help both researchers and practitioners to achieve a deeper and richer understanding of accounting within its social context.

Further reading on case study research

Books on case study and field research

Burgess, R. G. (1984) *In the Field: An Introduction to Field Research*. London: Allen and Unwin.
Hammersley, M. and Atkinson, P. (1995) *Ethnography: Principles and Practice*. London: Routledge.
Yin, R. K. (1994) *Case Study Research: Design and Methods*. 2nd edn. Beverly Hills, CA: Sage.

Learning Resources
Centre

Books on qualitative research

Flick, U. (1998) *An Introduction to Qualitative Research*. London: Sage.
Mason, J. (1996) *Qualitative Researching*. London: Sage.
Silverman, D. (1997) *Qualitative Research: Theory, Method and Practice*. London: Sage.

Papers on case studies in accounting

Atkinson, A. and Shaffir, W. (1998) Standards for field research in management accounting. *Journal of Management Accounting Research* 10: 41–68.
Humphrey, C. and Scapens, R. W. (1996) Theories and case studies of organizational accounting practices: limitation or liberation. *Accounting, Auditing and Accountability Journal* 9(4): 86–106.
Keating, P. J. (1995) A framework for classifying and evaluating the theoretical contributions of case research in management accounting. *Journal of Management Accounting Research* 7: 66–86.
Otley, D. T. and Berry, A. J. (1994) Case study research in management accounting and control. *Management Accounting Research* 5(1): 45–65.
Scapens, R. W. (1990) Researching management accounting research: the role of case study methods. *British Accounting Review* 22: 269–81.
Spicer, B. (1992) The resurgence of cost management accounting: a review of some recent developments in practice, theories and case research methods. *Management Accounting Research* 3(1): 1–37.

9

The research output

In this chapter, we will consider four ways of presenting and disseminating research. We will first examine the process of undertaking and presenting a postgraduate degree followed, in the second section, by an examination of the process of research publication in the academic literature. Third, we will discuss the role of publications in periodicals and, finally, the status of books in the publication of research in accounting and finance.

Each of the different ways of presenting research (or from the user's point of view, the different sources of research) has quite different characteristics and rules. Conducting research is just the first stage of the research process. The ideas which flow from an individual or group's research activity must go through a process of peer evaluation and criticism by the academic community before it can be accepted into the disciplinary body of knowledge.

Fundamentally, the academic community is a social system like any other social group. It has a certain structure, which is differentiated into levels and codes of conduct that govern behaviour. Individuals within an academic community are differentiated by reputation, and it is this reputation that represents the 'capital' of this particular social system. Individuals (and the academic institutions who employ them) gain their reputation from the perceived quality of their ideas and the contribution they make to the development of their discipline. In addition, they may also gain reputation through their teaching and communication skills. However, it is research output and its quality that is the dominant criterion for appointment and promotion decisions within higher education.

Postgraduate research

For those embarking upon an academic career, most academic institutions require formal research training before appointment. In the UK the shortage of suitably qualified applicants in the area of accounting and finance in the 1970s and 1980s resulted in many lecturers gaining their first academic appointment without a research degree. At that time, the possession of an appropriate professional qualification, together with a good first degree, was deemed sufficient for entry into academic life. This has now changed, and research-oriented accounting departments in the UK, partly because of the influence of other departments in the social sciences and partly because of the influence and opportunities offered in the USA, now require a doctoral degree before offering a permanent academic position.

Postgraduate research degrees can be obtained at two levels within most UK universities.[1] They are as follows:

- MPhil: Master of Philosophy, which requires one to two years' full-time, supervised postgraduate research
- PhD or D.Phil: Doctor of Philosophy, which requires a minimum of two to three years' full-time supervised research (depending upon previous academic training and qualifications).

The *UK Qualifications Framework*, published by the Quality Assurance Agency (QAA), describes a doctoral degree as follows:

> Doctorates are awarded for the creation and interpretation of knowledge, which extends the forefront of a discipline, usually through original research. Holders of doctorates will be able to conceptualise, design and implement projects for the generation of significant new knowledge and/ or understanding.
>
> (QAA 2001a)

and defines the outcomes of the degree as follows:

> i the creation and interpretation of new knowledge, through original research or other advanced scholarship, of a quality to satisfy peer review, extend the forefront of the discipline, and merit publication;
>
> ii a systematic acquisition and understanding of a substantial body of knowledge which is at the forefront of an academic discipline or area of professional practice;
>
> iii the general ability to conceptualise, design and implement a project for the generation of new knowledge, applications or understanding at the forefront of the discipline, and to adjust the project design in the light of unforeseen problems;
>
> iv a detailed understanding of applicable techniques for research and advanced academic enquiry.
>
> (QAA 2001b)

To gain an MPhil or PhD, the individual is required to go through a number of stages: first, acceptance by a department within a university (or other institute of higher education) for a research degree; second, registration within the chosen institution for the degree concerned; third, a period of supervised research; fourth, the writing up of the results of the research and, finally, examination.

The process of registration for a research degree can be complex and lengthy where the student, in discussion with members of staff, prepares a research proposal, which is sometimes referred to as the research 'title'. Most institutions require a full specification of the proposed project, a plan of work, the names of any collaborating institutions, the names of external sponsors (if any) and the names of the proposed supervisors. The supervisors will normally include at least one member of academic staff who is qualified to undertake such supervision. In some institutions, a supervision committee may be established consisting of a small number of relevant specialists who oversee the conduct of the research and provide a forum for the student and his or her supervisor to engage in regular review and debate. In the new UK universities,[2] this process can take between 12 and 18 months to complete, although in the older universities the process of registration can be far shorter.

The general UK practice is that upon registration and payment of the appropriate fees, the student will embark upon the research supported by a programme of classes in research methods and methodology as well as other subject areas that the student and the supervisor consider appropriate. It is not uncommon for entrants to PhD programmes to embark upon a taught masters programme in their specialist area and then, providing a satisfactory outcome is achieved (with overall scores in excess of 60 per cent being the norm), the student is allowed to proceed to register for the PhD. Again, practice varies, but many universities also insist that a student registers for an MPhil in the first instance, and then transfers to PhD once they have demonstrated satisfactory progress in their studies.

The first part of the research itself will normally be concerned with a thorough review of the relevant literature, and a process of refinement of the issues posed by the research problem. This is a crucial stage and the success of the whole enterprise depends upon the quality of this step.

It may be that after thorough investigation the student discovers that he or she is dealing with a problem that has already been addressed elsewhere in the literature or that the problem is in fact a 'non-issue'. In the social science disciplines and in accounting, in particular, this is not an uncommon event and is the downfall, or at least the reason for delay, of many postgraduate research projects. Chapter 10 on the analysis of research literature will set out some important criteria for this stage of the research process. The main point, however, is that the literature review and analysis should not be just a 'trawl' of everything written in the area. The construction of the literature review and the critical analysis of the state of knowledge within the area should be founded upon the student's perception of the research process in the subject area.

Following the initial stages of the research and the literature review, a specific research problem will be identified. After the problem has been identified and the position of that problem located within the subject area as a whole, the next stage will be to convert that problem into one or more research questions, either in the form of, or leading to, a series of hypotheses and to the design of the further research necessary to generate answers. In some cases, the research questions will lead to experiment or empirical methods, and in others to analytical discourse and, possibly, a series of thought experiments (perhaps using mathematics or some other formal system).

Many of the greatest intellectual leaps have been achieved in just this way. However, this latter type of research invariably requires great depths of intellectual intuition, which few individuals are lucky enough to possess. For this reason, the traditional empirical study of a narrowly defined set of research questions is regarded as the safest route to a research degree.

The final stage of the research process is the synthesis of results into a summary and conclusion leading to the presentation of the research as a dissertation. The word 'dissertation' means 'detailed discourse' (*Oxford English Dictionary*). Thus, it should be interpretive and dialectical, rather than purely descriptive.

Generally, dissertations contain the following elements:

- abstract (a short description of the project and its principal conclusions)
- contents page
- introduction (with a preview of the structure of the dissertation, the issues addressed and the conclusions reached)
- interpretive and critical 'reconstruction' of the relevant literature and an analysis of the research issues within that literature
- description and evaluation of the selected research methodology
- development of the research questions and, if appropriate, the hypotheses to be addressed
- description and evaluation of the research methods employed
- presentation of the results obtained and an evaluation of their significance in answering the research questions
- conclusion, with an indication of fruitful areas for future research
- bibliography

Research students are often interested in the final output they are expected to produce. In our experience, most PhD dissertations follow the above structure with the word counts indicated in Figure 9.1 (assuming a 75 000 word[3] thesis).

Figure 9.1 is indicative of the basic structure and weighting of the various components in the typical doctoral dissertation. The structure of a dissertation does not differ between an MPhil and a PhD, although the scope of the research at the two levels can be quite different, and some university regulations permit the MPhil standard to be reached by a thorough evaluation of the literature in a particular area. Originality is often specified at both levels, but is rarely defined except in a contextual sense. A literature review may well be original in that such a review has not been conducted before. It can also be original if it provides an interpretation and a critical commentary on the literature which has not been advanced before. At the doctoral level, the notion of originality is extended to include novel developments in either theory or method or both.

The final stage of the postgraduate research process is the examination. The examination for the MPhil and especially the PhD is conducted at two levels: first, the dissertation is examined by the internal and external examiners. In some universities internal examiners may include among their number the student's supervisor. However, the external examiner will be chosen for his or her independence from the research project, as well as for his or her experience. It is normal for only one external

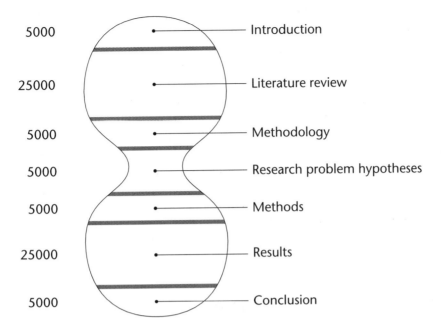

FIGURE 9.1 'Hour-glass' model of the standard PhD dissertation relying upon empirical evidence

examiner to be involved although practice varies from institution to institution. Second, a PhD candidate will be required to undertake a viva voce and this may also be required at MPhil level. During the viva voce examination the panel comprising the internal and external examiners will question the student in considerable depth about the research and related matters. As a result of this two-stage examination process the examiners will recommend pass or fail, or any number of conditions that must be fulfilled before the degree can be awarded. In continental Europe it is not uncommon for the oral examination to be conducted in public.[4] The viva voce is an important and exacting component of the examination and, even at this late stage, a candidate can find that the whole basis of his or her work is being questioned at a fundamental level. It is relatively rare for a research degree to be failed at the viva voce examination if a satisfactory dissertation has been submitted, although marginal students can be failed or subjected to stringent conditions for corrections and resubmission.

The process of gaining a research degree is an exhaustive one even in those discipline areas where there is a high degree of agreement among the academic community as to what constitutes appropriate research. In accounting, and to a lesser extent finance, such agreement has yet to be reached. As we have discussed in other chapters, there are a number of methodological positions held by different accounting researchers. These tensions pervade the discipline and present a challenge to all researchers irrespective of level. This inevitably adds an element of jeopardy to the PhD research process which can only be minimized by careful and expert supervision which will include, among the supervisor's duties, searching for examiners who are likely to be sympathetic to the research approach adopted.

As sources of research ideas, postgraduate research dissertations provide a fertile area for study although they are not always easily available. University libraries and the supervising departments will usually keep one copy of all successful dissertations. In many cases, however, the important results of postgraduate research find their way into the academic journals either during the course of the research or shortly after its completion. A significant proportion of the US accounting literature is represented by the output from the doctoral programmes of the major universities. An examination of the principal accounting and finance journals reveals a preponderance of papers acknowledging the debt the author owes to his or her doctoral research committee. Given the lower level of postgraduate research in the UK this is not so common. Finally, some postgraduate research finds its way, either in whole or in part, into books and we will examine this means of publishing postgraduate research later in this chapter.

Publication in research journals

Publication in the research journals is taken as a measure of achievement in academic life. In the UK's Research Assessment Exercise (RAE), which is conducted at approximately five-yearly intervals, all 'research active' staff are required to report their best four publications.[5] These publications are read by an expert panel who assess the quality of the research submitted. The results of this research directly influence the funding that universities receive from government via the Higher Education Funding Council. Although only about 10 per cent of total university funding is affected in this way, the RAE provides one of the few mechanisms whereby universities can improve their funding by their own efforts. For this reason, publication in the top research journals has become particularly important in accounting and finance.

The distinguishing characteristic of a research journal (compared with a periodical, for example) is that each submitted paper is subjected to a process of peer review, which is intended to be both independent and anonymous. This reviewing process commands wide support throughout the academic community, although it is acknowledged to have a number of deficiencies. The presumption is always that the independent reviewer is knowledgeable in the area concerned and will assess the research in an unbiased way. In addition, it is presumed that the journal's editors will exercise their judgement in a fair and unbiased manner.

Journals establish their reputation in a number of ways:

- the reputation of their editorial board
- the number of articles published that have made a significant contribution to the development of the particular literature
- the number of citations to that particular journal by authors writing in other journals.

There is considerable debate about the ways in which the impact of an individual piece of scholarly work and, indeed, the reputation of a journal can be measured. Clearly, journal reputation is based to a large extent on the intellectual impact of the articles published. There are two popular approaches to measuring this impact: the first employs what are known as 'bibliometric' methods, which involves the quantification of citations to an individual paper or to a journal as a whole. The second elicits the opinion of scholars working in the field.

Supporters of bibliometric techniques argue that the number of citations to an article or journal is a primary indicator of the importance of that research or the journal as a whole in the subsequent development of the literature. The most important source of citation data in accounting and finance is published in the *Social Sciences Citation Index*. However, this data can be unreliable for a number of reasons:

- Citations are only retrievable under principal author. This creates a problem in assessing the contribution of scholars who engage in significant joint work.
- Self-citations are not eliminated and thus it is open to authors to artificially boost their performance. There is also a pronounced tendency towards 'toadyism' with the editor receiving more citations than their work might strictly merit.
- Citation does not distinguish between a 'good' and a 'bad' publication. This criticism is rarely of great importance as most articles that have made a fundamental error or have asserted a theoretical or empirical conclusion which is unsupportable are quietly forgotten.
- The level of citation depends on the circulation of the journal. Journals with small circulations may publish outstanding work but will not attract the level of citation of a journal with greater international readership. The top US journals are often widely cited but UK and Australian journals may be undercited for this reason.
- There can be considerable variations in citation practice from journal to journal. Articles within the methodological mainstream tend to carry shorter bibliographies than those from areas exploiting social and organizational theory. There are a number of possible explanations for this but the most reasonable is that scholars in these areas tend to rely more upon the 'pedigree' of an argument than do those engaged in empirical work within the hypothetico-deductive tradition.

It is extremely difficult to identify the magnitude or the direction of the bias introduced by these effects and many critics respond by dismissing such studies out of hand. The UK Higher Education Funding Council has considered the use of citation indicators in the Research Assessment Exercise but has opted for a wide-ranging and comprehensive process of peer review. However, we would advocate that such studies if read with caution, and mindful of their inherent limitations, can give a guide to the reputation of particular journals although the value of any individual paper in the development of the literature can only be properly assessed by scholarly review and evaluation.

A number of studies have been published using both citation analysis and surveys of academic opinion which rank the accounting and finance journals. The consensus is that the most highly cited journals are ranked as follows (1) *Accounting Review*, (2) *Journal of Accounting and Economics*, (3) *Accounting, Organizations and Society*,

(4) *Journal of Accounting Research* and the (5) *Journal of Accounting and Public Policy.* This ordering is quite stable although since 1992 *JAR* has lost position to *AOS*. Most academics working in the finance area are in general agreement that the premier tier of finance journals comprises the *Journal of Finance*, the *Journal of Financial Economics* and the *Review of Financial Studies*. A number of subject-specific niche journals have developed in the finance area in recent years and specialists in derivatives, for example, would publish in the *Journal of Derivatives* and the *Journal of Future Markets*; specialists in mathematical aspects would publish in *Mathematical Finance*; specialists in emerging markets would publish in the *Pacific Basin Finance Journal* and microstructure specialists in the *Journal of Financial Markets*, for example.

In accounting there are many other journals of high repute such as *Abacus*, *Accounting and Business Research, Accounting, Auditing and Accountability Journal, British Accounting Review, Critical Perspectives in Accounting, Journal of Business Finance and Accounting* and *Management Accounting Research*. However, the accounting and finance disciplines now cover a very wide scope both in terms of subject matter and method, and these journals only represent a small fraction of the diverse and high-quality literature now being produced. There are a number of sources for journal rankings available on the Internet and elsewhere, although for the reasons we have outlined above we advocate a cautious approach to their use and, in the final analysis, quality cannot be measured by rankings but only by familiarity with the work or journal concerned.

The reviewing system as applied by all of these journals is anonymous, although many experienced and knowledgeable referees can often identify the author(s) from the subject matter and other contextual clues. Some authors, in their turn, attempt to reveal their identity by, for example, citing their own work and by other means. Each referee is required to produce a specific recommendation about the publishability of the research, as well as a critical report for the authors. However, with rejection rates on many journals in the range of 60 per cent to 80 per cent, even a favourable report may still lead to rejection by the editors on the grounds of relevance to the aims of the journal or for some other reason. Very few articles are published without revision, and in the major accounting journals it is not unusual for an article to go through three or four revisions before final acceptance. Following acceptance, the editors may still make significant modifications to enhance readability or to shorten the article.

The reasons for rejection of a journal article are various, but the most usual are:

- *Lack of originality in theoretical innovation.* Few journals accept papers of a purely theoretical nature but even those with the strongest empirical bias demand a certain degree of theoretical innovation to justify publication.
- *Lack of originality in the area of empirical study or in the methods of empirical analysis.* It is extremely rare in the accounting and finance areas for pure replication research to be published.
- *A fault in the experimental design in an empirical study.* Such faults can be: mis-specification of hypotheses, poorly targeted tests (that is, mismatch between what is being tested and the hypothesis under test), insufficient sample size to make sound inferences about the underlying populations and insufficient controls.

- *Lack of rigour in either formal or non-formal reasoning.* This can range from simple errors of logic to misapprehension of either empirical or theoretical facts. It is expected that analytical arguments, wherever presented, will be critically sound and where such arguments are supported by statistical techniques that they are of appropriate power and scope.
- *Lack of scholarship* in that important and relevant areas of the literature have been ignored or improperly interpreted.
- *Lack of clarity.* While clarity and ease of understanding are important virtues in any writing, they are always relative to the subject matter and the intended audience. Academic researchers, when reading the literature, usually appreciate economy of expression and do not need the lengthy explanations of underlying concepts that would be appropriate for a less knowledgeable audience.
- *Inappropriate subject matter for the journal concerned.*

Many editors also complain that authors fail to gain help and advice from colleagues and associates within the academic community before submitting articles for publication. Careful reading by colleagues within (and outside) the subject area can often reveal obvious defects in research design, analysis and conclusions that would render the material unpublishable. All journals set out in some way or other an editorial policy towards the subject matter which the editors are prepared to consider for publication.

Harre (1986) has made the point that the 'capital' of academic life is reputation and that the editors of journals hold a privileged position in the control of what is published and what is not. However, this does not necessarily imply that the discourse which is permitted is restricted in any significant way. All the journals mentioned earlier have high rejection rates and all insist on 'high quality' in terms of what is published. Quality, however, is not an objective criterion. It is dependent upon the methodological stance taken by the editorial boards. In order to form a view of the overt positions of the various editorial boards we will now consider the editorial policy statements (EPS) published by a number of journals in accounting and finance.

The senior journal, the *Accounting Review* (*AR*) (the journal of the American Accounting Association) commenced publication in 1926. Editors hold their tenure for three to six years and substantial changes have been made in the constitution of the editorial board over the years. The journal seeks to publish the 'results of systematic enquiries in any areas of accounting. The primary criterion for publication is the significance of the results as a contribution to accounting thought' (Editorial Policy Statement, 1988). In addition, the journal has also developed a stance favouring theoretical articles which can be seen to possess practical relevance: 'purely normative or descriptive articles generally will not be acceptable' (EPS, 1978). This has appeared to result in the publication of articles in a stereotyped format conforming to a hypothetico-deductive model of research. Authors are expected to define a relatively narrow problem area, cite important sources, develop one or more testable hypotheses, subject those hypotheses to test (using large, preferably unbiased samples and appropriate statistical method) and draw sound conclusions. Great emphasis is laid upon originality in problem specification and upon sound method, although well-justified innovation in the latter area is highly regarded.

Alongside the *AR*, other journals now published by the American Accounting Association, such as *Accounting Horizons*, *Issues in Accounting* and *Education and Management Accounting*, cover a wide range of topic areas but have not, as yet, published material within the social theory framework discussed in Chapter 2. Also, articles of a purely theoretical nature or which address methodological issues or issues which are not amenable to large sample methods stand a much lower chance of acceptance. Evidence of *AR*'s publishing history lends credence to the view that the journal predominantly supports two constituencies: established, highly cited academics and young non-tenured academics at the US ivy-league universities preparing papers from higher degree work with the support (and often co-authorship) of senior members of their supervision team.

Relatively few non-North American academics appear to meet the technical standards required by the *AR* (approximately 13 per cent of all manuscripts are received from non-North American sources).

The *Journal of Accounting and Economics* (*JAE*) was first published in 1979 in association with the Graduate School of Management, the University of Rochester. Under the leadership of Professors Watts and Zimmerman this journal has developed a distinctive style and policy:

> The Journal of Accounting and Economics encourages the application of economic theory to the explanation of accounting phenomena. The theories of the firm, public choice, government regulation and agency theory, in addition to financial economics, can contribute significantly to increasing our understanding of accounting problems ... A wide range of methodologies and topic areas are encouraged:
>
> (1) the determination of accounting standards;
> (2) government regulation of corporate disclosure;
> (3) the information content and role of accounting numbers in capital markets;
> (4) the role of accounting in financial contracts and in monitoring agency relationships;
> (5) the theory of the accounting firm;
> (6) government regulation of the accounting profession;
> (7) statistical sampling and the loss function in auditing;
> (8) the role of accounting within the firm.
>
> (EPS, 2001)

Much has already been written about Watts and Zimmerman's own perception of what constitutes sound research in accounting. The best summary of their position is given in Watts and Zimmerman (1986: 9–12) and they leave us in no doubt that their approach is very much in the instrumentalist tradition of positivism advocated by Friedman in his essay 'The Methodology of Positive Economics' (1953). A casual perusal of the published articles in *JAE* confirms the consistent application of their view in the editorial policy of the journal. The published articles in *JAE* follow the model discussed for the *AR* above: problem specification, hypothesis development, the identification of a set of testable implications, well-targeted and economical test design using appropriate mathematical or statistical methods and the derivation of valid conclusions concerning the hypotheses proposed. As with the *AR* and *JAR* (see below) a premium is placed on methodical innovation and rigour within a narrow methodological framework.

Accounting, Organizations and Society (*AOS*) commenced publication in 1976 under the editorship of Professor Anthony Hopwood. The *AOS* maintains a small but high reputation editorial team and has a specific editorial policy which states that the journal is 'devoted to the behavioural, organisational and social aspects of accounting' with the intention of providing a 'specialised forum' for research into those areas which foster 'new thinking, research and action' (EPS, 1976). In a letter from the editor of *AOS* to the then editor of the *AR* (quoted by Dyckman and Zeff, 1984) it was stated that: 'AOS was established, in part at least, because of the highly restrictive nature of [the] emphasis ... of JAR on human information studies which are only a part of behavioural research.'

Brown, Gardner and Vasarhelyi, (1987) provided a comparative analysis of the research contributions of *AOS*, *AR* and *JAR* over the first eight years of the existence of *AOS* from 1976 to 1984. They concluded that *AOS* provided a complementary outlet for research involving international, behavioural, organizational and social aspects of accounting. They identify distinct differences between *AOS* and the other two journals: *AOS* draws substantially more of its research from psychology, multiple disciplinary management and sociology/political science and substantially less from economics and finance, and mathematics/decision science/game theory than *AR* or *JAR*. Regarding research method, they found that the three journals are similar in that each journal's primary research methodology is analytical-internal logic (ibid.: 203). The publishing stance of *AOS* has remained broadly consistent although with the launch of *Critical Perspectives on Accounting* in 1986 it has tended to accept a greater proportion of material from the academic mainstream.

In addition, they commented that *AOS* is more likely to accept articles that employ opinion elicitation techniques as opposed to archival (database) type studies.

The *Journal of Accounting Research* (*JAR*) has been in existence since 1963 and was formed as a collaborative effort between the University of Chicago and the London School of Economics (LSE). The connection with the LSE was broken in 1975 with only Professor Baxter of the LSE remaining on the editorial board until 1977. Dyckman and Zeff (1984) note that when *JAR* came into existence in 1963 its main competitor was *AR*, which at that time contained a considerable amount of 'normative' research focusing on policy prescription and framework building. Very few empirical studies appeared and most that did were based upon either questionnaire studies or interviewing techniques. In its original statement of objectives, which has never been superseded, *JAR* was charged with reporting research 'in all areas of accounting' (EPS, 1963).

In discussing the origins of *JAR*, Davidson stated:

> The previous decade had seen substantial advances in the development of statistical techniques and quantitative analysis ... new information and theories on motivation and other aspects of behavioural science were developing ... a more scientific approach to accounting research was clearly on the horizon.
>
> (Davidson, 1984: 282)

Dyckman and Zeff (1984) conclude that during the years 1963–68 the content of *JAR* was similar to *AR* but that from that time *JAR* devoted 'increased attention to empirical forays (of a hypothesis testing kind) and to the application of mathematics and other disciplines to accounting questions' (ibid.: 245).

The *JAR*'s relative success appears to be attributable to the following:

- It promoted a 'scientific' style within the positivist 'hypothetico-deductive model' of scientific research with considerable weight being placed upon methodical innovation and rigour.
- It brought into the scope of accounting discourse areas such as human information processing, motivation theory and other topics which were often (mis)labelled as 'behavioural'.
- It pursued a policy of creating and maintaining a stable editorial team of high academic repute.

The journal commenced publication of an annual supplement containing selected conference papers in 1966. Over the first eight years these annual supplements published exclusively empirically based studies. Since 1985 the policy has been to 'choose conference papers which reflect special appeal because they illustrate either new approaches or controversial approaches to accounting research' (*JAR* Supp. Edn, 1985).

Without a doubt, the *JAR* has made an important contribution to the development of accounting thought, although the standards it demands have a particular focus towards highly sophisticated methods within a narrow methodological framework.

The journals mentioned above are important because of their long history in the publication of accounting and financial research and necessarily their record in publishing articles of outstanding importance in the development of the literature. However, not only are their standards high they do (apart from *AOS*) restrict acceptances to articles that fall within the prevailing orthodoxy. However, the wide range of other journals also provide an exacting refereeing process and an outlet for contributions from scholars with interests in critical research or, indeed, art and poetry (see, for example, *Critical Perspectives in Accounting*).

Publication in periodicals

Periodicals such as *Accountancy, The Accountant, Managerial Finance, Investors Chronicle* or *Financial Management* are not regarded as research publications within the academic community. The reason is that although there may be some system of editorial review, articles are not subjected to the independent and anonymous review process that is used for articles submitted to the research journals. However, this does not mean that the ideas presented in such periodicals are not worth while but, rather, that they have not been presented with the degree of rigour or the depth of argument required for publication in the research literature.

Periodicals serve a number of important purposes in the research process:

- They allow researchers to communicate their results to a wider audience than is possible with the academic literature.
- They permit a more discursive presentation of material than would be acceptable in the academic literature.
- They provide a forum for feedback of ideas from professionals and others who can make a valuable contribution to the research process.

Periodical publication is different in both style and content from journal publication. For example, it is not generally necessary to be exhaustive in citing the literature when developing an argument. Clearly, intellectual honesty demands that ideas are fully attributed but a full literature review is not usually necessary. Generally, most editors are seeking topical material and look for incisive writing that will stimulate interest in the uncommitted reader. Few people read the research literature with the same avid interest with which they read their daily newspaper, and the editors of periodicals are looking for the more stimulating reading found in the latter rather than the measured prose of the former. Finally, word budgets are likely to be more circumscribed in periodicals than in journals with 800 to 1500 words being the norm for publication in these sources.

Publication in books

The use of books for the publication of research in finance and accounting is not as widespread as in other disciplines. In philosophy and history, for example, books are at least as important as the journals for the publication of research.

Books can be categorized in three principal divisions:

(1) research monographs of usually 50 000–100 000 words
(2) teaching texts of usually between 150 000 and 250 000 words
(3) books of readings from the research literature or invited readings from scholars with a particular research interest.

A book requires the same order of commitment as a research degree and the refereeing process is just as rigorous as that pursued by the academic journals. However, books are sometimes referred to as 'secondary sources', as they are often used to disseminate work already published in research journals but within some larger theme developed by the author. In accounting and finance books are rarely used to publish the results of a single study, although there are notable exceptions.

In teaching texts, the research content will naturally vary with the level of intended audience. For a first-year text, for example, the research content will be entirely derivative but it may represent the fruits of considerable research into pedagogic issues. At the other extreme, a postgraduate text may contain a substantial component of new research, but pay little regard to the pedagogic needs of its readers.

The content of books of readings can range from compilations of new material from invited authors to selections of previously published articles. Compilations of new material offer an interesting insight into the development of a subject and can, through their bibliographies, offer an introduction into a new area of literature. However, they rarely offer novel research results in their own right as most academic authors gain greater credibility by publication in the primary literature. Generally, and it is only a generalization, books of invited readings rarely contain leading-edge research, although the material that is presented is more likely to be accessible to the non-specialist reader.

Books of readings from the existing journal literature, however, offer a very useful and convenient source of material around a particular theme. Indeed, the great articles in accounting and finance have received wide exposure through books of readings which, with the editorial commentaries that go with them, have made an immense impact upon the development of academic research and in certain cases the development of professional practice.

Summary

In this chapter, we have focused on the research output through dissertations, articles and books. The available literature is now expanding widely as new journals come on to the market, but there is, as always, a great shortage of quality research articles. The high rejection rates reflect not so much the low quality of the material submitted but the lack of proper development and exposure of the work concerned to comment by peers. Editors frequently remind contributors in their policy statements that premature submission is the most common cause of rejection. In this chapter we have outlined some of the issues in getting research published as well as the processes involved in obtaining research degrees. Since the first edition of this book the range of opportunities provided to scholars in the accounting and finance areas to publish original work has developed considerably, with many more outlets for research employing novel methods or derived from different methodological traditions than that currently accepted within the mainstream of the literature.

Notes

1 Continental European practice sometimes varies from the UK with the award of doctoral degrees for research, and in some cases a separate doctoral qualification in teaching is a prerequisite for an academic position. Indeed, it is not unusual for continental European academics to hold two or more doctoral qualifications.
2 These are the institutions awarded university status in 1992. Previously, the majority had been polytechnics, some of which had a distinguished record in applied research

and innovation. A small minority were former institutes of higher education whose size or scope had prevented them from attaining polytechnic status.

3 Different universities have different word counts and different rules for the counting of data in appendices.

4 There are arguments for and against public examinations. Advocates argue that it makes the award more open and subject to scrutiny. Opponents argue that many orals result in criticism of the supervisor as well as the student under fire and that this is best done in private.

5 For those unfamiliar with the UK's RAE exercise it should be noted that the requirements vary from subject to subject to subject. Accounting, finance and economics like the natural sciences place particular emphasis on refereed journal articles. In some other disciplines, other forms of submission such as books or original works of art or music are required.

Part Three

Techniques of critical analysis

10

The analysis of literature

Much of the literature on research method focuses on the issue of sound research design, hypothesis construction and testing, and the analysis and criticism of results. The methodology literature has, on the other hand, focused on rules for the evaluation of competing methods, the demarcation of good research from bad research and, in some cases, the critical analysis of argument. One area that most distinctively links methodology with method is the critical analysis of the literature. In this chapter, we provide some guidance on an effective framework for such critical analysis.

The distinguishing characteristic of academic research is the body of literature it creates and in which the reputations of scholars are vested. Some researchers have gone as far as to suggest that the single most important objective of the academic community is to generate research publications (Latour and Woolgar, 1979) rather than the search for ideal or true knowledge.

As Harre (1986) notes, it is extremely difficult to devise absolute standards for deciding whether or not the research process accumulates 'true' knowledge. One of the by-products of the revolution in thinking advanced by Einstein, Bohr and Heisenberg in the sciences and Fleck, Hanson and Kuhn in philosophy is that 'reality' is an attribute of relationships rather than objects. In the shifting sands of the meaning that we attach to language it is clear that the concepts and observations we describe by language are not objectively determinable facts of experience but are, at least to a degree, determined by our social and ideological preconceptions.

As we discussed in the last chapter, the importance of the literature within the academic community is well established at the institutional level as well as justified at the philosophical level. The reward systems for academic staff and the funding decisions for university departments are principally determined by published output through books and, in the majority of disciplines, through the academic journal literature. Some universities also consider citations to such published work as a primary measure of reputation. It is clear that the output of academics through the literature, and especially that literature controlled by independent refereeing processes, is of critical importance to the development of a discipline.

This fact is further recognized by the importance that is placed by university statutes upon the critical analysis of a literature as a necessary component of any programme of postgraduate research. Indeed, under the majority of research degree regulations in the UK, a critical and original literature review is a necessary and sufficient condition for the award of an MPhil degree and a necessary precondition for the award of a PhD. Further, in most disciplines a brief literature review is required in all articles other than notes submitted for publication in the academic literature.

Given the importance of the effective critical evaluation of literature it is somewhat surprising that so little has been written on this important topic. In this chapter we discuss the concepts of literature analysis and criticism in some detail, identifying the parameters of effective criticism. We then outline the elements of analysis from which an effective literature reconstruction can be achieved.

Criticism and rational reconstruction

Criticism always involves some inherent theory of truth and knowledge. Criticism, as defined by the *Oxford English Dictionary*, involves judgement of fault and censure. When such criticism is accompanied by remarks that suggest improvement or remedy, then the criticism is said to be 'constructive', otherwise it is destructive. Implicit in the notion of criticism, therefore, is the concept of fault or error. To judge error, in its turn, implies that the critic must have some criteria for determining whether a proposition is true or false. In terms of our discussion of realism in Chapter 1, such criteria might be established in terms of coherence with perceived reality. For those who accept that beliefs can only be justified by reference to prevailing social values and norms, criticism implies judgement of error relative to some 'consensus theory' of truth.

This idea that certain basic methodological and ideological positions must be identified before criticism can be undertaken is not new. What is not generally recognized is that this approach is demanded at the level of criticism of a literature as well as at the level of individual contributions to that literature. The goal of 'objective criticism' free of any methodological or ideological contamination is impossible to realize. For this reason the techniques of 'rational reconstruction' (RR) provide a useful starting point for analysis. Lakatos (1970) building upon the work of Popper (1959) argued that scientific (or social scientific) historical explanation can be developed at two levels: internal and external. Internal explanation relates to that component of history that can be explained within the terms of a particular methodology. External explanation relates to that component of history that is inexplicable in terms of that methodology. External history is idiosyncratic history in that it lies outside the scope of explanation by the chosen methodology. Any methodology can generate explanation although there are certain parameters that govern usefulness in this respect.

Some explanatory methodologies have high descriptive power but rather weak normative power. Popper's methodological falsificationism provides strict criteria for demarcating science from non-science and for determining good scientific practice from bad scientific practice. This methodology identifies the search for decisive experiments that have the potential to refute conjectured hypotheses as the objective of good scientific practice. However, the history of disciplinary developments has given few clear examples of this process being followed.

At the other extreme Kuhn's methodology of paradigm revolutions is descriptively very adaptable. Almost all scientific development can be classified as 'normal' or 'revolutionary' and clear examples in all fields can be offered for paradigm shifts. However, this methodology provides very weak guidance on what separates good from bad practice. An effective methodology must balance both prescriptive power (to establish criteria for criticism) and descriptive power (to gain general credibility in explanation and prediction).

To be effective as a framework for analysis, a methodology should offer a straightforward way of cognitively interpreting the development in any discipline. This notion, at its simplest, means that a methodology should lead to rules of criticism which are cognitively coherent to the analyst. Methodologies, which permit mappings, networks and other representational devices, are likely to be more effective and acceptable to the practitioners of the discipline concerned. The visual presentation of structure is usually easier to understand than more formal representations.

From the notions of internal and external history we can develop analogous concepts of internal and external criticism. By internal criticism we mean that criticism which presumes the methodological framework imposed either by the original researcher(s) or by the critic. Internal criticism within the original researcher's methodological frame is often labelled 'technical' criticism in that fundamental definitions and situational issues are taken for granted. However, technical criticism may not be possible where the original researcher's methodological position is unknown or has not been made explicit or, indeed, where the critic is unable to free himself or herself from methodological preconceptions. Effective internal criticism of the second type requires that the critic make the methodological position explicit.

External criticism targets issues outside the problem situation defined by the methodology chosen. Such issues include 'the importance of the problem ... the accuracy of the theorist's representation of the situational constraints facing him and of the (research) objectives themselves' (Wong, 1978). The scope of external criticism is defined by the scope of the internal criticism. Internal criticism of the 'technical' type leaves the greatest scope for debate of external issues.

In Figure 10.1 we articulate the process of rational reconstruction within the methodological framework outlined in Chapter 1. First, we define the methodology appropriate to the research programme and that may well be explicit, but more usually implicit, within the literature. The second stage is to define the key assumptions in which core terms are embedded within a 'proto-model' within the literature. The capital asset pricing model as originally defined and articulated by Sharpe (1964) is a good example of such a model. From that model certain modifications of its assumptions are possible and certain secondary models may be developed (see, for example, Brennan's 1970 adaptation of the capital asset pricing

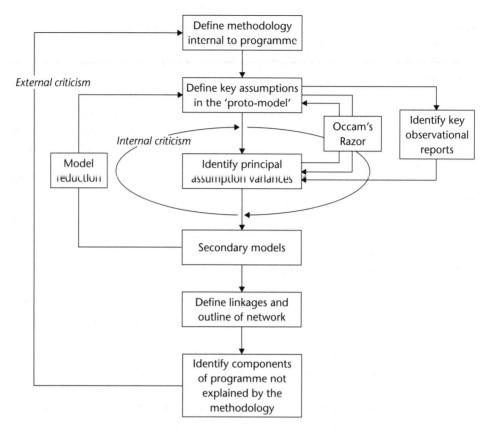

FIGURE 10.1 The process of reconstruction in the modelling framework

model for taxation). Alongside this process, a process of model reduction and validation by experiment also occurs (various observational reports will appear within the literature) causing progressive redefinition and economizing on the set of terms required for the particular model. Internal criticism will apply to this process and the creation of a network of interlinked core terms, assumptions and observation reports will form the elements of the internal history of the research programme.

External criticism examines the elements of the research process that cannot be defined within the methodology described by the internal history. The evidence of an accumulating external history through this critical process will result in a weight of evidence against the internal history and may lead to a redefinition of the methodological principles that led to its creation.

From this we can characterize the process of critical evaluation of a research literature as follows:

(1)   On the critic's part: self-evaluation of methodological preconceptions and beliefs. This can be a rather lengthy process of thinking through the critic's methodological presuppositions. In Chapter 1 we explored a number of different methodological positions.

(2) Review and evaluation of the methodological preconceptions of the researcher(s) contributing to the literature under study.

(3) Definition of the problem situation within the context of (1) or (2) above – this generates what is sometimes referred to as the 'reconstructed problem'.

(4) Evaluation of the internal consistency of the stated research objectives with any proposed solutions in the literature and the analysis of the logical coherence of arguments. In the next two chapters we will examine these areas in some depth.

(5) Evaluation of the differences between the critic's and the researcher's perceptions of the situational and methodological constraints binding the problem. At this point we are moving into the realm of external criticism with debate on such issues as shared understanding of the meanings of terms and the scope of the methodology (the role of theory formulation and testing in the research process, and criteria for demarcating 'good' from 'bad' research, for example).

When criticism is pursued in this manner, the critic will find himself or herself drawn into a dialectic with the literature under analysis. Starting with the initial process of evaluation, critical review should consist of a series of (more or less) carefully formulated propositions that are tested within and by the literature. By a process of stepwise refinement, the critic's initial position should become considerably modified and sharpened. By careful attention to the definition of the boundary between external and internal criticism, the force and effectiveness of the process is maximized.

Constructing the internal history of a literature review

The usual approach adopted by new students to research when reviewing a literature is to attempt to identify all writings which might possibly fall within the area of interest and then to describe the main thrust of the discussion as a temporal sequence of arguments. The more experienced researchers, when approaching a new area, follow essentially the same process but more efficiently identify the principal authors and papers by 'backtracking' from a known, and recent, contribution to the literature.

However, typically, such literature research relies on the identification of themes and issues based on a general sampling of the literature. The essential and implicit methodology adopted is inductive in that general conclusions about the development of the subject are drawn from a sample of literature observations and rarely are those conclusions subjected to testing within the literature itself. It may be that the sample of the literature chosen is believed to be exhaustive although, as we remarked in Chapter 1, induction as a methodology of research has a number of problems which apply whether it is applied in the realm of empirical testing, hypothesis development or literature analysis. These problems can be summarized as follows:

(1) General propositions about the development of a literature cannot, with certainty, be deduced from any number of singular observations. This is simply Popper's 'inductive' problem restated.

(2) This approach reinforces an empiricist perception of the literature with the belief that structures and meanings within a body of literature lie as empirical 'facts' and generalizations which can be found by 'objective' searching. This approach ignores the role of the literature analyst as an interpreter who contributes meaning to the literature under study.

(3) The absence of any structure on the search is particularly inefficient, because there are no rules for demarcating relevant from irrelevant elements within the literature.

Papineau's tree

A more efficient approach relies upon the creation of a network of core terms for the literature in question and is designed to represent the theoretical development within a particular research programme. This approach takes Papineau's (1979) concept of a descending order of core terms to demarcate those terms which are central to all researchers within a programme and those at the other extreme which are shared by a small group or school within the relevant research community. Papineau's concept of a hierarchy of core terms within a literature extends the work of Lakatos (1970) discussed in Chapter 1.

On the basis of a thorough understanding of the development of a particular literature, the various levels of core terms can be identified and used to provide a framework on which particular contributions to that literature can be placed and criticized. In Figure 10.2 we have indicated some levels of core terms within the finance literature, although these are only designed to illustrate the principle and do not represent a full exploration of the terms within the subject.

The natural extension of Papineau's tree is to couch each level and branch in terms of assumptions (which are complexities of core terms). This can be a simpler process where a literature has developed (as in finance) through a series of models containing a range of well-articulated assumptions and an extensive literature of observation reports.

Creating Papineau's tree can be difficult if the area is new to the student and the literature is being used as a fundamental learning exercise. It is a somewhat easier approach where the structure of the underlying discipline is well known and can be used as a framework to rationalize the existing literature.

The network theory of models

A simpler but more time-consuming approach relies upon the network theory of models developed by Hesse (1974, 1980). This technique is based upon the assumption that the literature represents a series of nodes in an interlinked network

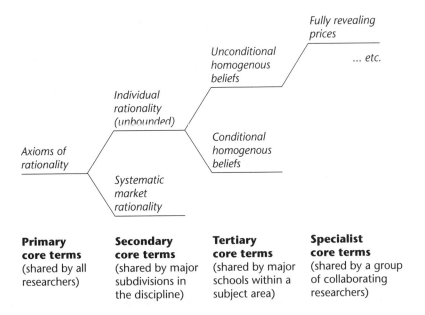

FIGURE 10.2 Papineau's tree

of theoretical and empirical developments. Certain articles will contain significant theoretical developments and will be at the core of the literature. These articles we refer to as 'grandmothers'. Other articles, which are still important in developing significant strands within the literature, we describe as 'mothers', and the remainder as 'daughters'. The researcher is, of course, free to devise his or her own nomenclature.

Within any well-established literature (such as the literature on capital asset pricing) only a relatively tiny number of articles will be defined as 'grandmothers' while there may well be many more articles in the mother category. However, beyond articles in both these categories there will be many more exploring their significance, corroborating (or otherwise) their results, criticizing their approach and extending their scope. Major articles (the 'grandmothers' of the literature) create what can almost amount to an intellectual industry. It is interesting to study, when creating such a network, the life cycle of interest in a given article and the sources (often PhD programmes) generating the bulk of the subsidiary literature.

The creation of a network is a surprisingly simple task although it is only a first stage in the process of analysis. The literature network overlays an underlying theoretical and empirical network and the second stage of analysis is to determine the reasons why certain articles appear when they do and the interlinkages that exist between them. In numerous trials, we have developed a simple procedure for the creation of the literature network:

(1)   In the most recent year a small number of high quality, representative journals should be selected. In one example, Cleaver (1990) selected just two journals: the *Journal of Finance* and the *Journal of Financial Economics*.

(2)   From a perusal of each article in that year in the selected journals the 'key' article(s) cited by the author(s) should be chosen. It takes just a few articles to develop the necessary skill to identify quickly that article (the primary citation) which the author(s) perceive as being principally generative for their own research. In our studies, in over 90 per cent of cases, one article was easily identified as predominant and in the balance it was rare to find more than two. Only review articles depart from this norm and they should be separated out for crosschecking at a later stage.

(3)   The primary articles identified in (2) above can be positioned on a time chart and the necessary linkages drawn in. It is important to stress that some inaccuracies in (1) and (2) will not invalidate the technique as most grandmothers and mothers will have adequate primary citations to locate them unambiguously.

(4)   The process above should be repeated back through time at between three- and five-year intervals. It is a matter of judgement to decide on the best time gap but we have found that a five-yearly interval is sufficient to ensure that all the principal nodes in the literature are effectively mapped. In Figure 10.3 we show a small portion of the mapping produced by Cleaver (1990).

(5)   It is sometimes questioned what should represent the vertical separation between nodes. In a study of the capital asset pricing literature, for example, a classification based upon assumptions was used while in the capital budgeting, literature a split on broad subject subdivisions was chosen. It is not particularly necessary to select any vertical separation, but to adopt the technique shown in Figure 10.3 with substantial annotation. In Figure 10.3, we have put the grandmother in the square box and have in indicated some of the linkages that were discovered.

The next stage in the analysis is to determine the motivation for each article, its literary antecedents and the methodological rationale that bind them together. In the finance literature, theoretical nodes are invariably bound to assumption changes and the scheme of reconstruction could proceed as we have described above. The existence of review articles in the literature should provide substantial corroboration of any network that is created, although in some cases this technique can seriously challenge the interpretation developed in a review.

The disadvantage of this technique is that in some poorly organized subject areas, where there is considerable methodological dispute, a network may be difficult to construct. However, this method has been used in areas as diverse as nursing studies, chemistry and law. In the last case the network was based upon principal precedents and a similar approach could be taken in quasi-legal areas such as standard-setting and regulation in financial accounting.

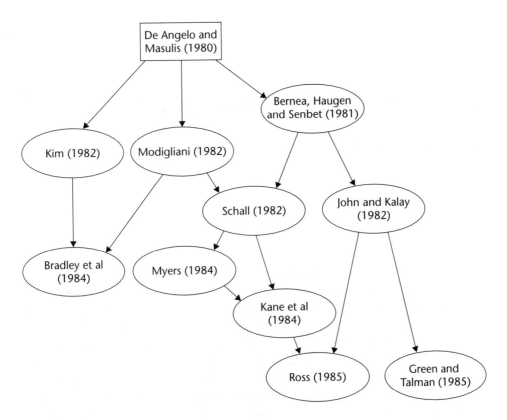

FIGURE 10.3 Main citations to De Angelo and Masulis (1980–1985)

Summary

In this chapter we have reviewed the process of criticizing literature and applied it to the important task of creating an effective, structured and comprehensive literature review. The techniques we have outlined are only a first stage in creating a methodologically sound basis for interpreting the literature and are not an end in themselves. In the next two chapters we refine our discussion of critical analysis by looking at deeper levels of interpretation.

11

The critical analysis of reasoning

In this, the second of three chapters on techniques of analysis, we discuss methods for the analysis of natural language arguments (NLA). In the next chapter we will outline the techniques of symbolic logic concerned with the formal analysis of arguments expressed in the meta-language of propositional and predicate calculus.

As we will discover, the precision of expression and argument necessary for symbolic logic is both the strength and weakness of the technique. The weakness arises because of the problems of translating arguments in natural language into the symbols required for analysis. People use natural language in both idiosyncratic and ambiguous ways and it is for this reason that the methods of natural language reasoning (NLR) have been developed.

In this chapter we will discuss the distinction between argument and rhetoric, and the rules for assessing arguments, the analysis of the structure of an argument, the notion of strength of reasoning and the problems of suppositional reasoning. In addition, we will also consider two fundamental problems in research: the determination of the standard of proof and the degree of support needed for a conclusion.

In order to give an insight into the power of NLR techniques we will examine some extracts from the accounting literature. The NLR techniques offer particular benefits when analysing this type of textual material: first, they clarify the structure of the argument; second, they help identify the background knowledge and research which is necessary to become convinced of the truth of the assertions made; and, third, they allow a provisional test of validity and a judgment of the strength of an argument to be made.

Argument and rhetoric

Natural language reasoning is concerned with discourse that contains reasoning. Reasoning leads to conclusions which are supported by statements consisting of justifications and explanations put forward in order to 'prove' or 'make' more probable the truth of those conclusions. Reasoning is designed to encourage the modification of beliefs through argument and judgement. Some types of argument allow us to form completely certain beliefs given acceptance of one or more assumptions or premises about the state of the world. For such an argument to succeed it must bring us to the judgement that it is impossible to accept the premises of such an argument as true and yet deny the conclusion. Such an argument is said to be deductively valid. On the contrary, an argument, which leads to a certainly false conclusion while its premises are true is invalid.

However, not all arguments lead to certainty in their conclusions. With the majority of NLAs, belief in the truth or falsity of their conclusions is either strengthened or weakened rather than proved or disproved. The standards of proof for different subject areas are, however, very different. The standards of proof in (say) pure mathematics are quite different from what may be acceptable in law or accounting.

Rhetoric is discourse whose purpose is to impress others and by so doing modify or condition their beliefs without recourse to reason. Notions of rhetoric are somewhat confused among different disciplines, although there is a school of thought that all scientific and technical discourse is rhetorical. The justification for this position is that it is very difficult to establish objective criteria for determining whether one type of discourse (labelled reasoning) is any better than another (labelled rhetoric). Ultimately, it is up to the reader to decide this issue – as we have indicated in Chapter 1, we take the view that this position is overly nihilistic and pessimistic.

To illustrate an example of reasoning, consider the following extract from the first edition of a highly cited text in accounting:

> There is evidence that private producers of public goods have been able to contract to receive payment from some of the users of those goods (Coase, 1974; Cheung, 1973). Further, there is evidence that firms provided accounting reports long before those reports were required by law (Benston, 1969a). If private producers contract for payment from some of those who receive benefits from the public good, why don't they contract with those who 'free ride'? One answer, of course, is the cost of contracting with those individuals. Presumably, the payment (benefit) the private producer would receive from contracting with those individuals exceeds the cost of contracting with them. By definition, this is why these consumers are 'free riders'.
>
> (Watts and Zimmerman, 1986: 167)

In this short extract of text we are invited by the authors to consider what is often regarded as a particular difficulty in the economics of public goods. Why is it that private producers of public goods do not seek to engage in contracts for production with all consumers of that good? This question, justified by the first two sentences, forms the conclusion of an argument for which reasons are advanced in the latter part of the example. Some important questions can be raised about this example which apply more generally:

- What makes it an example of reasoning rather than mere rhetoric?
- How can its structure as an argument be analysed?
- How can we distinguish between good reasoning and bad?

In order to examine these questions we introduce two important principles into our discussion. The first of these is the *principle of charity*. The function of analysis is to extend and justify our knowledge, rather than to engage in destructive criticism. The principle of charity, as formulated by Thomas (1986), is that we should always place the most favourable interpretation on a piece of text as is possible. In other words, if it appears difficult to decide whether an argument is presented as reasoning or rhetoric we should always presume the former as our working hypothesis.

The second important principle (after Fisher, 1988 and Thomas, 1986) is used to test the strength of a particular argument. This principle is known as the *assertability principle* and is an important test of the validity of an argument in context: if we are able, in a particular example of reasoning, to assert that the premises are true and the conclusion false judging by appropriate standards of evidence or appropriate standards of what is possible then that reasoning is invalid.

Clearly, this principle must be supported by a test of what constitutes an appropriate standard. This principle of assertability can be reframed as a question (sometimes referred to as the *assertability question*): what argument or evidence would justify asserting the conclusion within the context of reasonable and accepted norms for the area of discourse from which the text under analysis has been drawn (Fisher, 1988)?

Natural language logicians see the question of what is reasonable to assert as a contextual issue. In this respect, they diverge in a most important way from formal logic. As we shall see in the next chapter, formal logic applies a strictly unqualified approach to validity. Either an argument is deductively valid (a position of complete certainty) or it is not. Inductive arguments, for instance, where conclusions are not completely justified by their premises, are completely disregarded in formal logic, but are amenable to treatment by NLR methods.

Finally, before moving to examples of NLR it is appropriate to suggest some criterion that would allow us to assert a conclusion as true in the fields of finance and accounting. It is generally accepted that when attempting to resolve such questions as 'is the capital market efficient' or 'is the APT testable' or 'are holding gains distributable' different criteria may be appropriate when deploying the assertability criterion. However, with many questions of this type, the issue can be adjudicated by appeal to standards invoking consensus agreements and/or to a standard of materiality. In many areas where statistical inference is employed anything in excess of a 5 per cent chance of error (that is, a 95 per cent confidence level) is usually taken as sufficient to reject a hypothesis. The test of when it is reasonable to believe the truth or otherwise of an assertion is often couched in terms of what is commonly accepted as standards of proof in law – in our case what would answer a question beyond reasonable doubt for a group of qualified individuals in the field in question? Objectivity, likewise, is often taken to be assured when a group of such individuals separately answering a particular question based on the same data or justifications produce the same answer.

We must emphasize that these are simply suggested criteria that might be employed when applying the assertability question. In the area of NLR the choice of criteria is, we emphasize, a contextual issue which depends upon the norms applicable for the area concerned. Any criteria, which are adopted, should always be open to criticism and revision.

The analysis of natural language reasoning

The first practical question which must be answered when examining a piece of text is whether or not reasoning is present. In NLR this is accomplished by a two-stage process of analysis:

(1) The presence and categorization of provisional reasoning indicators (PIUs). These PIUs are words or phrases that in their normal grammatical usage are taken to mean that either a reason, justification or conclusion is being asserted.

(2) The construction of a reasoning structure upon the text and a critical examination of that structure.

Stage 1: identification of reasoning indicators

Some typical reasoning indicators are given in Table 11.1. This list is not exhaustive and many of the indicators must be treated with caution. Of particular interest are the presence of the words 'because' and 'then' in an extract of text. 'Because' can indicate a causality. For example: 'the accounts were qualified because a principal subsidiary was not consolidated' is an assertion of a causal connection. Whereas 'the accounts must be qualified because the fixed assets have not been valued on a going concern basis' is an assertion of reasoning.

The word 'then' in a statement usually signals that a conclusion is indicated, and that reasons are within the text. However, if the 'then' is preceded by an 'if' reasoning is not indicated.

The example from Watts and Zimmerman (1986) cited above gives an example: 'If private producers contract for payment from some of those who receive benefits from the public good, [then] why don't they contract with those who "free ride"?' The comma in this sentence marks the position of the implicit [then] that can be added to make the conditional nature of this question clear. In a statement such as this, the consequent (the part following the 'then') is not intended to follow as a matter of logic from the antecedent. It is couched as a question, which is conditional upon the first part of the sentence, but it cannot be logically inferred from the antecedent clause.

Examining the Watts and Zimmerman argument we can identify a number of PIUs which indicate the presence of reasons and conclusions in the argument they present. In Figure 11.1 we show the example marked up for analysis. Words or phrases which appear to be acting as PIUs have been ringed. Candidates for reasons or justifications for conclusions have been underlined and the conclusions themselves

TABLE 11.1 Provisional inference indicators

Conclusion indicators	Reason indicators	Suppositional indicators	Modal terms (indicating that a conclusion is forced by certain preceding reasons)
therefore	assuming	assume that	must
hence	because	presume that	can
thus	since	let us assume	cannot
so	for	for the sake of argument	impossible
consequently	follows from	let us say	necessarily
which proves that	first, second, third	consider the theory/ hypothesis/model	
proving	may be inferred from	let us postulate	
justifies	it follows from the fact		
in conclusion	it may be deduced (concluded) from		
implies			
leads us to believe			
infer			
demonstrates			
establishes			
and, as a result			
entails that			
it follows that			
then (without a preceding 'if')			

(There is evidence) **R1** that private producers of public goods have been able to contract to receive payment from some of the users of those goods (Coase, 1974; Cheung, 1973). (Further, there is evidence) **R2** that firms provided accounting reports long before those reports were required by law (Benston, 1969). If ⟨ **C1** private producers contract for payment from some of those who receive benefits from the public good, ⟩ ⟨ **C2** why don't they contract with those who 'free ride'. ⟩ (One answer,) **R3** of course, is the cost of contracting with those individuals. (Presumably) **R4** the payment (benefit) the private producer would receive from contracting with those individuals exceeds the cost of contracting with them. By definition, this is why these consumers are 'free riders'.

(Watts and Zimmerman, 1986, p.167)

FIGURE 11.1 Watts and Zimmerman argument marked up for analysis

have been bracketed $\langle\rangle$. The principal conclusion is couched as a question (C2) which is necessarily entailed by a preliminary conclusion (C1). If it is true that private producers contract for the supply of a public good with only some of those who receive benefit from its consumption, then it necessarily follows that they fail to contract with some others who also benefit (the so-called 'free riders'). The conclusion C1 is supported by two observations R1 and R2 and the second stage of the analysis will be to test the strength of this assertion. Finally, a further link of reasons R3 and R4 are used to support the conclusion C2.

Stage 2: analysis of the reasoning structure

The steps that we have gone through now lead us to formulate a structure of the reasoning in this text.

$$R1^* + R2^*$$
$$\underline{\qquad\qquad} \qquad \underline{\qquad} \; R4$$
$$C1 + R3$$
$$\underline{\qquad}$$
$$C2$$

The first question we should ask in analysing this argument is do the two reasons R1 and R2 (which are presented as assertions of facts) support the conclusion C1? In other words, do:

> R1* there is evidence that private producers of public goods have been able to contract to receive payment from some of the users of those goods and
>
> R2* there is evidence that firms provided accounting reports long before those reports were required by law

support the conclusion C1:

> C1 private producers contract for payment from some of those who receive benefits from the public good.

We have asterisked the reasons R1 and R2 to show that they are evidential claims rather than suppositions or assumptions. Now, on the basis of the assertability question, what evidence would be required to accept beyond reasonable doubt (the standard of acceptability we have chosen) the truth of C1? The authors of this passage offer their evidence in two ways. First, they argue that C1 is directly confirmed by the evidence presented within the research literature. Is this the case? One question to be answered, for example, is whether or not the evidence was restricted to a sample of private producers of whom all were shown to have entered contracts with users or only some? In the former case, the evidence does not exclude the possibility that no 'free riders' might exist in which case the 'some' in C1 would have to be replaced with 'all' and hence C2 would not be entailed.

Reason R2 is slightly less satisfactory in that it requires us to establish that accounting reports have the nature of a public good, and that prior to regulation by law they fell into the hands of individuals who gained benefit from using them even though they had no contractual relationship with the company providing those reports.

However, given that the evidence referred to in R1 supports the authors' case, it would not be unreasonable to believe that at some place and at some time *some* individuals gained benefits from public goods even though they had not entered into any contractual arrangement with the supplier. Our everyday experience testifies to the fact that individuals enjoy the benefits of such things as newspapers as well as accounting reports without paying for them. On this basis, preliminary conclusion C1 appears well justified by R1* and R2*.

Finally, what can we say about the strength of the explanatory argument presented as R3? Does this argument support C2 which appears to be well supported by the evidence? It should be clear that the link R4–R3–C2 is an example of reasoning as opposed to evidential justification. The PIU 'one answer' could be just as easily substituted by 'one reason is' and the sense of the argument would still stand. But how good is this explanatory argument? Is it possible that R3 (as amplified by R4) could be true while C2 is false? As R3 stands it is neither an answer nor a reason – the reader is meant (in the light of R4) to come up with something such as:

> C2 (restated) private suppliers of public goods do not contract with those who free ride

because

> R3 and R4 the cost of contracting with those free riders exceeds the benefits the private suppliers would receive from those contracts.

Note how we have reworded R4; it is quite evident that the authors have mis-stated their argument and given the obvious nature of their error (they argue that suppliers do not contract with free riders because the benefit of contracting *exceeds* the cost) the principle of charity dictates that we should correct the error and then attempt to construct the strongest reasoning that we can.

Given our rewording would there be any other reason why a supplier might fail to contract with a free rider than merely the balancing of costs and benefits? The answer to this question lies in the definition of 'cost' and 'benefit'. If we define cost and benefit purely in terms of what is financially measurable, then the answer is transparently no. It might be that the supplier, for reasons of public service or plain altruism, permits some individuals to enjoy the benefit of the public good without paying for it even though, if they were forced to pay, the benefit received by the supplier would outweigh the cost of enforcement. In this case we could have grounds for believing that R3 and R4 (modified) are true but still reject C2, and thus the argument is invalid, However, if we relax the definition of cost and benefit to include all non-financial costs and benefits which accrue to a supplier, then the argument is much stronger. The only element of doubt which remains is whether or not such contracting arrangements are made on the basis of the rational evaluation of (broadly defined) costs and benefits. Our analysis of the Watts and Zimmerman argument reveals the nature of the hidden assumption or 'supposition' which is fundamental to their case. We will discuss the importance of such suppositional arguments later in this chapter.

Structures and strength of argument

In formal logic there are three important logical primitives – negation, disjunction (signified by the word 'or', or equivalent) and conjunction (signified by 'and', or equivalent). We will explore the full logical significance of these terms in the next chapter. However, for present purposes it is important to note an important characteristic which distinguishes arguments based upon reasons in disjunction and reasons in conjunction. In NLR we refer to the former as 'independent' reasons in that the truth of the conclusion of an argument is only dependent upon the truth of one or other of the reasons (but not necessarily both) and the latter as 'joint' reasons in that the truth of the conclusion is dependent upon both being true together.

In the Watts and Zimmerman argument above, R1* and R2* are presented by the authors as joint reasons supporting the conclusion C1. However, is it necessary to hold R1* and R2* true together in order to support C1? Would the conclusion C1 be invalidated if R1* and/or R2* were false? The answer to this depends on the nature of R1* and R2*. Remember that both of these reasons are cited as evidential justification. The authors are not expecting us to accept C1 as a logical consequence of accepting R1* and/or R2*. In this case, therefore, NLR introduces a concept which is alien to traditional logic, namely 'degree of support' for a conclusion. Thomas offers four levels which are sufficient for most purposes:

- nil – where the reasons provide no support for the conclusion
- weak – where even though one or more true reasons provide some support for a conclusion, a number of probable circumstances can be envisaged where the conclusion could still be false. In this case the onus of proof still lies with advocates of the particular conclusion
- moderate – where support is provided for a conclusion which turns the onus of disproof against those who would wish to contradict the conclusion
- strong – where a conclusion would be deemed supported by its reasons beyond reasonable doubt. In this case it is extremely difficult to establish a scenario where the conclusion was false whilst its supporting reasons remained true.

With each of these four levels the standards of support are taken in the context of the normal standards applied to the subject matter concerned – what might be deemed strong support within one area may be regarded as moderate, or indeed weak, in another.

Suppositional arguments

In accounting and finance many theories are developed in the context of a series of assumptions which are taken to be true for the sake of the argument concerned. In NLR such assumptions are termed suppositions and arguments containing them suppositional arguments. In general, a suppositional reason contaminates an entire argument rendering the conclusion suppositional also. However, if (1) suppositional reason R^S leads to conclusion C^S, then the conditional statement 'if R then C' is true even given the suppositional nature of R and C. If (2) $R1^S$, R2 and R3 are joint reasons supporting C, then C will be suppositional and 'if R1 then C' will be true given R2 and R3 are themselves true. However, if (3) $R1^S$, $R2^S$ and R3 are joint reasons supporting C, then 'if R1 then C' will also be suppositional, but 'if R1 and R2 then C' will be true providing that R3 is true. The structure of these three cases is shown below:

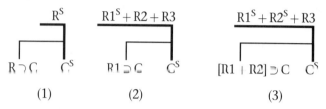

Whenever a single suppositional reason is used to support a conclusion (whether or not other non-suppositional reasons are present) then a conditional statement of the type 'if R then C' can be added as a separate conclusion of the argument. This provides a powerful means for clarifying arguments. Table 11.1 includes some indicators that suppositional reasoning is present in an argument.

An illustration of natural language reasoning

In the first part of this chapter we have used NLR techniques to analyse a small fragment of text within a much larger body of argument. However, much more substantial arguments can also be analysed. In order to give a more comprehensive insight into the power of NLR techniques we use as an illustration a substantial piece of reasoning put forward by William Beaver in his text: *Financial Reporting: An Accounting Revolution* (1981). In this extract Beaver is proposing that the assumption that (at least) some sophisticated investors are required for market efficiency to hold is unnecessary.

> The crux of a theory of market efficiency which does not rely upon the existence of a set of 'experts' is that the level of knowledge reflected in prices is greater than merely the 'average' level of knowledge in the market. Some simple analogies illustrate this point. Consider each individual containing a 'small' amount of knowledge and a considerable amount of idiosyncratic behaviour. This can be modelled as each individual receiving a garbled signal from an information system that provides an ungarbled signal disguised by a 'noise' component. The garbling is so large that any inspection of that individual's behaviour provides little indication that such an individual is contributing to the efficiency of the market with respect to the ungarbled information system. Moreover, assume that this is true for every individual who comprises the market. However, the idiosyncratic behaviour, by definition, is essentially uncorrelated among individuals. As a result, security price, which can be viewed as a 'consensus' across investors, is effectively able to diversify away the large idiosyncratic component, such that only the knowledge (i.e., the ungarbled signal)

persists in terms of explaining the security price. By analogy, the individual investor beliefs can be viewed akin to individual securities and the security price can be viewed as an aggregate akin to a portfolio.

The small amount of knowledge is the systematic component across investors. Although it is dwarfed by the idiosyncratic behaviour at the individual investor level, it is the only portion that persists at the security price level. This does not require the existence of any 'experts'. Moreover, the quality of the knowledge reflected in prices is considerably higher than the average quality of knowledge across the individuals who comprise the market. Analogously, in portfolio theory the variance of return of any portfolio is strictly less than the average variance of the securities' returns that comprise the portfolio, if securities returns are uncorrelated with one another.

This is an important piece of reasoning which by appealing to analogy and some well-known properties of multivariate behaviour is offering a somewhat counter-intuitive conclusion.

The first stage in the analysis of this argument entails identifying the PIU's and marking off the reasons and conclusions which appear in the text. In any exercise of analysis it is necessary to accept that mistakes are inevitable and to be prepared to modify and self-critically reinterpret the provisional structure imposed upon the text (see Figure 11.2).

As is common with many examples of NLR, the principal conclusion opens Beaver's argument. His contention is that market efficiency does not rely, necessarily, upon the existence of a pool of sophisticated investors. The opening words, 'The crux of a theory', indicate that the following statement is central to the argument. The main component of the conclusion which his argument seeks to establish is summarized by:

C10 the level of knowledge reflected in prices is greater than merely the 'average' level of knowledge in the market

We have labelled this as C10 to refer to the reasoning structure derived below. Beaver then engages directly in the argument with the statement:

R1^S Consider each individual containing a 'small' amount of knowledge and a considerable amount of idiosyncratic behaviour.

It is not clear whether Beaver is asking us to accept this as a supposition or as a statement of fact about individual behaviour. The inclusion of quotation marks around 'small' acts as a defuser and is a common device by authors who wish to remove an assertion from the area of criticism. As a literary device, it is designed to indicate that what is enclosed should not be given a specific meaning but rather be interpreted within the context of the argument. The use of the opening words 'Consider each' and 'small' justify the initial categorization of this statement as suppositional. We may decide in the light of further analysis to revise this interpretation.

(The crux of a theory) of market efficiency which does not rely upon the existence of a set of 'experts' is that the ^{C10} ⟨level of knowledge reflected in prices is greater than merely the 'average' level of knowledge in the market.⟩ Some simple analogies illustrate this point. ^{R1} (Consider) each individual containing a 'small' amount of knowledge and a considerable amount of idiosyncratic behaviour. ^{C1} (This can be modeled) as each individual receiving a garbled signal from an information system that provides an ungarbled signal disguised by a 'noise' component. The garbling is so large ^{R2} (that) ^{C2} ⟨any inspection of that individual's behaviour provides little indication that such an individual is contributing to the efficiency of the market with respect to the ungarbled information system.⟩ (Moreover, assume that) ^{C3} ⟨this is true for every individual who comprises the market.⟩ (However) ^{R3} the idiosyncratic behaviour, by definition, is essentially uncorrelated among individuals. (As a result,) ^{C4} ⟨security price, which can be viewed as a 'consensus' across investors, is effectively able to diversify away the large idiosyncratic component⟩ (such that) ^{C5} ⟨only the knowledge (i.e., the ungarbled signal) persists in terms of explaining the security price.⟩ (By analogy) ^{R4} the individual investor beliefs can be viewed akin to individual securities (and) the ^{R5} security price can be viewed as an aggregate akin to a portfolio. ^{C6} ⟨The small amount of knowledge is the systematic component across investors.⟩ (Although it is) ^{R1} dwarfed by the idiosyncratic behaviour at the individual investor level, ^{C7} ⟨it is the only portion that persists at the security price level.⟩ (This) does not ^{C8} require the existence of any 'experts'. (Moreover,) ⟨the quality of the knowledge reflected in prices is considerably higher than the average quality of knowledge ^{C10} across the individuals who comprise the market.⟩ (Analogously,) ^{C9} ⟨in portfolio theory the variance of return of any portfolio is strictly less than the average variance of the securities' returns that comprise the portfolio⟩ (,) if securities ^{R6} returns are uncorrelated with one another.

FIGURE 11.2 Beaver's argument marked up for analysis

The phrase 'This can be modeled as' in the next sentence refers to Beaver's use of the notion of analogy referred to earlier in the text. However, as a statement $R1^S$ is not identical to, nor can it be restated as:

> $C1^S$ [as] each individual receiving a garbled signal from an information system that provides an ungarbled signal disguised by a 'noise' component

Indeed, for this statement to act as a model of the behaviour described by $R1^S$, $C1^S$ must represent a conclusion derived from $R1^S$ acting jointly with a number of other unstated assumptions about individual behaviour. The structure of this element of reasoning can be represented as:

$$\frac{R1^S + U_1^S + U_2^S + \ldots}{}$$

$$\{R1 + U_1 + U_2 + \ldots\} \supset C1 \qquad C1^S$$

where the U_n^S represent the unstated assumptions. The branched conditional specifies the truth that C1 is only true if supposition $R1^S$ and all of the assumptions (U_n^S) are both independently and jointly true. In order to deploy the assertability question we must eventually make some judgment as to what these assumptions might be. We will return to this point later.

$C1^S$ plus reason R2:

> R2 the garbling is so large

leads to a further inference:

> C2 any inspection of that individual's behaviour provides little indication that such an individual is contributing to the efficiency of the market with respect to the ungarbled information system.

The next stage of this analysis now brings in an additional level of supposition where Beaver explicitly assumes that C2 is generalizable to all individuals within the market. This is a crucial step in the argument as it takes us from an analysis of the behaviour of an individual to the behaviour of the market and opens the possibility of conclusions concerning market efficiency. We label this market-wide generalization of behaviour $C3^{SS}$:

> $C3^{SS}$ this is true for every individual who comprises the market

which when coupled with the asserted behaviour in R3:

> R3 the idiosyncratic behaviour ... is essentially uncorrelated among individuals

leads to two derived conclusions $C4^{SS}$ and $C5^{SS}$:

> $C4^{SS}$ security price, which can be viewed as a 'consensus' across investors, is effectively able to diversify away the idiosyncratic component

such that:

> C5^{SS} only the knowledge (that is, the ungarbled signal) persists in terms of explaining the security price

The ss superscript is somewhat cumbersome but serves the purpose of reminding us that we have two levels of supposition in operation in this argument and that a complex conditionality has been developed. We can now represent the argument as it has developed as follows:

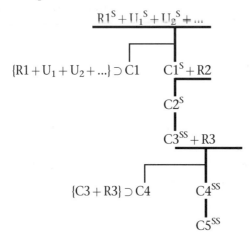

This structure leads to two important observations: first, the strength of the argument so far developed depends upon the reasonableness of the initial assumptions and the generalization which takes us from C2 to C3 and, second, more crucially, the validity of the argument hinges upon the truth of R2 and R3.

At this stage, assuming the reasoning is sound, Beaver has concluded that idiosyncratic interpretations of information are 'diversified away' in the pricing process leaving only the rational evaluation of the economic content of the information as the determinant of price. However, he has not, as yet, demonstrated his principal conclusion that this process produces a level of knowledge in prices which is greater than the average level of knowledge in the market. He attempts to do this in the final stage of his argument by an appeal to analogy. To make this analogy work, Beaver asks the reader to accept that the private beliefs based upon information signals by investors is the 'atom' of economic value:

> R4^S the individual investor beliefs can be viewed akin to individual securities

and that a security's price is a market derived consensus of these beliefs analogous to a portfolio representing an aggregation of individual securities' performance:

> R5^S the security price can be viewed as an aggregate akin to a portfolio.

Because idiosyncratic beliefs are asserted to be uncorrelated with one another (R3) only reasonable beliefs based upon the ungarbled signals coming from the information system remain as the systematic component of investor behaviour in the market:

C6^S The small amount of knowledge is the systematic component across investors.

This conclusion jointly with C5 and a restatement of R1:

R1 it (the small amount of knowledge) is dwarfed by the idiosyncratic behaviour at the individual investor level

leads to the conclusion:

C7^S it (the small amount of knowledge) is the only portion that persists at the security price level.

From this, Beaver deduces C8^S:

C8^S this does not require the existence of any experts.

By an implicit line of reasoning he argues that it is unnecessary to assume the existence of a small group of specialist information evaluators (experts) operating in the market if a process for transferring knowledge into prices based upon the ungarbled component of market signals can be derived. However, Beaver has not quite accomplished his objective because expertise normally implies better than the normal (average) performance we would expect from investors in general. He achieves this final step by linking conclusion C7 with the notion that the 'quality' of knowledge reflected in price can be described by the concept of variance (analogously with variance of portfolio return) in an implicit but unstated assumption. The final conclusion of this argument is established from the conjunction of C7 and the well-known multivariate property of uncorrelated, normally distributed variables expressed in intermediate conclusion C9:

R6 if security returns are uncorrelated with one another

then

C9 in portfolio theory the variance of return of any portfolio is strictly less than the average variance of the securities' returns that comprise the portfolio.

This result obtains from the fact that the variance of a multivariate distribution of uncorrelated, normally distributed variables is less than the average of the variances of those variables because for a two component portfolio:

$$[x_a^2 s_a^2 + x_b^2 s_b^2] < [x_a s_a^2 + x_b s_b^2]$$

where: $x_a + x_b = 1$ (the weights of the component variables). At this point Beaver has completed his argument with:

C10^S the quality of knowledge reflected in prices is considerably higher than the average quality of knowledge across the individuals who comprise the market.

We complete our analysis with a complete specification (see diagram) of the reasoning structure in this argument (the dashed lines indicate the connections between the portion of analysis shown in diagram form above and the last part of the argument just discussed).

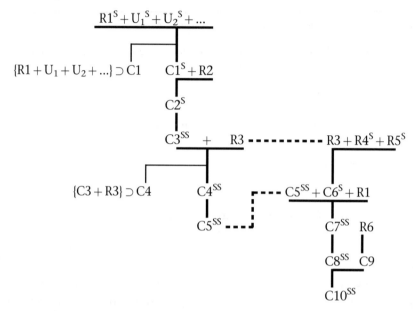

Once this stage is accomplished it is necessary to engage in a critique of the validity and strength of the argument structure using the assertability question as a guide. In order to use the assertability question effectively we move backwards from the final conclusion assessing the strength and validity of each inference. In the final representation of the argument we have omitted a number of the conditional assertions which flow from the various suppositions and many of the unstated assumptions implicit in the argument. You may like to attempt the final embellishment of the diagram yourself.

Rather than provide a detailed critique, we suggest a number of points which emerge from the process of analysis we have just gone through:

(1)　The final argument hinges on a chain of suppositional reasoning. Each of these suppositions differs in strength and, in addition, these suppositions are often supported by analogy. Indeed, the final conclusion is drawn from reasons concerning the type of knowledge which emerges in the price setting process and an analogy with the multivariate behaviour of a portfolio assuming normal and uncorrelated share prices. However, is the analogy sufficiently robust to support the conclusion? That depends on whether you are prepared to believe that the knowledge possessed by an individual can be represented by a normal distribution of beliefs. This is contradicted by the wide body of evidence that individual judgement is consistently flawed in ways which overweight the probabilities of certain types of events and underweight others.

(2)　Proceeding backwards through the structuring of reasoning we notice that conclusion C5 is important both in its own right as well as supporting the analogical reasoning given later. Using the assertability question is it possible to argue the case that C5 is false while the reasons upon which it is based are true? We could argue that prices can diversify away chaotic behaviour and settle at a level which represents investor beliefs which are congruent with one another (that is, C4 be held to be true). However, it is not necessarily true that those beliefs are founded on the 'ungarbled' component of the information system. It may be, for some reason, that large groups of investors consistently misinterpret market information or, indeed, read information into signals which are irrelevant to the economic performance of a company.

(3) C3 requires us to make an assumption about generalized behaviour. Generalizations such as this introduce a very weak supposition into any argument and can only be supported if the rationale is particularly strong. In this case, it only represents an amplification of the generalization implicitly referred to in R1. It is usually easier to accept a generalization of assumed behaviour (which is an extension of the assumption) than a generalization of observed behaviour from a single instance (weak induction).

Moving back through the reasoning chain the assertability question forces the analyst to test the strength of each supporting reason and on that basis to assess the overall strength of the argument. This particular argument appears weak because of the strong (and compounded) thread of suppositional argument which runs throughout its length and because at its heart lies the notion that beliefs are of two separable types: one of which is lost through the process of price-setting and the other which persists to determine the price.

Summary

In this chapter we have introduced a technique for the analysis of arguments expressed in natural language. This technique clarifies the process of argument in that it permits a structure to be drawn and provides a test, contained within the assertability question, which allows the process of asking the 'right questions' to commence. Unlike the formal methods of symbolic logic discussed in the next chapter, NLR cannot unambiguously prove an argument valid or invalid. It does, however, allow us to form a judgement about the strength of reasoning in a particular argument and may give some insights into how arguments can be strengthened.

· · · · · 12

Formal methods of analysis

In this chapter we consider the use of formal logic as a tool in the analysis of arguments. We will consider four important topic areas which give the researcher the tools needed for the formal analysis of arguments: the logic of (1) simple and (2) general propositions, (3) the simple logic of relations and (4) the analysis and interpretation of complex arguments. In the previous chapter we introduced an outstandingly powerful tool for the analysis of arguments in natural language. Those were the sorts of natural language arguments which are used within the literature to represent arguments about experimental design, the interpretation of results and so forth. Symbolic logic is also an extremely powerful technique but it has a much narrower application. Generally, it is restricted to specialist arguments within a literature which are designed to be interpreted in a rigorous and axiomatic way. At the end of this chapter we will examine various techniques for the analysis of assumptions within models.

The belief that arguments should be logical is well entrenched within the social as well as the natural sciences. Some philosophers and sociologists of science make a strong case that logic is simply a rhetorical device for adding credibility to writings (see Harre, 1986). However, we are of the view that for active researchers a basic knowledge of the methods of symbolic logic can be important for a number of reasons.

For researchers who accept that their scientific beliefs are grounded in reality, the transmission of truth value from one proposition to another is obviously important. In other words, the realist will wish to ensure that the implications of the truth content within one proposition can be transferred through logic to other propositions. Furthermore, for researchers who believe that logic is a rhetorical device it is important to know the techniques that others are using. Those whose interests lie in the area of computing will notice considerable similarity between the logic of propositions outlined below and Boolean algebra. We will not discuss formal deductive method in this chapter but rather introduce a simple tree technique for determining the validity and consistency of logical arguments.

The logic of propositions

We can define a proposition as any unit of meaning which cannot be reduced to component parts and a statement as a series of propositions connected by grammatical terms which govern their logical relationship. Our concern, when analysing the logical form of particular statements, is not with their meaning per se or with the truth or otherwise of particular propositions. Indeed, we are not particularly concerned with the meaning of particular words except those which govern the logical sense of statements or arguments.

The three most important logical primitives are negation, conjunction and disjunction. These three primitives emerge from Aristotle's three laws of thought: any proposition is identical with itself (x is x – the law of identity), a proposition cannot be both true and false at the same time (nothing can be both x and not x – the law of non-contradiction) and every proposition is either true or not true (that is, is either x or not x – the law of excluded middle). These three logical primitives, supplemented with the notions of exclusive disjunction, implication and equivalence, form our tool kit for simple propositional logic.

Propositions are the basic elements of meaning and when we are concerned with the logical connections between propositions being used in a general sense we symbolize them with lower case characters. Where it is important to indicate singular instances of a proposition we will designate them with upper case letters. We use the symbols in Table 12.1 to designate the five principal logical connectives.

The symbols p and q indicate 'any proposition p' and 'any proposition q', and ¬ represents negation. If 'p' means 'p is true' then '¬p' means 'not p is true'.

In English usage, the existence of a logical connection may be very subtle and difficult to interpret. By and large the skill of the logician comes not in formal analysis but rather in interpreting the logical form of natural language.

The logical character of a statement is determined by its truth value given different states of the world derived from the truth values of its constituent propositions. If a statement or argument consists of only two propositions then four states of the world can exist: where both are true, where both are false and where only one is true (there are two options here). In Table 12.2 we show the truth value of the logical connectives listed in Table 12.1.

TABLE 12.1 Symbols designating the five principal logical connectives

Primitive	Symbol	Example	Example indicators in English usage
negation	¬	¬p	not, neither, never, impossible
conjunction	&	p&q	and, but, yet
disjunction	v	pvq	either, or
implication	>	p>q	if ... then, it follows that
equivalence	≡	p≡q	same, equivalent to, identical

TABLE 12.2 Truth values of the principal logical connectives

p q	Negation ¬p	Conjunction p&q	Disjunction pvq	Exclusive Disjunct (pvq)& ¬ (p&q)	Implication p>q	Equivalence p≡q
T T	F	T	T	F	T	T
T F	F	F	T	T	F	F
F T	T	F	T	T	T	F
F F	T	F	F	F	T	T

Negation has the simple effect of reversing the truth value of a given proposition, so if p is true, ¬p is false and vice versa. A conjunction, from the Law of Non-Contradiction, can only be true when both of its constituent propositions are true. Thus the conjunction p&q can only be true when both p and q are true together.

The requirement for truth in a disjunction is less stringent than in a conjunction in that the disjunction as a whole will be true if either of its constituent propositions are true. The simple disjunction (symbolized by v, from the Latin *'vel'* or *'or'*) covers the case where either p or q or both can be true. For example the statement: 'to practise as a chartered accountant you must be a member of either the English or Scottish Institute' would not preclude the possibility of members of both being able to practise. In the situation where only one of two possibilities is allowed we must invoke disjunction in its *exclusive* sense. For example, take a statement which would normally be interpreted in its exclusive form: 'shareholders may elect for payment either in shares or in cash but not both'. This statement is equivalent to: '*either* shareholders may elect to take their payment in shares *or* shareholders may elect to take their payment in cash *but not* [shareholders may elect to take their payment in shares *and* shareholders may elect to take their payment in cash]'. The defining truth table for this statement is shown in Table 12.3.

where: p = shareholders may elect to take their payment in shares
          q = shareholders may elect to take their payment in cash

TABLE 12.3 The defining truth table

p	q	pvq	p&q	¬(p&q)	(pvq)&¬(p&q)
T	T	T	T	F	F
T	F	T	F	T	T
F	T	T	F	T	T
F	F	F	F	T	F

There are two points to note here: (1) n propositions generate 2^n possible states of the world or possible conjunctions of being true or false and (2) in symbolizing this statement we have invoked certain conventions concerning the scope of the operators and the hierarchy of analysis:

(1) Propositions, statements and operators within brackets are analysed within the bracket and then treated as a single entity.

(2) The negation sign operates on the smallest component possible. For example, the negation in ¬pvq relates to the p only, while in ¬(p&q) it relates to the bracketed term as a single entity.

Implication is indicated by the presence of the structure 'if ... then' in a statement. Symbolically we will represent implication with >, so the statement '*if* a false return of income is made (p) *then* the taxpayer will be liable to prosecution (q)' can be represented as p>q. An implication can be seen to be false if the antecedent (p) is true and the consequent (q) is false, i.e., if p&¬q is false. Conversely, an implication must be true if ¬(p&¬q) is true. Therefore p>q is identical to the statement ¬(p&¬q) in the truth table shown in Table 12.2

Equivalence holds when two propositions have the same truth value. Equivalence can be restated as p is equivalent to q if and only if p is true when q is true and false when q is false. Thus, in Table 12.2 we show the truth table for this logical connective. An equivalence is said to be 'tautological' if it is true under all possible states of the world. To demonstrate this we show in Table 12.4 the truth table for the equivalence ¬(p&q)≡(¬p v¬q).

TABLE 12.4 Truth table for ¬(p&q)≡(¬p v¬q)

p	q	¬p	¬q	p&q	¬(p&q)	¬pv¬q	¬(p&q)≡ (¬p v¬q)
T	T	F	F	T	F	F	T
T	F	F	T	F	T	T	T
F	T	T	F	F	T	T	T
F	F	T	T	F	T	T	T

You may like to confirm that the equivalence (¬p&¬q)≡¬(pvq) is also tautological. These two equivalences are particularly important in logical analysis and are known as 'deMorgan's theorem'.

In order to deploy the propositional logic outlined above we need to define certain properties of statement sets. For the sake of precision we can define any statement as S_n; thus statement 1 is s_1, statement 2 is s_2 and so on. In general a statement set can be represented as:

$$S = (s_1, s_2, s_3, ... s_n)$$

and an argument A is defined as a statement set where a concluding statement s^* is believed to be entailed by $s_1, s_2, s_3 ... s_n$, that is,

$$A = (s_1, s_2, s_3, ... s_n \mid s^*)$$

The bar symbol (|) can be taken to represent $s_1, s_2, s_3 .. s_n$, *implies* s^*.

There are a number of important properties of statements and statement sets:

(1) Any statement is tautological if it is true under all possible states of the world. Conversely,

(2) Any statement is contradictory if it is false under all possible states of the world.

(3) Any statement is *consistent* if there is at least one state of the world (row of a truth table of $s_1, s_2, s_3, ... s_n$) where each statement in the set S is true. An inconsistent set is one where no such state of the world exists.

(4) An argument A is said to be valid if it is impossible to assert $s_1, s_2, s_3 ... s_n$ as true whilst holding the conclusion s^* false. Thus a row in an argument's truth table which consisted of all true states except for the conclusion would render the argument invalid.

There is one interesting property of an invalid argument which we will put to considerable use later on. If the conclusion of an invalid argument is negated all previously consistent rows within its truth table become inconsistent (see 3 above) as all true elements in the conclusion's column of the truth table become false and vice versa. However, one row of the truth table will become consistent – the original invalid row (see 4 above). Thus we can test for invalidity by negating the conclusion of an argument and then looking for consistency in the revised argument A'. An absence of consistency in such a revised argument is evidence that an invalidating row did not exist in the original argument and hence the original must have been valid.

To understand the use of the propositional logic we will consider a simple argument and analyse it using the truth table technique:

> If investors are rational then we would expect them to prefer return and be averse to risk. Experimental evidence confirms our expectations that investors prefer return and are averse to risk which leads to the conclusion that investors are rational.

The initial step in assessing such an argument is one of interpretation. The first sentence of this natural language argument (NLA) contains both implication and conjunction in what is termed the 'major premise'. The second sentence of the NLA is what is referred to in formal logic as the 'minor premise' and simply asserts that the consequent in the major premise is true. Finally, the conclusion appears to be a

TABLE 12.5 Truth table

p	q	r	q&r	p>(q&r)	p
T	T	T	T	T	T
T	T	F	F	F	T
T	F	T	F	F	T
F	**T**	**T**	**T**	**T**	**F**
F	F	T	F	T	F
F	T	F	F	T	F
T	F	F	F	F	T
F	F	F	F	T	F

reassertion of the antecedent in the major premise. If we define 'investors are rational' as 'p', 'investors prefer return' as 'q' and 'investors are risk averse' as 'r' then the argument is of the general form {p>(q&r); (q&r); therefore p}. Referring to Table 12.2 we can construct a truth table as in Table 12.5.

The final three columns in Table 12.5 represent the truth table for the argument. Note that the fourth row (emboldened) is an invalidating row although the argument (through the first row) is consistent. This can be demonstrated if we reverse the conclusion to ¬p and recast the truth table; the first consistent row becomes inconsistent and the original invalidating row (emboldened) becomes consistent (see Table 12.6).

The use of truth tables becomes more cumbersome as the number of propositions increases. A five-proposition argument would generate a truth table with 32 rows. To surmount this problem we can use a simple tree technique which makes use of the properties of consistency and reduction.

This technique removes the necessity for complete enumeration of all possible states of the world and focuses upon possible consistency within an argument. To employ this technique:

(1) List all statements in A and then negate the conclusion to create A'.
(2) Convert all statements to their simplest form as either conjunctions or disjunctions.
(3) Create a tree structure for A and A' regarding disjunctions (or) as forks and conjunctions (and) as branch extensions starting with the statement which brings elimination most quickly within the tree.
(4) Eliminate branches as soon as an inconsistency is revealed. An inconsistency is revealed when a contradiction occurs, e.g., p and ¬p appearing on the same branch would be contradictory and, therefore, inconsistent.
(5) Add reduced forms of statements successively on to each unreduced branch.
(6) A final tree using A which has one or more unclosed routes to its extremity indicates consistency in A.
(7) A final tree using A' which has one or more unclosed routes to its extremities indicates consistency in A' and hence invalidity in A.

TABLE 12.6 Revised truth table

q&r	p>(q&r)	¬p
T	T	F
F	F	F
F	F	F
T	**T**	**T**
F	T	T
F	T	T
F	F	F
F	T	T

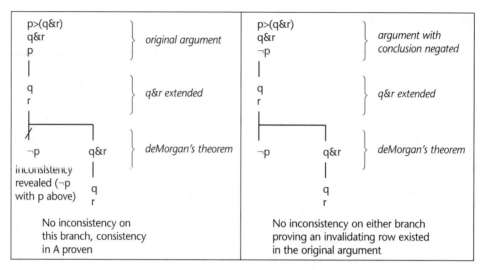

FIGURE 12.1 Trees for the argument A and the modified argument A'

In Figure 12.1 we show the trees for the argument A and the modified argument A' (that is, A with its conclusion negated). The first step is to show the conclusion at the head of the tree. As the conclusion is a single proposition no reduction into simpler propositions is necessary. We then extend the trunk downwards showing the statement p&q as a sequence (see 3 above). The implication, p>(q&r), is broken down by the following chain of equivalence:

$$p>(q\&r)\equiv(p\&\neg(q\&r))\equiv\neg pv\ (q\&r)\ (\text{by deMorgan's theorem})$$

We can show the disjunction as a fork in the tree. The left hand branch in the tree for A shows a contradiction ¬p against p and is thus closed. However, as we extend the right hand branch down the tree is not closed indicating that a consistent route has been found. The tree for A' shows consistency again revealing invalidity in the original argument.

In the use of trees the following replacement rules are extremely important in simplifying arguments. Figure 12.2 shows the tree element which is generated by the right-hand side of each equivalence.

We will now apply the tree technique to a much more complex statement set:

A = {pv(q>r); ¬s>(r>t); p>s; ¬s | q>t}.

In Figure 12.2 we show the decomposition of A' to prove validity. As all the branches are closed, there is no consistent branch in A' (that is, there is no consistent row within this argument's truth table) and so we can conclude that the original argument was valid.

Notice the sequence of decomposition chosen to reduce the complexity of tree construction. Inspection of the argument usually indicates the most appropriate statement to bring next into the decomposition process. The best strategy is always to choose statements with disjunctions which permit one of the two branches to be eliminated quickly.

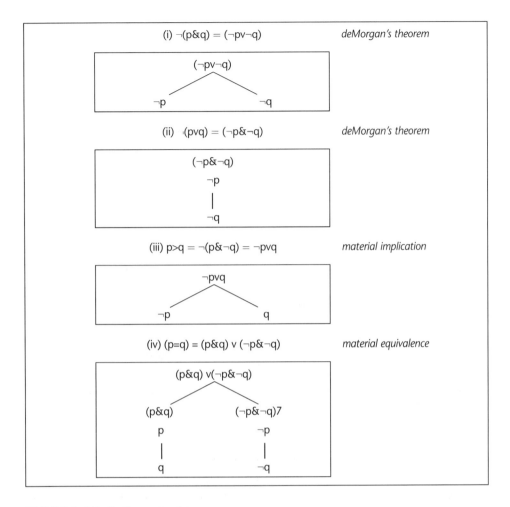

FIGURE 12.2 Elements of trees

You may like to rework Figure 12.3 to check for consistency in the original argument. It is possible to construct a consistent argument which is invalid and vice versa.

The logic of general propositions

The principal difficulty with the technique outlined above is that it does not permit statements of the type 'all individuals are rational utility maximizers' or 'some costs are sunk costs'. In the first case we are making a universal statement consisting of an exhaustive set of individual propositions of the type: x is a rational utility maximizer. In the second case we are making a statement about the existence of one or more (that is, at least one) sunk costs. The first case is called a 'universal' proposition and the second case an 'existential' proposition.

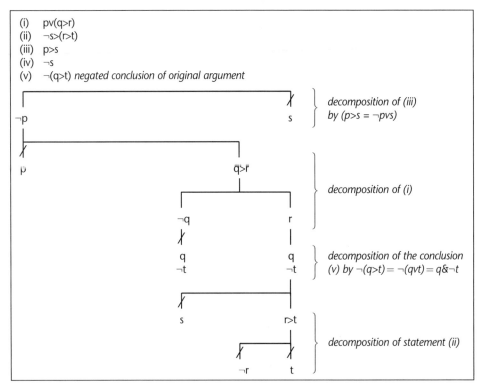

FIGURE 12.3

The symbolism for a universal is fairly straightforward. Consider the statement 'All accountants are boring'. We are concerned with the logical structure of such a statement rather than its particular meaning or, indeed, whether it is true or false. We can replace this statement with the following: (for any x whatsoever)[If x is an accountant then x is boring] which can be symbolized as (x)[Ax>Bx].

The (x) is referred to as the 'universal quantifier' (UQ), A and B refer to the general attributes in question (in this case the attributes of being an accountant and being boring) and the postscript x refers to the general instantiation of those attributes.

'Some accountants are women' can be interpreted as (there is at least one x) [which is an accountant and a woman]. This is an example of existential quantification which we symbolize as (∃x)[Ax&Wx] where ∃x means 'there is at least one instance of x'.

There are four rules for dealing with universal and existential quantification in trees:

(1) Instantiating a universal: if (x)Ux appears in an argument any singular term may be used in its place. Because, if (x)Ux is true the specific instances Ua, Ub, Uc . . . must also be true. Replacement of a universal generalization can be done any number of times throughout a reduction process. For example:

All accountants are wealth maximizers	$(x)(Ax > Wx)$
All wealth maximizers are rational	$(x)(Wx) > Rx)$
Bob Ryan is an accountant	Ab
Therefore not all accountants are irrational	$\neg(x)(Ax > \neg Rx)$
To test for invalidity we negate the conclusion	$\neg\neg(x)(Ax > \neg Rx)$

and take a specific instance (b) of each universal (see Figure 12.4).

As all branches are inconsistent there can be no invalidating row in a truth table for the original argument.

(2) Decomposing an existential quantifier $(\exists x)Ux$: because an existential quantifier only necessarily binds a single instance we may only place that instance once on a given branch.

(3) Decomposing the negation of an existential quantifier $\neg(\exists x)Ux$: because $\neg(\exists x)Ux$ has the same logical sense of $(x)\neg Ux$ then $\neg(\exists x)Ux$ can be replaced by the specific instances $\neg Ua$, $\neg Ub$, $\neg Uc$ as many times as we like. This equivalence can be seen with a simple example: 'there is not at least one thing which is an exciting accountant' is equivalent to saying 'there are no exciting accountants' which can be replaced by the statement 'for all x there is no instance of x which is an exciting accountant'.

(4) Decomposing the negation of a universal $\neg(x)Ux$: can be replaced by a singular instance, for example, $\neg Ua$ but only once on each branch, that is, $\neg(x)Ux \equiv (\exists x)\neg Ux$.

These four rules give us a complete system for determining the validity of an argument by looking for inconsistency in A'. However, with arguments containing quantifiers the tree reduction technique is more restricted than is the case with the simple propositional logic in that it is impossible to determine consistency in A. This is because, as you may remember, checking for consistency relies on finding at least one branch which is not closed by the reduction technique. With universal instantiation, the possibility of creating an infinite set of specific instances only

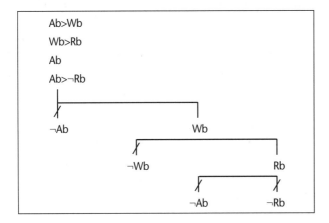

FIGURE 12.4

permits us to prove that an argument is inconsistent (by closure) but not consistent, which would entail complete enumeration of all possibilities. However, because proof of inconsistency in A′ allows us to prove validity in argument A we still have a very powerful analytical tool at our disposal.

We will restrict further discussion on the analysis of quantified terms and, in particular, the problems of instantiating such terms until we have discussed the important area of relations. The combination of these three areas of logic offer us a powerful calculus for the analysis of natural language statements and arguments.

The logic of relations

Relations do not present too many difficulties for analysis given the methods already discussed. Indeed, the main difficulty in the analysis of terms involving relationships is one of representation rather than interpretation.

Relationships are categorized along a number of dimensions:

- dyadic – 'n'adic (for example, 'triadic')
- symmetrical – non-symmetrical
- transitive – non-transitive
- reflexive – non-reflexive.

A dyadic relationship is of the type: 'return is always preferred to risk' which is symbolized as $(x)(y)Pxy$ where P is the relational operator, x is return and y is risk. We have shown the relationship with the universal quantifiers (x) and (y) because of the use of the word 'always'.

A triadic relationship is of the type: 'Bob Ryan, Mike Theobald and Bob Scapens wrote this book together' which is symbolized as $Wrts$ where W is the relational operator and r, t and s represent the individuals related. Note we have not used the universal quantifiers as this is a simple relationship between three authors. Higher-order relationships can also be expressed in the same way (with additional terms).

Symmetry in a relationship is where the relationship is bi-directional and equivalent. For example the statement 'the English (e) and Scottish (s) Institutes have the same entry (E) requirements' is a symmetrical relationship in that the order can be reversed and the statement has exactly the same truth content, that is, $Ees > Ese$ holds. A relationship is defined as asymmetrical if the order is unidirectional. 'Return is always preferred to risk' is asymmetrical in the $(x)(y)$ $[Pxy > \neg Pyx]$. This can be loosely translated as if return (x) is always preferred to risk (y) then it is not true that risk is preferred to return. Non-symmetrical relationships are where the relationship is ambiguous, for example, 'the training to become an accountant is no more onerous than that required to become a doctor', can be interpreted as meaning that the training is of the same duration or of less duration for accountants than for doctors.

Transitivity, as a concept, relates to sets of dyadic relationships and is most familiar in the finance and economics fields as transitivity in preferences. The concept in logic asserts that common dyadic relationships are transitive if the following is true: Rxy&Rxz then Rxz, that is, (x)(y)(z)[(Rxy&Ryz) > Rxz]. Thus, in preference theory, if a is preferred to b and b is preferred to c then a will be preferred to c if the preferences are transitive. Intransitivity occurs when a relationship will not extend through the order and (x)(y)(z)[(Rxy&Ryz) > ¬Rxz] holds. An example is: if a is the father of b and b is the father of c then a is not the father of c. Non-transitivity occurs when the relationships are ambiguous. For example, if Co. a is an associate of Co. b and Co. b is an associate of Co. c then it is possible that a is an associate of c but not necessarily so.

Reflexivity refers to the situation where a relational operator can be self related. For example, the term 'is identical with' indicates total reflexivity in that (x)Rxx is true. An irreflexive relation is where (x) ¬Rxx is true. Ordinarily reflexivity indicates the situation where something is related to itself or where either Rab or Rba is true. A relationship such as 'the English Institute has the same entry qualifications as the Scottish Institute' is ordinarily reflexive as all of the following are true Eee, Ess, Ees or Ese. Formally, a relationship is reflexive if (x)[(∃y)(Rxy v Ryx) > Rxx] is true. All totally reflexive relationships are ordinarily reflexive but not vice versa.

Finally, before leaving our general discussion of the logical properties of relations we need to define the concept of identity. This is a simple idea which is formalized by Leibnitz's principle of identity: two entities are identical if and only if (usually written as 'iff') every attribute of one is present in the other and vice versa.

Identity is symbolized by '=' and formally (x)(x=x); (x)(y)[(x=y) > (y=x)]; (x)(y)(z){[(x=y)&(y=z)] > (x=z)}. Identities are, therefore and trivially, totally reflexive, symmetrical and transitive.

The relationship between the various relational attributes outlined above can be tested. For example, it is straightforward to prove that asymmetrical relationships are irreflexive (see Figure 12.5). Because inconsistency is demonstrated (that is, the absence of a consistent line in the corresponding truth table) then no invalidating line exists in the original argument and hence that argument is valid.

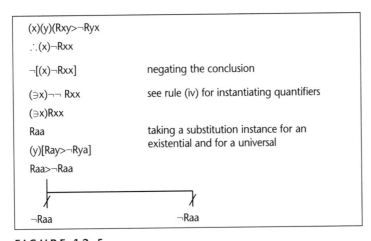

FIGURE 12.5

The problem of interpretation

In the field of logic, interpretation is the most difficult problem faced by the analyst. Natural language grammars are particularly subtle and are invariably used by individuals in idiosyncratic ways. As we have seen, the grammatical constructions in our logical meta-language are small in number and have definite and precise meanings. For this reason we have to decide upon the degree of violence we must do to an NLA to translate its meaning into logical form. We can identify two levels at which this can be undertaken in critical analysis:

Level 1: the general construction of a paper

At this level we can usually discern two types of argument:

(1) Given $F = \{f_1, f_2, f_3 \ldots f_n\}$ (assumptions)
     then $M = \{m_1, m_2, m_3 \ldots m_n\}$ (models)
     and, given M
     then $I = \{i_1, i_2, i_3 \ldots i_n\}$ (implications)

or

(2) Given $H = \{h_1, h_2, h_3, \ldots h_0\}$ (hypotheses)
     and $T = \{t_1, t_2, t_3 \ldots t_m\}$ (test conditions)
     then $P = \{p_1, p_2, p_3 \ldots p_0\}$ (predictions)

In the case of (1), the translation $F \rightarrow M$ may well entail the use of mathematical reasoning which can only be validated within the context of the mathematical system chosen. As we shall see when we come to examine the construction of assumptions and the deduction of implications, logic can be used to determine the consistency and validity of such arguments. However, one important point should be noted: if any one of a model's implications can be falsified then that falsifies both the model and its assumptions. Taking the NLA 'if model (m) is derived from two assumptions (f_1 and f_2) alone and that model produces two implications (i_1 and i_2) then if either of the two implications are false then both the model and either one or other of the two assumptions are false'. It can be demonstrated that this argument

$$A = \{(f_1 \& f_2) > m; \; m > (i_1 \& i_2) \mid (\neg i_1 v \; \neg i_2) > (\neg m \; \& (\neg f_1 v \neg f_2))$$

is valid, as shown in figure 12.6.

That is, as no consistent combination of truth values can be found in A' an invalidating row in the equivalent truth table does not exist in A and hence the argument is valid.

The validity of this argument points to the fact that if any of the implications of a theoretical model can be shown to be either empirically or logically false then one can safely conclude that both the model and one or more of its assumptions are also false.

In the case of (2), (H&T) > P, the linkages may well be expressed as natural language arguments and some form of logical analysis employed. Within,

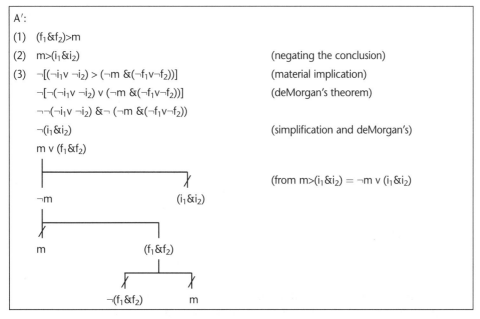

FIGURE 12.6

experimental work it is rare that a valid confirmatory argument can be constructed on the basis of outcomes determining the truth or otherwise of $p_1, p_2, p_3 \ldots p_0$. The Fallacy of Affirming the Consequent where $A = \{h > p;\ p\ |\ h\}$ is an easy trap to fall into, although Popper's falsificationist strategy only works when the *modus ponens* $A = \{h > p;\ \neg p\ |\ \neg h\}$ can be unambiguously identified in an experimental structure. Even the introduction of a single test condition (t) into conjunction with a single hypothesis (h) is sufficient to remove the possibility of valid refutation as while: $A = \{(h \& t) > p;\ \neg p\ |\ \neg h\}$ is a consistent argument it is invalid.

At the construct level, type (2) research can never be used to determine that a hypothetical proposition is necessarily true from the experimental truth of one of its conclusions. Experimental research of this type does not generate formal certainties but is, as we pointed out in the Introduction, a process in the modification of beliefs. Type (2) research can be fruitfully described as a Bayesian process where prior beliefs (expressed as subjective probabilities attaching to states of the world hypothesized in H) are revised to give posterior beliefs on the basis of our conditional expectations about the significance of affirming or disconfirming empirical tests (Figure 12.7).

Level 2: the construction of particular arguments embedded within elements of text

It may be necessary to symbolize certain portions of text and to subsequently test them for inconsistency and validity. For example, the following extract of text is taken from Sharpe's classic paper 'Mutual fund performance' (*Journal of Business,* January 1966):

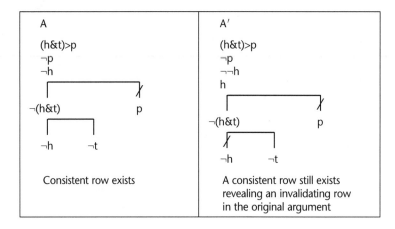

FIGURE 12.7

If all funds hold properly diversified portfolios and spend the appropriate amount for analysis and administration, they should provide rates of return giving Ai, Vi values lying generally along a straight line. () On the other hand, if some funds fail to diversify properly, or spend too much on research and/or administration, they will persistently give rates of return yielding inferior Ai, Vi values.

A sentence, (), has been omitted for the sake of simplicity (it makes a note about transitory performance and does not affect the logical meaning of the remainder of the extract).

We can restructure the two conditionals in this extract as follows:

Statement (1)
If *all* funds hold properly diversified portfolios
    and spend the appropriate amount for analysis
    and (spend the appropriate amount for) administration
    (then) they (all funds) should provide rates of return giving Ai, Vi values
    lying generally along a straight line.
Statement (2)
If *some (not all)* funds (do not hold properly diversified portfolios),
    or spend too much on research
    and/or (spend too much on) administration,
    then *they* will persistently give rates of return yielding inferior Ai, Vi values.

We have emboldened those words which appear to serve as logical connectives, italicized those words which indicate quantification and bracketed the additional interpretations we have made.

This example introduces a particularly difficult problem in logical interpretation, namely, that of scope. Scope relates to the range of operation of a connective or quantifier. In some cases (the first 'if', for example) the scope can be easily determined from the sense of what is written, although we have had to interpret the implicit position of the consequent in both statements. However, the scope of the quantification of each term must be carefully defined. From the sense of the text we interpret that the *all* at the start of statement (1) quantifies the implicit references to funds throughout that statement but not through statement (2). The following would appear to be a reasonable symbolic interpretation of statement (1):

$$(x) [(Fx\&Dx\&Rx\&Ax)>Px]$$

Statement (2) could be interpreted as follows:

$$(\exists y) [(Fy \& (\neg Dy \lor \neg Ry \lor \neg Ay))>(\neg Py)]$$

In this interpretation we have ignored the relationship of research expenditure, administration expenditure and the anticipated performance to the funds covered in statement (1). The negation signs merely indicate that the expenditure levels are not appropriate and that the optimal level of return will not be earned. You may like to consider how this could be introduced into the analysis using a relationship operator of the type Lzy or Gzy to represent 'less than' or 'greater than'. Two existential operators will be required: one for those funds which are behaving optimally and one for those which are not. Finally, the symbolic form of this statement would need to indicate that all funds (x)Fx are identical to those funds which do operate optimally $(\exists y)(Fy \ldots)$ and those which do not $(\exists z)(Fz \ldots)$. You may like to consider whether the two statements (1 and 2) are inconsistent and whether that inconsistency is caused by the way the author has quantified each statement or by the way we have chosen to translate each statement into symbolic form.

There are rules concerning scope within all natural language grammars, although different individuals invariably interpret those rules idiosyncratically. Each individual has what is often referred to as a 'private language' consisting of their own interpretation of the rules and meanings within the language. This makes our problem of interpretation particularly difficult as it appears that the widest divergences in personal usage exist in the area of scope. Translation involves the following steps:

- interpreting the meaning of an individual's private language into the common grammar of the natural language, the paraphrasing of the natural language into a form where the logical terms are exposed and, finally, (what is usually the easy part) the abstraction of the resultant pseudo-language into symbolic form.
- the detailed analysis of statements within arguments and particularly the logical analysis of assumptions. For example, consider the following two assumptions taken from Merton's (1973b) 'An intertemporal capital asset pricing model':

    Assumption 1: *All assets have limited liability.*
    Assumption 2: *There are no transactions costs, taxes, or problems with the indivisibility of assets.*

These can be translated into symbolic form:

Assumption 1 = (for all x)[If x is an asset then x has limited liability]
A1 = (x)[Ax>Lx]

Assumption 2 = (for all y)(for all x)[(if y is a trade in asset x then (there are no transactions costs on trade y) and (there are no taxes on trade y)) and x is divisible]
A2 = (y)(x)[(Tyx > (¬Cy & ¬Ky)) & Dx]

It is a lengthy and exhausting task to interpret a full set of assumptions in a research paper into symbolic form although the process can be well worth while if some inconsistency is suspected. In addition, the full interpretation of a set of assumptions in conjunction with a model's implications may well reveal routes for the elimination of unnecessary clauses and indeed the reduction of the number of necessary assumptions. This process is what is known as the application of Occam's Razor to a set of assumptions and is an important step in any theoretical development.

Summary

In this chapter we have outlined a system of propositional and predicate logic which permits the analysis of complex natural language statements and arguments. We have made a case for the use of logic on two grounds: first, it can help in the identification of inconsistency and invalidity in statements and arguments in the research literature and, second, it forces a careful interpretation of what is presented. Within the accounting and finance literature the use of language can be rather opaque and logic is an important tool in gaining economy and clarity of expression. However, the weakness of formal logic is that it is only as strong as the translation from the natural language in which the original argument appears. It is not a simple task and it is for this reason that the use of logical analysis of this type is restricted to sections of text containing arguments and assumptions. It is also true to say that much of the benefit of analysis of this type is in the process rather than the result, because it is in the process of carefully thinking about meaning that inconsistency, invalidity and ambiguity become apparent.

..... 13

Conclusion

Accounting and finance are important subjects for research within any economic system. The output of research can take a considerable time to penetrate into professional practice and to become an established part of our teaching. Research into these subjects is not free from criticism by professionals. They often complain that they cannot understand it, or the language is obscure or that it is 'too simplistic'. However, research in accounting and finance is typical of research in other disciplines – only a small proportion stands the test of time and is judged to have made a substantial contribution to the literature. Criticism is inevitable and although we may all wish from time to time that it was better informed, it is generally to be welcomed as adding to the debate rather than detracting from it.

Method depends on methodology, and inadequacy of either will lead to deficient research. We also believe that research requires systematic training beyond a sound understanding of the subject. Skills of intuition, analysis and discourse can be developed, and to that end we have chosen our topics to give a broad coverage of the sort of material which would be suitable for such a training programme. We hope that these topics will stimulate debate and through that lead to more effective research.

Finally, much of what we have said, especially in the methodological area, is the subject of fierce debate and is wrapped round by personal belief systems which are unlikely to be altered by rational debate. There is a large majority of researchers in accounting and finance who are committed to the positivist programme because they believe that that programme is the surest way to true knowledge of financial phenomena. Others hold divergent views, in some cases through conviction and in others through a personal realization that they do not have the skills to undertake research with the formal rigour demanded by those who control the positivist programme. But for whatever reason researchers take up the positions they do, there can be no doubt that research thrives and is at its best in a community of critical but tolerant scholarship. Ideas should stand or fall on their own merits. Research is necessarily conditioned by our values of what is important, but there is no place for dogma.

References

Abdel-khalik, A. R. and Ajinkya, B. B. (1979) *Empirical Research in Accounting: A Methodological Viewpoint*. Sarasota, FL: American Accounting Association.

AICPA (1994) *Improving Business Reporting – A Customer Focus: Meeting the Information Needs of Investors and Creditors. Comprehensive Report of the Special Committee on Financial Reporting* (The Jenkins Report). New York: American Institute of Certified Public Accountants.

American Accounting Association (1936) *Accounting Principles Underlying Corporate Financial Statements*. Sarasota, FL: American Accounting Association.

American Accounting Association (1966) *A Statement of Basic Accounting Theory*. Sarasota, FL: American Accounting Association.

Amihud, Y. and Mendelson, H. (1986) Asset pricing and the bid–ask spread. *Journal of Financial Economics* 17: 223–50.

Amin, K. and Jarrow, R. (1992) Pricing options on risky assets in a stochastic interest rate economy, *Mathematical Finance* 2: 217–37.

Amin, K. and Ng, V. (1993) Option valuation with systematic stochastic volatility, *Journal of Finance*, 48: 881–910.

Amir, E. and Lev, B. (1996) Value-relevance of nonfinancial information: the wireless communications industry. *Journal of Accounting and Economics* 22.

Anthony, R. N. (1960) The trouble with profit maximization. *Harvard Business Review* 38, November–December: 126–34.

APB (1999) *Statement of Principles for Financial Reporting*. London: Accounting Standards Board.

Argyris, C. (1952) *The Impact of Budgets on People*. New York: The Controllership Foundation.

Ariel, R. (1987) A monthly effect in stock returns, *Journal of Financial Economics* 18: 161–74.

Arnold, V. and Sutton, S. E. (eds) (1997) *Behavioral Accounting Research: Foundations and Frontiers*. Sarasota, FL: American Accounting Association.

ASSC (1975) *The Corporate Report*. London: Accounting Standards Steering Committee.

Atkinson, A. and Shaffir, W. (1998) Standards for field research in management accounting. *Journal of Management Accounting Research* 10: 41–68.

Audi, R. (1995) *The Cambridge Dictionary of Philosophy*. Cambridge: Cambridge University Press.

Audi, R. (1998) *Epistemology – a Contemporary Introduction to the Theory of Knowledge*. London: Routledge.

Ayer, A. J. (1936) *Language, Truth and Logic*. London: Pelican.

Baiman, S. (1982) Agency research in managerial accounting: a survey. *Journal of Accounting Literature* 1.

Baker, C. R. and Bettner, M. S. (1997) Interpretive and critical research in accounting: a commentary on its absence from mainstream accounting research. *Critical Perspectives on Accounting* 8: 293–310.

Bakshi, G., Cao, C. and Chen, Z. (1997) Empirical performance of alternative option pricing models, *Journal of Finance* 52: 2003–49.

Ball, R. (1978) Anomolies in relationships between security yields and yield surrogates. *Journal of Financial Economics* 6.

Ball, R. and Brown, P. (1968) An empirical evaluation of accounting income numbers. *Journal of Accounting Research* 6.

Ball, R., Kothari, S. and Shanken, J. (1995) Problems in measuring portfolio performance: an application to contrarian investment strategies. *Journal of Financial Economics*, 35: 40–66.

Banergie, A., Colado, J., Galbraith, J. and Hendry, D. (1993) *Co-integration Error-Correction, and the Econometric Analysis of Non-stationary Data*. Oxford: Oxford University Press.

Banz, R. W. (1981) The relationship between return and market value of common stocks. *Journal of Financial Economics* 9: 3–8.

Barron, O. E., Kile, C. O. and O'Keefe, T. B. (1999) MD&A quality as measured by the SEC and analysts' earnings forecasts, *Contemporary Accounting Research* 16(1).

Barth, M., Beaver, W. and Landsman, W. (2001) The relevance of the value relevance literature for financial accounting standard setting: another view. *Journal of Accounting and Economics*, (31) 1–3: 77–104.

Barth, M. E. and Landsman, W. R. (1995) Fundamental issues related to using fair value accounting for financial reporting. *Accounting Horizons* 9(4).

Barth, M. E., Clement, M. B., Foster, G. and Zasznik, R. (1998) Brand values and capital market valuation. *Review of Accounting Studies* 3(1/2).

Basu, S. (1977) Investment performance of common stocks in relation to their price. *Journal of Finance* 32: 663–82.

Bates, D. (1991) The crash of 87: was it expected? The evidence from options markets. *Journal of Finance* 46: 1009–44.

Bates, D. (1996) Testing option pricing models, in G. Maddala and C. Rao (eds) *Handbook of Statistics*, vol 15: *Statistical Methods in Finance*. Amsterdam: North Holland.

Baxter, W. T. (1938) A note on the allocation of on-costs between departments. *Accountant* 99.

Beattie, V. A. (2000) The future of corporate reporting: a review article. *Irish Accounting Review* 7(1).

Beattie, V. A. and Jones, M. J. (2000) Changing graph use in corporate annual reports: a time series analysis. *Contemporary Accounting Research* 17(2).

Beaver, W. (1981) *Financial Reporting: An Accounting Revolution*. Englewood Cliffs, NJ: Prentice-Hall.

Bedford, N. M. (1965) *Income Determination Theory: an Accounting Framework*. London: Addison Wesley.

Bell, D. (1981) Models and reality in economic discourse, in D. Bell and J. Kristol (eds) *The Crisis in Economic Theory*. New York: Basic Books.

Bell, D. and Kristol, I. (eds) (1981) *The Crisis in Economic Theory*. New York: Basic Books.

Berg, J., Dickhaut, J. and McCabe, K. (1995) The individual versus the aggregate, in R. H. Ashton and A. H. Ashton (eds) *Judgment and Decision-Making Research in Accounting and Auditing*. New York: Cambridge University Press.

Berry, A. J., Capps, T., Cooper, D., Ferguson, P., Hopper, T. and Lowe, E. A. (1985) Management control in an area of the NCB: rationales of accounting in a public enterprise. *Accounting, Organizations and Society* 10(1).

Bhaskar, R. (1997) *A Realist Theory of Science*. London: Verso.

Bhattacharya, S. (1976) Imperfect information, dividend policy and the bird in the hand fallacy. *Bell Journal of Economics* 10.

Black, F. (1972) Capital market equilibrium with restricted borrowing. *Journal of Business* 45: 444–54.

Black, F. and Scholes, M. (1973) The pricing of options and corporate liabilities. *Journal of Political Economy* 81: 637–54.

Black, F. and Scholes, M. (1974) The effect of dividend yield and dividend policy on common stock prices and returns. *Journal of Financial Economics* 1: 1–22.

Black, F., Jensen, M. C. and Scholes, M. (1972) The CAPM: some empirical tests, in M. C. Jensen (ed.) *Studies in the Theories of Capital Markets*. New York: Praeger

Bloomfield, R. and O'Hara, M. (1999) Market transparency: who wins and who loses? *Review of Financial Studies* 12: 5–35.

Blume, M. E. and Stambaugh, R. F. (1983) Biases in computed returns. *Journal of Financial Economics* 12: 387–404.

Blumer, H. (1969) *Symbolic Interactionism: Perspective and Method*. Englewood Cliffs, NJ: Prentice-Hall.

Boland, R. J. Jr (1993) Accounting and the interpretive act. *Accounting, Organizations and Society* 18(1): 1–24.

Boness, A. (1964) Elements of a theory of stock-option value. *Journal of Political Economy* 72: 163–75.

Botosan, C. A. (1997) Disclosure level and the cost of equity capital. *Accounting Review*, 72(3).

Box, G. and Jenkins, G. (1970) *Time Series Analysis: Forecasting and Control*. San Francisco: Holden Bay.

Boyle, P. (1988) A lattice framework for option pricing with two state variables. *Journal of Financial & Quantitative Analysis* 23: 1–12.

Bracht, G. and Glass, G. (1968) The external validity of experiments. *American Educational Research Journal*.

Braverman, H. (1974) *Labor and Monopoly Capital*. New York: Monthly Review Press.

Brennan, M. J. (1970) Taxes, market valuation and corporate financial policy. *National Tax Journal* 23(4).

Brisley, N. and Theobald, M. (1996) A simple measure of price adjustment coefficients: a correction. *Journal of Finance* 51: 381–2.

Broadie, M., Glasserman, P. and Kou, S. (1998) Connecting discrete and continuous path dependent options. *Mathematical Finance* 2: 1–28.

Brown, D. and Jennings, R. (1989) On technical analysis. *Review of Financial Studies* 2: 527–52.

Brown, L. D., Gardner, J. C. and Vasarhelyi, M. A. (1987) An analysis of the research contributions of accounting organisation and society, 1976–1984. *Accounting, Organizations and Society* 12.

Brown, S. and Warner, J. (1985) Using daily stock returns: the case of event studies. *Journal of Financial Economics* 14: 3–31.

Brown, S., Goetzmann, W. and Ross, S. (1995) Survival. *Journal of Finance* 50: 853–73.

Burchell, S., Clubb, C., Hopwood, A., Hughes, J. and Nahapiet, J. (1980) The roles of accounting in organizations and society. *Accounting, Organizations and Society* 5(1): 5–27.

Burgess, R. G. (1984) *In the Field: An Introduction to Field Research*. London: Allen and Unwin.

Burns, J. and Scapens, R. (2000) Conceptualising management accounting change: an institutionalist framework. *Management Accounting Research* 11(1): 3–25.

Burns, T. and Stalker, G. M. (1961) *The Management of Innovation*. London: Tavistock.

Burrell, G. and Morgan, G. (1979) *Sociological Paradigms and Organisational Analysis*. London: Heinemann.

Campbell, D. and Stanley, J. (1963) *Experimental and Quasi-experimental Designs for Research.* Chicago: Rand McNally.

Campbell, J. (2000) Asset pricing at the millenium. *Journal of Finance* 55: 1515–67.

Campbell, J. and Kyle, A. (1993) Smart money, noise trading and stock price behaviour. *Review of Economic Statistics* 60: 1–34.

Campbell, J., Lo, A. and MacKinlay, C. (1997) *The Econometrics of Financial Markets.* Princeton, NJ: Princeton University Press.

Canning, J. B. (1929) *The Economics of Accountancy: A Critical Analysis of Accounting Theory.* New York: Ronald Press.

Caporaso, J. (1973) Quasi-experimental approaches to social sciences, in J. Caparosa and L. Ross (eds) *Quasi Experimental Approaches.* Evanston, IL: Northwestern University Press.

Chambers, R. J. (1966) *Accounting Evaluation and Economic Behaviour.* Englewood Cliffs, NJ: Prentice-Hall International.

Chandler, A. D. (1977) *The Visible Hand: The Managerial Revolution in American Business.* Cambridge, MA, and London: Harvard University Press.

Chartered Institute of Management Accountants (CIMA) (1996) *Management Accounting Official Terminology.* London: Chartered Institute of Management Accountants.

Chen, N. F. (1983) Some empirical tests of the theory of arbitrage pricing. *Journal of Finance* 38: 1393–414.

Chen, N. F. and Ingersoll, J. E. (1983) Exact pricing in linear factor models with finitely many assets: a note. *Journal of Finance* 38: 985–8.

Chen, N., Roll, R. and Ross, S. (1986) Economic forces and the stockmarket. *Journal of Business* 59: 383–404.

Chopra, N., Lakonishok, J. and Ritter, J. (1992) Measuring abnormal performance: Do stocks overreact? *Journal of Financial Economics* 31: 235–68.

Christenson, C. (1982) The methodology of positive accounting. *Accounting Review* 58(1): 1–22.

Christie, A. A. (1990) Aggregation of test statistics: an evaluation of the evidence on contracting and size hypotheses. *Journal of Accounting and Economics* 12.

Christie, A. A. and Zimmerman, J. L. (1994) Efficient and opportunistic choices of accounting procedures: corporate control contests. *Accounting Review* 69(4).

Chua, W. F. (1986) Radical developments in accounting thought. *Accounting Review* 61.

Clarke, J. M. (1923) *Studies in the Economics of Overhead Costs.* Chicago: University of Chicago Press.

Clarkson, P. M., Kao, J. L. and Richardson, G. D. (1999) Evidence that management discussion and analysis (MD&A) is a part of a firm's overall disclosure package. *Contemporary Accounting Research* 16(1).

Cleaver, E. E. (1990) Financing strategies of large UK corporations, 1979–88. MPhil dissertation, University of Southampton.

Coase, R. H. (1937) The nature of the firm. *Economica* November: 386–405.

Cochrane, J. (1999) *Asset Pricing.* Working paper, University of Chicago.

Cohen, K. J. and Cyert, R. M. (1975) *Theory of the Firm: Resource Allocation in a Market Economy.* New York: Prentice-Hall.

Connor, G. (1984) A unified beta pricing theory. *Journal of Economic Theory* 34: 13–31.

Connor, G. and Korajczyk, R. (1988) Risk and return in an equilibrium APT: application of a new test methodology. *Journal of Financial Economics* 15: 373–94.

Connor, G. and Korajczyk, R. (1993) A test for the number of factors in an approximate factor structure. *Journal of Finance* 48: 1263–91.

Cooper, D. and Sherer, M. J. (1984) The value of corporate accounting reports: arguments for a political economy of accounting. *Accounting, Organizations and Society.*

Cooper, D., Scapens, R. and Arnold, J. (1983) *Management Accounting: Research and Practice.* London: Chartered Institute of Management Accountants.

Copeland, T. E. and Friedman, D. (1987) The effect of sequential information arrival on asset prices: an experimental study. *Journal of Finance* 42: 763–97.

Core, J. E. (2001) A review of the empirical disclosure literature. *Journal of Accounting and Economics*, (31) 1–3: 441–56.

Cox, J. and Ross, S. (1976) The valuation of options for alternative stochastic processes. *Journal of Financial Economics* 3: 125–44.

Cox, J. C., Ingersoll, J. E. and Ross, S. A. (1977) A theory of the term structure of interest rates and the valuation of interest dependent claims. *Journal of Financial and Quantitative Analysis* 12: 112–21.

Cox, J. C., Ingersoll, J. E. and Ross, S. A. (1981) The relationship between forward and future prices. *Journal of Financial Economics* 9: 321–46.

Cox, J., Ingersoll, J and Ross, S. (1985) An intertemporal general equilibrium model of asset prices, *Econometrica* 53: 363–84.

Cox, J., Ross, S. and Rubinstein, M. (1979) Option pricing: a simplified approach. *Journal of Financial Economics* 7: 229–64.

Cyert, R. M. and March, J. G. (1963) *A Behavioural Theory of the Firm*. Englewood Cliffs, NJ: Prentice-Hall.

Daft, R. L. and Macintosh, N. B. (1978) A new approach to design and use of management information. *California Management Review* Fall: 82–92.

Damadaran, A. (1993) A simple measure of price adjustment coefficients. *Journal of Finance* 48: 387–99.

Daniel, K., Hirshleifer, D. and Subrahmanyam, A. (1998) A theory of overconfidence, self attribution and security market under- and over-reactions. *Journal of Finance* 53: 1839–85.

Daniel, W. (1978) *Applied Non-parametric Statistics*. Boston, MA: Houghton Mifflin.

Davidson, S. (1984) The origins of the Journal of Accounting Research. *Journal of Accounting Research* 22.

DeAngelo, H. and Masulis, R. W. (1980a) Optimal capital structure under corporate and personal taxation. *Journal of Financial Economics* 8.

DeAngelo, H. and Masulis, R. W. (1980b) Leverage and dividend irrelevancy under corporate and personal taxation. *Journal of Finance* 35.

DeBondt, W. and Thaler, R. (1995) Financial decision making in markets and firms: a behavioural perspective, in R. Jarrow *et al.* (eds), *Handbooks in OR and MS*, vol 9. Amsterdam: Elsevier.

DeBondt, W. F. M. and Thaler, R. (1985) Does the stock market overreact? *Journal of Finance* 40: 793–805.

Dechow, P., Sloan, R. and Sweeney, A. (1995) Detecting earnings management, *Accounting Review*, 70.

DeGroot, M. (1989) *Probability and Statistics* Boston, MA: Addison-Wesley.

DeLong, J., Schleifer, A., Summers, L. and Waldman, R. (1990) The economic consequences of noise traders. *Journal of Political Economy* 98: 703–38.

Demski, J. S. (1967) An accounting system structured on a linear programming model. *Accounting Review* 43(3): 669–79.

Demski, J. S. (1972) Optimal performance measurement. *Journal Accounting Research* 10(2).

Demski, J. S. and Feltham, G. A. (1976) *Cost Determination: A Conceptual Approach*. Ames, IA: Iowa State University Press.

Dhrymes, P. J., Friend, I. and Gultekin, N. B. (1984) A critical reexamination of the empirical evidence on the arbitrage pricing theory. *Journal of Finance* 39: 323–46.

Diamond, D. and Verrecchia, R. (1981) Information aggregation in a noisy rational expectations economy. *Journal of Financial Economics* 9: 221–35.

Dickey, D. and Fuller, W. (1981) Likelihood ratio statistics for autoregressive time series with a unit root. *Econometrica* 49: 1057–72.

Diebold, F. and Nerlove, M. (1990) Unit roots in economic time series: a selective survey, in T. Formby and G. Rhodes (eds) *Advances in Econometrics* vol 8. London: JAI Press.

Dimson, E. and Marsh, P. (1986) Event study methodologies and the size effect: the case of UK press recommendations. *Journal of Financial Economics* 17: 209–31.

Drury, C. (1996) *Management and Cost Accounting.* London: Thomson.

Duffie, D. (1992) *Dynamic Asset Pricing Theory.* Princeton, NJ: Princeton University Press.

Duhem, P. (1962) *The Aim and Structure of Physical Theory.* New York: Atheneum.

Dumas, B., Fleming, J. and Whaley, R. (1998) Implied volatility functions: empirical tests. *Journal of Finance* 53: 2059–106.

Dyckman, T. K. and Zeff, S. A. (1984) Two decades of the Journal of Accounting Research. *Journal of Accounting Research* 22.

Dyvbig, P. H. and Ross, S. A. (1985) Yes – the APT is testable. *Journal of Finance* 40: 1173–88.

Edwards, E. O. and Bell, P. W. (1961) *The Theory and Management of Business Income.* Berkeley, CA: University of California Press.

Edwards, R. S. (1939) The nature and measurement of income. *Accountant* 99.

Eichner, A. S. (1983) *Why is Economics not a Science?* London: Macmillan.

Engle, R. and Granger, C. (1987) Co-integration and error correction: Representation, estimation and testing. *Econometrica* 49: 251–76.

Engle, R., Hendry, D. and Richard, J. (1983) Exogeneity. *Econometrica* 51: 277–304.

Fama, E. F. (1970) Efficient capital markets: a review of theory and empirical work. *Journal of Finance* 25: 383–417.

Fama, E. (1991) Efficient capital markets: II. *Journal of Finance* 46: 1575–617.

Fama, E. (1998) Market efficiency, long term returns and behavioural finance. *Journal of Financial Economics* 49: 283–306.

Fama, E. and French, K. (1992) The cross-section of expected stock returns. *Journal of Finance* 47: 427–66.

Fama, E. and French, K. (1996) Multifactor explanations of asset pricing anomalies. *Journal of Finance* 51: 55–84.

Fama, E. F., Fisher, L., Jensen, H. C. and Roll, R. (1969) The adjustment of stock market prices to new information. *International Economic Review* 10: 1–21.

FASB (2001) *Business and Financial Reporting, Challenges from the New Economy.* Special report, Norwalk, CT: Financial Accounting Standards Board.

Ferson, W. E., Kandel, S. and Stambaugh, R. W. (1987) Tests of asset pricing with time varying expected risk premiums and market betas. *Journal of Finance* 42.

Feyerabend, P. (1970) *Against Method.* Minneapolis, MN: University of Minnesota Press.

Fisher, A. (1988) *The Logic of Real Arguments.* Cambridge: Cambridge University Press.

Fisher, I. (1906) *The Nature of Capital and Income.* London: Macmillan.

Fleck, L. (1935) *Genesis and Development of a Scientific Fact.* Chicago: Chicago University Press.

Flood, M., Huisman, R., Koedjik, K. and Mahieu, R. (1999) Quote disclosure and price discovery in multiple-dealer financial markets. *Review of Financial Studies* 12: 37–59.

Foster, G. (1977) Quarterly accounting data; time series properties and predictive-ability results. *Accounting Review* 52.

Foster, G., Olsen, C. and Shevlin, T. (1984) Earnings releases, anomalies and the behaviour of security returns. *Accounting Review* 59(4).

Francis, J. and Schipper, K. (1999) Have financial statements lost their relevance? *Journal of Accounting Research* 37(2).

Frankel, R., McNichols, M. and Wilson, G. P. (1995) Discretionary disclosure and external financing. *Accounting Review* 70(1).

French, K. (1980) Stock returns and the weekend effect. *Journal of Financial Economics* 8: 55–70.

Friedman, M. (1953) *Essays in Positive Economics.* Chicago: University of Chicago Press.

Froud, J., Haslam, C., Johal, S. and Williams, K. (2000) Shareholder value and financialization. *Economy and Society* 29(1).

Gaffikin, M. J. R. (1988) Legacy of the golden age, recent developments in the methodology of accounting. *Abacus* 24.

Gernon, H. and Wallace, R. S. O. (1995) International accounting research: a review of its ecology, contending theories and methodologies. *Journal of Accounting Literature* 14.

Geske, R. and Roll, K. (1983) The fiscal and monetary linkage between stock and inflation. *Journal of Finance* 38.

Gibbins, M., Richardson, A. J. and Waterhouse, J. (1990) The management of corporate financial disclosure: opportunism, ritualism, policies, and processes. *Journal of Accounting Research* 28(1).

Gibbins, M., Richardson, A. J. and Waterhouse, J. (1992) *The Management of Financial Disclosure: Theory and Perspectives*. Research Monograph Number 20. Vancouver, BC: Canadian Certified General Accountants' Research Foundation.

Gibbons, M. (1982) Multivariate tests of financial models – a new approach. *Journal of Financial Economics* 10: 3–27.

Gibbons, M. R. and Ferson, W. (1985) Testing asset pricing models with changing expectations and unobservable market portfolio. *Journal of Financial Economics* 14: 217–36.

Giddens, A. (1979) *Central Problems in Social Theory: Action, Structure and Contradiction in Social Analysis*. London: Macmillan.

Giddens, A. (1984) *The Constitution of Society*. Cambridge: Polity Press.

Gilovich, T., Griffin, D. and Kahneman, D. (eds) *Heuristics and Biases*. Cambridge: Cambridge University Press. (2002 forthcoming).

Glosten, L. (1999) Introductory comments: Bloomfield and O'Hara, and Flood, Huisman, Koedjik and Mahien. *Review of Financial Studies* 12: 1–3.

Goffman, E. (1959) *The Presentation of Self in Everyday Life*. New York: Doubleday.

Golden-Biddle, K. and Locke, K. (1993) Appealing works: an investigation of how ethnographic texts convince. *Organization Science* 4(4): 595–616.

Granger, C. (1969) Investigating causal relationships by econometric models and cross spectral methods. *Econometrica* 37.

Graves, O. F., Flesher, D. L. and Jordan, R. E. (1996) Pictures and the bottom line: the television epistemology of U.S. annual reports. *Accounting, Organizations and Society* 21(1).

Grossman, S. (1976) On the efficiency of competitive stock markets where traders have diverse information. *Journal of Finance* 31.

Grossman, S. and Zhou, Z. (1996) Equilibrium analyses of portfolio insurance. *Journal of Finance* 51: 1379–403.

Habermas, J. (1972) *Knowledge and Human Interests*. London: Heineman.

Hanson, N. R. (1958) *Patterns of Discovery*. Cambridge: Cambridge University Press.

Harre, R. (1986) *Varieties of Realism*. Oxford: Blackwell.

Harris, R. and Raviv, A. (1991) The theory of capital structure. *Journal of Finance* 46: 297–355.

Harrison, J. and Pliska, S. (1979) Martingales and arbitrage in multiperiod securities markets. *Journal of Economic Theory* 20: 381–408.

Healy, P. M. and Palepu, K. G. (2001) Information asymmetry, corporate disclosure, and the capital markets: a review of the empirical disclosure literature. *Journal of Accounting and Economics*, (31) 1–3: 405–40.

Healy, P. M., Hutton, A. P. and Palepu, K. G. (1999) Stock performance and intermediation changes surrounding sustained increases in disclosure. *Contemporary Accounting Research* 16(3).

Heath, D., Jarrow, R. and Morton, A. (1992) Bond pricing and the term structure of interest rates: a new methodology for contingent claims valuation. *Econometrica* 60: 77–105.

Hesse, M. (1974) *Models and Analogies in Science*. London: Sheed and Ward.

Hesse, M. (1980) *Revolutions and Reconstructions in the Philosophy of Science*. Brighton: Harvester Press.

Heston, S. (1993) A closed form solution for options with stochastic volatility with applications to bond and currency options. *Review of Financial Studies* 6, 327–43.

Heuristics and Biases. Cambridge: Cambridge University Press.

Hinkelheim, K. and Kempthorne, O. (1994) *Design and Analysis of Experiments*. New York: John Wiley.

Hirst, M. K. (1981) Accounting information and the evaluation of subordinate performance: a situational analysis. *Accounting Review* 57(3): 477–505.

Ho, T. and Lee, S. (1986) Term structure movements and pricing interest rate contingent claims. *Journal of Finance* 41: 1011–29.

Hodgson, G. M. (1988) *Economics and Institutions: A Manifesto for a Modern Institutional Economics*. Cambridge: Polity Press.

Hofstede, G. (1968) *The Game of Budget Control*. London: Tavistock.

Hogarth, R. (1987) *Judgement and Choice*, Chichester: John Wiley. .

Holthausen, R. and Watts, R. (2001) The relevance of the value-relevance literature for financial accounting standard-setting. *Journal of Accounting and Economics*, (31) 1–3: 3–75.

Hong, H. and Stein, J. (1999) A unified theory of underreaction, momentum trading and overreaction in asset markets. *Journal of Finance* 54: 2143–84.

Hopper, T. and Powell, A. (1995) Making sense of research into organizational and social aspects of management accounting: a review of its underlying assumptions. *Journal of Management Studies* 22(5): 429–65.

Hopper, T., Cooper, D., Lowe, T., Capps, T. and Mouritsen, J. (1986) Management control and worker resistance in the National Coal Board: financial controls in the labour process, in D. Knights and H. C. Willmott (eds) *Managing the Labour Process*. London: Gower.

Hopwood, A. G. (1972) An empirical study of the role of accounting data in performance evaluation. *Journal Accounting Research* supplement: 156–93.

Hopwood, A. G. (1987) The archaeology of accounting systems. *Accounting, Organizations and Society* 13(3): 207–34.

Horngren, C. T. (1975) Management accounting: where are we? in W. A. Albrecht (ed.) *Management Accounting and Control*. Madison, WI: University of Wisconsin-Madison.

Horngren, C. T., Bhimani, A., Foster, G. and Datar, S. M. (1999) *Management and Cost Accounting*. London: Prentice-Hall Europe.

Huberman, G. (1982) A simple approach to arbitrage pricing theory. *Journal of Economic Theory* 28: 183–91.

Hughes, K. E. (2000) The value relevance of nonfinancial measures of air pollution in the electric utility industry. *Accounting Review*, 75(2).

Hull, J. (2000) *Options, Futures and Other Derivatives*. 4th edn. Upper Saddle River, NJ: Prentice-Hall.

Hull, J. and White, A. (1987) The pricing of options on assets with stochastic volatilies. *Journal of Finance* 42: 281–300.

Hull, J. and White, A. (1990) Pricing interest rate derivative securities. *Review of Financial Studies* 4: 573–92.

Humphrey, C. and Scapens, R. (1996) Theories and case study of organizational accounting practices: limitation or liberation. *Accounting, Auditing and Accountability Journal* 9(4): 119–22.

ICAEW (1999) *Inside Out: Reporting on Shareholder Value*. London: Institute of Chartered Accountants in England and Wales.

ICAS (1999) Business reporting: the inevitable change? V. Beattie (ed.). Edinburgh: Institute of Chartered Accountants of Scotland.

Ijiri, Y. (1967) *The Foundations of Income Measurement*. Englewood Cliffs, NJ: Prentice-Hall International.

Ittner, C. D. and Larcker, D. F. (1998) Are nonfinancial measures leading indicators of financial performance? An analysis of customer satisfaction. *Journal of Accounting Research* 36.

Jackwerth, J. and Rubinstein, M. (1996) Recovering probability distributions from option prices, *Journal of Finance* 51: 1611–31.

Jacobs, F. H. (1978) An evaluation of the effectiveness of some cost variance investigation models. *Journal of Accounting Research* Spring: 190–203.

Jagannathan, R. and Wang, Z. (1996) The conditional CAPM and the cross-section of expected returns. *Journal of Finance* 51: 3–53.

Jegadeesh, N. and Titman, S. (1993) Returns to buying winners and selling losers: implications for stock market efficiency. *Journal of Finance* 48: 65–91.

Jensen, M. C. (1972) *Studies in the Theories of Capital Markets*. New York: Praeger.

Jensen, M. C. (1978) Some anomalous evidence regarding market efficiency. *Journal of Financial Economics* 2.

Jensen, M. C. (1983) Organisation theory and methodology. *Accounting Review* 58.

Jensen, M. C. and Meckling, W. H. (1976) Theory of the firm: managerial behaviour, agency costs and ownership structure. *Journal of Financial Economics* 3.

Johnson, K. T. and Kaplan, R. S. (1987) *Relevance Lost – the Rise and Fall of Management Accounting*. Cambridge, MA: Harvard Business School Press.

Johnston, J. (1972) *Econometric Methods*. Tokyo: McGraw-Hill Kogakusha.

Jones, J. (1991) Earnings management during import relief investigations. *Journal of Accounting Research* 29.

Jorion, P. and Goetzman, W. (1999) Global stockmarkets in the twentieth century. *Journal of Finance* 54: 953–80.

Kaplan, A. (1964) *The Conduct of Enquiry*. San Francisco: Chandler Press.

Kaplan, R. S. (1984) The evolution of management accounting. *Accounting Review* 59(3).

Kaplan, R. S. (1986) The role of empirical research in management accounting. *Accounting, Organizations and Society* 11(4/5): 429–52.

Kaplan, R. S. (1998) Innovation action research: creating new management theory and practice. *Journal of Management Accounting Research* 10: 89–118.

Kassem, S. (1977) Organisation theory: American and European styles. *Management International Review* 17.

Keim, D. B. (1983) Size related anomalies and stock return seasonality. *Journal of Financial Economics* 12.

Kemna, A. and Vorst, A. (1990) A pricing method for options based on average asset values. *Journal of Banking and Finance* 14: 113–29.

Kleidon, A. W. (1986) Bias in small sample tests of stock price rationality. *Journal of Business* 59: 953–1001.

Kothari, S., Shanken, J. and Sloan R. (1995) Another look at the cross section of stock returns. *Journal of Finance* 50: 185–224.

Kothari, S. P. (2001) Capital markets research in accounting. *Journal of Accounting and Economics*, (31) 1–3: 105–231.

Kraus, A. and Litzenberger, R. H. (1976) Skewness preference and the valuation of risk assets. *Journal of Finance* 31: 1085–100.

Kristol, I. (1981) Rationalism in economics, in D. Bell and J. Kristol (eds) *The Crisis in Economic Theory*. New York: Basic Books.

Kuhn, T. S. (1962) *The Structure of Scientific Revolutions*. 2nd edn. Chicago: Chicago University Press.

Lakatos, I. (1970) Falsification and the methodology of research programmes, in I. Lakatos and A. Musgrave *Criticism and the Growth of Knowledge*. Cambridge: Cambridge University Press.

Lang, M. and Lundholm, R. (1993) Cross-sectional determinants of analyst ratings of corporate disclosures. *Journal of Accounting Research* 31.

Latour, B. (1987) *Science in Action.* Cambirdge, MA: Harvard Business School Press.

Latour, B. and Woolgar, S. (1979) *Laboratory Life.* London: Sage.

Laughlin, R. (1995) Empirical research in accounting: alternative approaches and a case for 'middle-range' thinking. *Accounting, Auditing and Accountability Journal* 8(1): 63–87.

Laughlin, R. C. (1987) Accounting systems in organisation contexts: a case for critical theory. *Accounting, Organizations and Society* 12.

Leibenstein, H. (1976) *Beyond Economic Man.* Cambridge, MA: Harvard University Press.

Leroy, S. (1976) Efficient capital markets: comment. *Journal of Finance* 31.

Lev, B. (2000) New accounting for the new economy. Available at www.stern.nyu.edu/~blev/.

Lev, B. (2001) *Intangibles: Management, Measurement and Reporting.* Washington, DC: Brookings Institution Press.

Lev, B. and Zarowin, P. (1999) The boundaries of financial reporting and how to extend them. *Journal of Accounting Research* 37(2).

Levitt, A. (1998) The numbers game. Speech delivered at the New York Center for Law and Business, 28 September.

Libby, R., Bloomfield, R. and Nelson, M. W. (2001) Experimental research in financial accounting. Revised version of a paper presented at the Accounting, Organizations and Society 25th Anniversary Conference, July 2000.

Lincoln, Y. S. and Guba, E. G. (1985) *Naturalistic Inquiry.* Beverly Hills, CA: Sage.

Lintner, J. (1965) Security prices, risk and maximal gains from diversification. *Journal of Finance* 20: 587–615.

Lintner, J. (1969) The aggregation of investor's diverse judgements and preferences in purely competitive security markets. *Journal of Financial and Quantitative Analysis* 4: 347–400.

Lo, A. and MacKinlay, C. (1990) Data snooping biases in tests of financial asset pricing models. *Review of Financial Studies,* 3: 431–68.

Longstaff, F. (1995) Option pricing and the martingale restriction. *Review of Financial Studies* 8: 1091–124.

Lowe, E. A., Puxty, A. G. and Laughlin, R. C. (1983) Simple theories for complex processes: accounting policy and the market for myopia. *Journal of Accounting and Public Policy* 2.

Lukka, K. and Kasanen, E. (1995) The problem of generalizability: anecdotes and evidence in accounting research. *Accounting, Auditing and Accountability Journal* 8(5): 71–90.

MacBeth, J. and Merville, L. (1979) An empirical examination of the Black–Scholes call option pricing model. *Journal of Finance* 34: 1173–86.

Machlup, F. (1967) Theories of the firm, marginalist, behavioural and managerial. *American Economic Review* 57(1).

Macintosh, N. B. Scapens, R. W. (1990) Structuration theory in management accounting. *Accounting, Organizations and Society* 15(5): 455–77.

MacKinlay, C. (1995) Multifactor models do not explain deviations from the CAPM, *Journal of Financial Economics* 38: 3–28.

Maddala, G. (1992) *Introduction to Econometrics.* 2nd edn. New York: Macmillan.

Maddala, G. and Kim, I. (1998) *Unit Roots, Cointegration and Structural Change.* New York: Cambridge University Press.

Magee, R. P. (1976) A simulation analysis of alternative cost variance investigation models. *Accounting Review* 52(2): 529–44.

Maines, L. A. (1995) Judgment and decision-making research in financial accounting: a review and analysis, in R. H. Ashton and A. H. Ashton (eds) *Judgment and Decision-Making Research in Accounting and Auditing.* New York: Cambridge University Press.

Maines, L. A. and McDaniel, L. S. (2000) Effects of comprehensive-income characteristics on nonprofessional investors' judgments: the role of financial statement presentation format. *Accounting Review* 75(2).

Markowitz, H. (1953) Portfolio selection. *Journal of Finance* 7.

Mattessich, R. (1964) *Accounting and Analytical Method*. London: Irwin.

Mayers, D. (1972) Nonmarketable assets and capital markets equilibrium under uncertainty, in M. C. Jensen (ed.) *Studies in the Theory of Capital Markets*. New York: Praeger.

Mei, J. (1993) A semiautoregression approach to APT. *Journal of Finance* 48: 599–620.

Merquior, J. G. (1985) *Foucault*. London: Fontana.

Merton, R. (1990) *Continuous-Time Finance*, Oxford University Press.

Merton, R. C. (1973a) The relationship between put and call option prices: a comment. *Journal of Finance* 28: 867–87.

Merton, R. C. (1973b) An intertemporal capital asset pricing model. *Econometrica* 41(5): 141–83.

Merton, R. C. (1987) A simple model of capital market equilibrium with incomplete information. *Journal of Finance* 42.

Mill, J. S. (1874) *A System of Logic*. New York: Harper.

Miller, M. H. (1977) Debt and taxes. *Journal of Finance* 32.

Miller, M. H. and Modigliani, F. (1961) Dividend policy, growth and the valuation of shares. *Journal of Finance* 17.

Miller, M. H. and Modigliani, F. (1966) Some estimates of the cost of capital to the electrical utility industry (1954–57). *American Economic Review* 56(3).

Miller, M. H. and Scholes, M. (1972) Rates of return in relation to risk: a reexamination of some recent findings, in M. C. Jensen (ed.) *Studies in the Theory of Capital Markets*. New York: Praeger.

Miller, M. H., Muthuswamy, J. and Whaley, R. (1994) Mean reversion of Standard and Poor's 500 index basis changes: arbitrage induced or statistical illusion? *Journal of Finance* 49: 479–514.

Miller, P. and O'Leary, T. (1987) Accounting and the construction of the governable person. *Accounting, Organizations and Society* 12(3): 235–61.

Miller, P. and O'Leary, T. (1997) Capital budgeting and the transition to modern manufacture. *Journal of Accounting Research* 35(2): 257–71.

Modigliani, F. and Miller, M. H. (1958) The cost of capital, corporation finance and the theory of investment. *American Economic Review* 48.

Morgan, G. and Smircich, L. (1980) The case for qualitative research. *Academy of Management Review* 5(4): 491–500.

Mossin, J. (1966) Equilibrium in capital asset markets. *Econometrica* 34: 768–83.

Nagel, E. (1961) *The Structure of Science*. London: Routledge and Kegan Paul.

Neftci, S. (1996) *An Introduction to the Mathematics of Financial Derivatives*. San Diego, CA, and London: Academic Press.

Nelson, C. L. (1973) A-priori research in accounting, in Dopuch and Revsine (eds) *Accounting Research 1960–70: A Critical Evaluation*. Urbana, IL: Centre for International Education and Research in Accounting, University of Illinois Press.

Neu, D. (1992) The social construction of positive choices. *Accounting, Organizations and Society* 17(3/4).

O'Hara, M. (1998) *Market Microstructure Theory*. Oxford: Blackwell Business.

O'Hara, P. A. (1993) Methodological principles of institutional political economy: holism, evolution and contradiction. *Methodus* June: 51–71.

Ohlson, J. (1995) Earnings, book values and dividends in equity valuation. *Contemporary Accounting Research* 11.

Otley, D. (1980) The contingency theory of management *accounting: achievement and prognosis*. Accounting, Organizations and Society 5(4): 413–28.

Otley, D. T. (1984) Management accounting and organisation theory: a review of their interrelationship, in R. W. Scapens, D. T. Otley and R. J. Lister (eds) (1987) *Management Accounting, Organisation Theory and Capital Budgeting*. London: Macmillan/ESRC.

Papineau, D. (1979) *Theory and Meaning*. Oxford: Clarendon Press.

Papineau, D. (1987) *Reality and Representation*. Oxford: Blackwell.

Parker, L. D. (1994) Professional accounting body ethics: in search of the private interest. *Accounting, Organizations and Society* 19(6).

Pastor, L. (2000) Portfolio selection and asset pricing models. *Journal of Finance* 55: 179–223.

Pastor, L. and Stambaugh, R. (1999) Costs of equity capital and model mispricing, *Journal of Finance* 54: 67–121.

Poincare, H. (1905) *Science and Hypothesis*. London and New York: Walter Scott.

Popper, K. R. (1959) *The Logic of Scientific Discovery*. Oxford: Clarendon Press.

Popper, K. R. (1972) *Objective Knowledge*. Oxford: Oxford University Press.

Poterba, J. M. and Summers, L. H. (1988) Mean reversion in stock prices: evidence and implications. *Journal of Financial Economics* 22: 27–60.

Power, M. K. (1988) Educating accountants: towards a critical ethnography. Paper presented at the Interdisciplinary Perspectives on Accounting Conference, Manchester.

Preston, A. M., Cooper, D. J. and Coombs, R. W. (1992) Fabricating budgets: a study of the production of management budgeting in the national health service. *Accounting, Organizations and Society* 17(6): 561–93.

Preston, A. M., Wright, C., Young, J. J. (1996) Imag[in]ing annual reports. *Accounting, Organizations and Society* 21(1).

Pukelsheim, F. (1993) *Optimal Design of Experiments*. New York: John Wiley.

Puxty, A. G. and Laughlin, R. C. (1983a) Accounting regulation: an alternative perspective. *Journal of Business Finance and Accounting* 10(3).

Puxty, A. G. and Laughlin, R. C. (1983b) A rational reconstruction of the decision usefulness criterion. *Journal of Business Finance and Accounting* 10(3).

Puxty, A. G, Willmott, H., Cooper, D. and Lowe, E. A. (1987) Modes of regulation in advanced capitalism: locating accountancy in four countries. *Accounting, Organizations and Society* 12(3): 273–92.

QAA (2001a) *UK Qualifications Framework*. Executive Brief, January. London: Quality Assurance Agency.

QAA (2001b) *QAA Qualifications Framework*. Qualifications Descriptors, January. London: Quality Assurance Agency.

Ramstad, T. (1986) A pragmatic quest for holistic knowledge: the scientific methodology of John R. Commons. *Journal of Economic Issues* 20, December: 1067–105.

Reinganum, M. R. (1981) The misspecification of capital asset pricing empirical anomalies based on earnings yields and market values. *Journal of Financial Economics* 10: 19–46.

Robson, K., Willmott, H., Cooper, D. and Puxty, T. (1994) The ideology of professional regulation and the markets for accounting labour: three episodes in the recent history of the U.K. accountancy profession. *Accounting, Organizations and Society* 19(6).

Roll, R. (1977a) A critique of the asset pricing theory's tests. *Journal of Financial Economics* 4: 129–76.

Roll, R. (1977b) An analytic formula for unprotected American call options on stocks with known dividends. *Journal of Financial Economics* 5: 251–8.

Roll, R. (1981) A possible explanation of the small firm effect. *Journal of Finance* 36: 879–88.

Roll, R. (1983) On computing mean returns and the small firm premium. *Journal of Financial Economics* 12: 371–86.

Roll, R. (1986) The hubris hypothesis of corporate takeovers. *Journal of Business* 59.

Roll, R. and Ross, S. (1994) On the cross-sectional relation between expected returns and betas. *Journal of Finance* 49: 101–22.

Roll, R. and Ross, S. A. (1980) An empirical investigation of the arbitrage pricing theory. *Journal of Finance* 35: 1073–103.

Roll, R. and Ross, S. A. (1984) A critical reexamination of the evidence on the arbitrage pricing theory: a reply. *Journal of Finance* 39: 347–50.

Roslender, R. (1992) *Sociological Perspectives on Modern Accountancy*. London: Routledge.

Roslender, R. (1996) Relevance lost and found: critical perspectives on the promise of management accounting. *Critical Perspectives on Accounting* 7.

Roslender, R. and Dillard, J. F. (2001) Reflections on the interdisciplinary perspectives on accounting project. *Critical Perspectives on Accounting*, forthcoming.

Ross, S. A. (1976) The arbitrage theory of capital asset pricing. *Journal of Economic Theory* 13: 341–60.

Ross, S. A. (1977) The determination of financial structure – the incentive signalling approach. *Bell Journal of Economics* 8.

Rubinstein, M. (1976) The strong case for the generalised logarithmic utility model as the premier model of financial markets. *Journal of Finance* 31: 407–25.

Rubinstein, M. (1985) Non-parametric tests of alternative option pricing models using all reported trades and quotes on the 30 most active option classes from August 23, 1976 through August 31, 1978. *Journal of Finance* 40: 455–80.

Russell, B. (1961) *History of Western Philosophy*. 2nd edn. London: Allen and Unwin.

Ryan, R. J. (1982) Capital market theory – a case study in methodological conflict. *Journal of Business Finance and Accounting* 9(4).

Scapens, R. W. (1984) Management accounting – a survey paper, in R. W. Scapens, D. T. Otley and R. J. Lister, *Management Accounting, Organisation Theory and Capital Budgeting – Three Surveys*. London: Macmillan/ESRC.

Scapens, R. W. (1999) Broadening scope of management accounting: from a micro-economic to a broader business perspective. *Maandblad voor Accountancy en Bedrijfseconomie* 73(12): 638–49.

Scapens, R. W. and Arnold, J. A. (1986) Economics and management accounting research, in M. Bromwich and A. Hopwood (eds) *Research and Current Issues in Management Accounting*. London: Pitman.

Schiff, M. and Lewin A. Y. (1970) The impact of people on budgets. *Accounting Review* 46(1): 259–68.

Scholes, M. and Williams, J. (1977) Estimating betas from non-synchronous data. *Journal of Financial Economics* 5: 309–28.

Scott, L. (1997) Pricing stock options in a jump-diffusion model with stochastic volatility and interest rates, *Mathematical Finance* 7: 413–26.

Scott, W. R. (1995) *Institutions and Organizations*. London: Sage.

Shanken, J. (1982) The arbitrage pricing theory: is it testable? *Journal of Finance* 37: 1129–40.

Shanken, J. (1985) Multi beta CAPM or equilibrium APT? *Journal of Finance* 40: 1189–96.

Shanken, J. (1992a) The current state of the arbitrage pricing theory. *Journal of Finance* 47: 1569–74.

Shanken, J. (1992b) On the estimation of beta pricing models. *Review of Financial Studies* 5: 1–34.

Sharpe, W. (1964) Capital asset pricing: a theory of market equilibrium under conditions of risk. *Journal of Finance* 19: 425–42.

Shefrin, H. and Statman, M. (1985) The disposition to sell winners too early and ride losers too long: theory and evidence. *Journal of Finance* 40.

Shields, M. D. (1997) Research in management accounting by North Americans in the 1990s. *Journal of Management Accounting Research* 9: 3–61.

Shleifer, A. (2000) *Inefficient Markets: An Introduction to Behavioural Finance*, Oxford and New York: Oxford University Press.

Shleifer, A. and Vishy, R. (1997) A survey of corporate government. *Journal of Finance* 52: 738–83.

Simon, H. A. (1957) *Administrative Behaviour*. 2nd edn. New York: Macmillan.

Simon, H. A. (1959) Theories of decision making in economics and behavioural science. *American Economic Review* 49.

Simon, H. A. (1979) Rational decision making in business organisations. *American Economic Review* 69.

Smith, C., Whipp, R. and Wilmott, H. (1988) Case study research in accounting: methodological breakthrough or ideological weapon. *Advances in Public Interest Accounting* 2: 95–120.

Soros, G. (2000) *Open Society – Reforming Global Capitalism*. London: Little Brown.

Spence, M. (1973) Job market signalling. *Quarterly Journal of Economics* 87.

Stambaugh, R. F. (1983) Arbitrage pricing with information. *Journal of Financial Economics* 12: 235–68.

Stapleton, R. C. and Subrahamanyam, M. G. (1983) The market model and capital asset pricing theory: a note. *Journal of Finance* 38.

Sterling, R. R. (1970) *Theory of the Measurement of Enterprise Income*. Lawrence, KA: University Press of Kansas.

Sterling, R. R. (1990) Positive accounting: an assessment. *Abacus* 26(2).

Stuart, A. (1984) *The Ideas of Sampling*. London: Charles Griffin.

Summers, L. H. (1986) Does the stock market rationally reflect fundamental values? *Journal of Finance* 41.

Sundaram, R. (1997) Equivalent martingale measures: an expository note. *Journal of Derivatives* 5: 85–98.

Sundaresan, S. (2000) Continuous-time methods in finance: a review and an assessment. *Journal of Finance* 55: 1569–622.

Tabachinck, B. and Fidell, L. (2001) *Using Multivariate Statistics*. Boston, MA: Allyn and Bacon.

Theobald, M. and Price, V. (1984) Seasonality estimation in thin markets. *Journal of Finance* 39: 377–92.

Thomas, S. (1986) *Practical Reasoning in Natural Language*. Englewood Cliffs, NJ: Prentice-Hall.

Tinker, A. M., Marino, B. D. and Neimark, M. D. (1982) The normative origins of positive theories – ideology and accounting thought. *Accounting, Organizations and Society*.

Tinker, T. and Neimark, M. (1987) The role of annual reports in General Motors: 1917–1976. *Accounting, Organizations and Society* 12(1): 71–88.

Tomkins, C. and Groves, R. (1983) The everyday accountant and researching his reality. *Accounting, Organizations and Society* 8(4): 361–74.

Trueblood Report (1973) *Objectives of Financial Statements*. New York: American Institute of Certified Public Accountants.

Verrecchia, R. E. (1978) On the choice of accounting methods for partnerships. *Journal of Accounting Research* 16.

Wagenhofer, A. (1990) Voluntary disclosure with a strategic opponent. *Journal of Accounting and Economics* 12.

Walker, M. (1996) Management accounting and the economics of internal organization. *Management Accounting Research* 9(1): 21–30.

Walker, S. P. and Shackleton, K. (1995) Corporatism and structural change in the British accountancy profession, 1930–1957. *Accounting, Organizations and Society* 20(6).

Watts, R. L. (1978) Systematic abnormal returns after quarterly earnings announcements. *Journal of Financial Economics* 7.

Watts, R. L. and Zimmerman, J. L. (1978) Towards a positive theory of the determination of accounting standards. *Accounting Review* 53.

Watts, R. L. and Zimmerman, J. L. (1979) The demand and supply of accounting theories: the market for excuses. *Accounting Review* 54.

Watts, R. L. and Zimmerman, J. L. (1986) *Positive Accounting Theory*. Englewood Cliffs, NJ: Prentice-Hall International.

Watts, R. L. and Zimmerman, J. L. (1990) Positive accounting theory: a ten year perspective. *Accounting Review* 65(1).

Whaley, R. (1981) On the valuation of American call options on stocks with known dividends. *Journal of Financial Economics* 9: 207–11.

Whittington, G. (1986) Financial accounting theory – an overview. *British Accounting Review*, 18(Autumn).

Wiles, P. (1983) Ideology, methodology and neoclassical economics, in A. S. Eichner (ed.) *Why is Economics not a Science?* London: Macmillan.

Williamson, O. E. (1975) *Markets and Hierarchies: Analysis of Antitrust Implications*. New York: Free Press.

Williamson, O. E. (1985) *The Economic Institutions of Capitalism: Firm, Markets and Rational Contracting*. New York: Free Press.

Willmott, H. (1990) Beyond paradigmatic closure in organizational enquiry, in J. Hassard and D. Pym (eds) *The Theory and Philosophy of Organizations*. London: Routledge.

Wong, S. (1978) *The Foundations of Paul Samuelson's Revealed Preference Theory*. London: Routledge and Kegan Paul.

Wonnacott, T. and Wonnacott, W. (1990) *Introduction to Statistics*. New York: Wiley.

Woodward, J. (1958) *Management and Technology*. London: HMSO.

Xu, X. and Taylor, S. (1994) The term structure of volatility implied by foreign exchange options. *Journal of Financial and Quantitative Analysis* 29: 57–74.

Yin, R. K. (1984) *Case Study Research, Design and Methods*. Beverly Hills, CA: Sage.

Zeff, S. A. (1978) The rise of economic consequences. *Journal of Accountancy* November.

Zellner, A. (1979) Causality and econometrics, in K. Brunner and A. Meltzer (eds) *Carnegie–Rochester Conference Series*. Amsterdam: North Holland.

Zimmerman, J. L. (1979) The cost and benefits of cost allocations. *Accounting Review* 54.

Zingales, L. (2000) In search of new foundations, *Journal of Finance* 55: 1623–53.

Index

Learning Resources
Centre